CHICKEN SOUP FOR THE SHOPPER'S SOUL

CHICKEN SOUP
FOR THE
SHOPPER'S SOUL

Celebrating Bargains, Boutiques
& the Perfect Pair of Shoes

Jack Canfield
Mark Victor Hansen
Theresa Peluso

Health Communications, Inc.
Deerfield Beach, Florida

www.hcibooks.com
www.chickensoup.com

We would like to acknowledge the many publishers and individuals who granted us permission to reprint the cited material. (Note: The stories that were penned anonymously, that are in the public domain or that were written by Jack Canfield, Mark Victor Hansen or Theresa Peluso are not included in this listing.)

Introduction. Excerpt adapted and reprinted by permission of Pamela N. Danziger. ©2006 Pamela N. Danziger, *Shopping: Why We Love It and How Retailers Can Create the Ultimate Shopping Experience* (Kaplan).

Shopping for Dancing Shoes. Reprinted by permission of Morgan St. James. ©2006 Morgan St. James.

The Perfect Present. Reprinted by permission of Terri Duncan. ©2006 Terri Duncan.

Comfy Pajamas. Reprinted by permission of Jodie Haley. ©2006 Jodie Haley.

Mistaken Identity. Reprinted by permission of D. K. Abbott. ©2005 D. K. Abbott.

Parting Gifts. Reprinted by permission of Dianna Graveman. ©2006 Dianna Graveman.

(Continued on page 307)

Library of Congress Cataloging-in-Publication Data
is available from the Library of Congress.

©2006 Jack Canfield and Mark Victor Hansen
ISBN 0-7573-0552-0

Publisher: Health Communications, Inc.
3201 S.W. 15th Street
Deerfield Beach, FL 33442–8190

Cover design by Andrea Perrine Brower
Illustrations by Kevin Stawieray
Inside book design and formatting by Lawna Patterson Oldfield

We dedicate this book to our
forebears who roamed the Earth,
hunting and gathering,
before there were malls, super stores,
home-shopping channels and infomercials.

Contents

Contents

2. THE QUEST FOR A BARGAIN

3. SHOP TILL YOU DROP

4. MALLS, MAIL ORDER, AND MOM & POP SHOPS

5. SEAMLESS CUSTOMER SERVICE

Acknowledgments

Compiling, editing and publishing a book requires the energy and expertise of many people. It begins with the support of our families, who are a perpetual source of joy and love. Thank you, Inga, Christopher, Travis, Riley, Oran, Kyle, Patty, Elisabeth, Melanie and Brian.

Behind the scenes, there are dozens of talented, enthusiastic staff members, freelancers and interns who keep the wheels turning smoothly at Chicken Soup for the Soul Enterprises, Self-Esteem Seminars, Mark Victor Hansen and Associates, and Health Communications, Inc.

The vision and commitment of our publisher, Peter Vegso, brings *Chicken Soup for the Soul* to the world.

Patty Aubery and Russ Kalmaski of Chicken Soup for the Soul Enterprises have shared this journey with love, laughter and endless creativity.

Patty Hansen has handled the legal and licensing aspects of each book thoroughly and competently, and Laurie Hartman has been a precious guardian of the *Chicken Soup* brand.

Barbara LoMonaco and D'ette Corona bring their endless cooperation and incredible coordination and organization of a million details to the table, time and again.

Veronica Romero, Teresa Esparza, Robin Yerian, Jesse Ianniello, Lauren Edelstein, Jody Emme, Debbie Lefever, Michelle Adams, Dee Dee Romanello, Shanna Vieyra, Lisa Williams, Gina Romanello, Brittany Shaw, Noelle Champagne, Tanya Jones and Mary McKay support Jack's and Mark's businesses with skill and love.

Allison Janse, our editor, makes every book a joy to work on with her sense of humor and her extraordinary gift with words.

The staff of Health Communications, Inc. (all hundred-plus of you!), from the creative production team and editorial department to management, sales, marketing, public relations and fulfillment, gets all of our books into readers' hands, copy after copy, with exacting standards and professionalism.

Readers around the world enjoy *Chicken Soup* in over thirty-six languages because of the efforts of Claude Choquette and Luc Jutras at Montreal Contacts.

And our thanks and appreciation go out to Katherine Bontrager, Amanda Capelli, Marianne Davidson, Scott Dooley, Dara Fleischer, Debbie Hill, Deb Karpek, Karen Paulson Miller, Alicia Newland, Evelyn Oster, Marjorie Oppenheim, Jennifer Reinsch, Sally Rodman, Diane Smith, Heather Turlington, Marsha Tyson and Dave Wilkins for helping us select the stories for this book by generously giving their time and sharing their feedback.

To everyone who submitted a story, we deeply appreciate your letting us into your lives and sharing your experiences with us. For those whose stories were not chosen for publication, we hope the stories you are about to enjoy convey what was in your heart and in some way also tell your story.

And last, but certainly not least, to our readers. You are the reason we strive for the best and continue to bring you the magic of *Chicken Soup for the Soul*.

Introduction

When I was growing up, I had three pairs of shoes—my "Sunday" shoes, my school shoes and a pair of bright, white, canvas Keds. Today, as my husband will attest, things have changed. I now have a closet full of shoes in every color (several shades of the same color, in fact), and all manner of heels, toes and comfort.

With all of that, living in South Florida and working from a home office, I'm usually barefoot, which delights my pedicurist to no end. Ironically, none of that stops me from shopping for, or stopping to ogle, shoes. I am not alone. And no, thank you, I'm not interested in doing any spring-cleaning of my psyche to "resolve my issues." I'm a happy shopper.

We all shop. For the essentials and the not-so-essential. Many of us shop with great satisfaction; others only when absolutely necessary and with great exasperation. For some, shopping seems as necessary as breathing, eating and sleeping. The process by which we acquire things that help us define our identity and establish, maintain (or defy) social norms didn't actually have a name until the late 1700s, but shopping is surely encoded in our DNA. That we must find and possess things that make us feel secure and happy drives one of the largest industries in the world economy.

In ancient Greece and medieval Europe, people bartered for goods that they produced themselves in open-air markets. Then one day an entrepreneurial trader established a "shop." Bakers, butchers and grocers soon followed, and modern man became a shopper. In those early days, the shopkeeper retrieved the goods a customer requested and often delivered the purchases to the customer's home. In the next evolution in our shopping DNA, the industrial revolution produced a plethora of consumer goods, and the department store was born. Stores became larger and less specialized. Self-service was introduced, and we took our goods with us. When suburban sprawl began, the shopping mall was spawned. Then came shoppertainment centers, lifestyle centers, outlet mill malls and festival marketplaces. Contemporary shoppers can select the products they desire from the comfort of their home, *dot.com* shopkeepers retrieve them, and a man in a big brown (or white or yellow) truck delivers them.

But why do we shop? Are we driven by our desire to "have" or to "get"? Certainly, we shop because we need basic necessities like food, clothing and household items. But we also shop recreationally for fashion, furnishings, entertainment, hobby-related products and decorative items for our homes. We browse, explore and hunt for bargains. We build vacations around shopping. And we do it to the tune of about $4 trillion a year. That's a lot of caching! Shopping makes the economic world go round, and many people very happy.

Experts are hard at work to help us understand the complexity of our shopping impulses. Not surprisingly, men and women are motivated to shop for different reasons. Women are driven more to express love and nurturing by shopping for their homes and family. They reinforce or initiate change in their social relationships by shopping: Is that perfect gift meant to show how much they care or perhaps motivated by a need to be liked more by the recipient? Men approach shopping as an achievement, as proof of their ability to succeed—by getting the best deal on the latest tool, car or tech gadget.

We also shop to fulfill needs. In her new book, *Shopping: Why We Love It and How Retailers Can Create the Ultimate Shopping Experience,* Pamela Danziger, founder of Unity Marketing, recently defined five types of shoppers. We have Ursula, the *Uber Shopper,* who is a highly involved shopper and gets the greatest enjoyment out of the shopping experience. While Ursula spends more, she is also an active bargain shopper. The *Therapeutic Shopper,* Theresa, shops as a form of therapy, as an escape, and enjoys browsing almost as much as buying. Theresa represents the second most active type of shopper. Next is Diana, the *Bargain Huntress,* who carefully researches her purchases, comparison shops and doesn't let impulsive buying enter the equation. Diana rarely pays full price, knows where the discounts can be found and is always on the hunt for good buys. Denise, the *Discerning Shopper,* is older and at a life-stage where she is more likely to be downsizing her life rather than acquiring more material goods. And last, but not least, there is Les, the *Least Enthusiastic Shopper.* Les requires a bit of coaxing to get him into a store, but once there, he enjoys the shopping experience as much as a woman. Les spends the least amount of money shopping for fun and shops less often than the other personalities.

We shop because we want to relate to our peers—to eat what they eat, to wear what they wear, to feel accepted. And we also shop to define ourselves. The buttoned-down business woman by day transforms herself into a free spirit by night through the clothes and accessories for which she very deliberately shops. We socialize, bond, chase away the blues, solve problems and relax by shopping.

Dissecting our shopping personalities and motivations is very interesting and helpful for the marketers trying to sell us products. As long as we are aware they are hard at work serving their business models, their efforts are welcome and ultimately benefit shoppers—we get what we want, sooner and more efficiently.

But when all the research models, sociological theses and economic impact studies are complete, any true shopper knows the object matters less than the experience. After all is said and done, we shop because it is fun.

So, allow us to entertain you with some of those experiences in *Chicken Soup for the Shopper's Soul*. Our writers bring you stories of love, laughter and lessons learned from their living rooms, malls, flea markets, exclusive boutiques and markets around the world. And we've included some tips and interesting facts about shopping that will help you sharpen your skills and have more fun at the game. We invite you to sit back, relax and enjoy *Chicken Soup for the Shopper's Soul*—and then, of course, *go shopping!*

Theresa Peluso

Share with Us

We would love to hear your reactions to the stories in this book. Please let us know what your favorite stories were and how they affected you.

We also invite you to send us stories you would like to see published in future editions of *Chicken Soup for the Soul.* You can send us either stories you have written or stories written by others. Please send submissions to:

Chicken Soup for the Soul
P.O. Box 30880
Santa Barbara, CA 93130
Fax: 805-563-2945

You can also access e-mail or find a current list of planned books at the *Chicken Soup for the Soul* Web site at *www. chickensoup.com.*

We hope you enjoy reading this book as much as we enjoyed compiling, editing and writing it.

chapter 1

Born to Shop

I will buy any cream,
cosmetic or elixir from a woman
with a European accent.

ERMA BOMBECK

Shopping for Dancing Shoes

The great use of life is to spend it for something that will outlast it.

WILLIAM JAMES

Mom sat on the slightly worn floral sofa in the reception room of the nursing home watching the door like a sentinel standing guard. She was going shopping. Anyway, that's what the nurse told her. Her silver-white hair was set off by a pretty lavender pantsuit and on her feet, a slightly worn pair of athletic shoes.

I smiled and kissed her on the cheek. "Come on, Mom, we're going to the May Company to buy you a new pair of shoes. Then we'll stop and get some of that Chinese food you love. Okay?"

She stood up and smoothed her outfit. I marveled at how erect she was for a woman nearly ninety. "New shoes. Oh, boy." Then she looked at me with confusion mirrored in her kind hazel eyes. "By the way, you're a pretty young lady. Do I know you?"

She clutched a small leather handbag that contained Grandma's External Hard Drive as my son called it . . . a book my sister and I created to help her remember who people were and why she lived at the nursing home.

"I can't forget my purse, you know. It has all my important information." She took the book out and looked through it. She read in a clear voice, "'My name is Rosetta Lachman, and I moved here after I had mini strokes.' See," she said, "that's what I mean. Important information. You're a pretty young lady. Do I know you?" There it was again, reminding me that I was the adult now, and she was the child.

I took her arm, and as we walked to the car, I said, "Actually, you do know me. I'm your daughter, and I love you very much. You have another daughter who lives in Alaska."

"How lucky. Two pretty daughters. What do you know." She settled into the car, and we drove the short distance to the shopping center. Her attention span was growing very short these days, so I knew it had to be a quick excursion. Not like in the old days, when we would spend a whole day looking for great bargains, trying on clothes and shoes for hours, and then packing up our purchases and heading for the Chinese restaurant. I felt a little catch in my throat.

Once I settled her into a chair in the shoe department, she chatted away with the clerk. Since he didn't know her, he had no idea that mini strokes had robbed this charming woman of her memory. He was very gentle as he slipped various styles of shoes on her fragile feet. She would stand for a moment, walk around a bit and try on the next pair, thanking him each time for being so helpful.

"She's such a sweet lady," he said to me. "How old is your mom?"

"She'll be ninety next month," I said, taking her hand in mine and patting it.

"Wow. I thought she was in her seventies. Ninety. Wow." He prepared to take her selection to the desk to ring it up.

"Young man," she said in a voice that belied her age, "I like those shoes, but how am I going to dance in them? When they play that rock and roll music, I just have to dance." He smiled broadly and removed the shoes from the box. Then he put them on for her and took her around in a dance position.

"Let's just try them out, okay?" So Mom and the young man danced to silent music as he carefully led her through some simple steps in the shoe department of the May Company. She smiled up at him. "Thank you, young man. These will do just fine."

STAYING POWER

There's room in everyone's wardrobe for fun, trendy styles, but if you spend more on classic pieces, whether it's clothing, shoes or furniture, your style will be timeless.

I could feel tears welling in my eyes as I said, "Are you ready for that Chinese food?"

"I sure am. You're a pretty young lady. Do I know you?"

That was the last time I was able to take Mom out shopping, and it will stay with me forever. A few months later, she broke her hip and never danced again. She's ninety-six now and confined to a wheelchair, but she still has her "dancing shoes."

Morgan St. James

The Perfect Present

. . . teach me still to be thankful for life and for time's oldest memories that are good and sweet . . .

MAX EHRMANN

I am a born shopper. Like my mother, who shops with unbridled enthusiasm, and especially my grandmother, who derived great pleasure from purchasing, I shop with passion for bargains and deals, for gifts and gadgets. But shopping took on a new and very different meaning during the Christmas season of 1991.

For the first time, shopping for the perfect present was not simply a Christmas cliché. We discovered in early spring that my father had inoperable lung cancer, and he was sent home with little hope. Prayers and miracles were the only possible cure. The weeks that followed the diagnosis were melancholy, and the Christmas season, a time of year that my entire family usually looked forward to and embraced, brought little cheer. We knew that this Christmas would in all likelihood be our father's last, and our hearts were heavy. The last thing that anyone in the family felt like doing was decorating and shopping.

But I had a two-year-old daughter and a newborn son, Daddy's only grandchildren, and I knew that he would never want their Christmas ruined, especially not because of him and his illness. So, I shopped. I did so, not because I wanted there to be piles of presents under the tree on Christmas morning, but because I wanted to create a lasting memory for my father, one he would recall vividly for the rest of his life, no matter how limited that span of time might be.

As I wandered the aisles, I pondered each purchase carefully. *What would Dad want to see his grandchildren play with? Would he like seeing his grandson dressed in a little sailor suit? Would he enjoy reading this story to them or watching this particular video as his granddaughter sat, curled up in his lap? Would he have the strength to play this game with her, or would it be better to choose another?* Each purchase was an act of love, an incredibly meaningful purchase meant to make Dad's last days with us as memorable as possible.

Shopping for Dad's gift also took on new meaning. The days of giving power tools and fishing equipment were over. Daddy was now confined to a much smaller world,  one that simply did not include such pastimes. My sister, brother and I discussed the options for days and days. Our conversations were guarded and stilted, and more was left unspoken than spoken. None of us could verbalize the real reason that this shopping expedition was so important. It was as if we believed that if we did not actually say the words, then perhaps it was not true.

We were not the only ones desperately trying to determine the perfect gift for someone we loved. Dad was also in a quandary. He knew that he was facing his final holiday with my mother, his high-school sweetheart and wife of nearly thirty years. With his usual enthusiasm and determination, he secretly spoke to us about what he should get for Momma. Though he was unable to drive, and very limited physically, he wanted to make sure that she had a spectacular gift under the tree Christmas morning. His excitement was contagious and was the best antidote for our Christmas blues. My siblings and I plotted and planned with Daddy, and helped him shop for a very special gift for Momma.

Shopping for the perfect Christmas gifts became a catharsis for all of us that year. With each purchase, I closed my eyes and imagined the smile on my father's face. It was the memory of that smile that would carry me through the many rough days ahead. Sadly, Dad passed away the following fall at the far-too-young age of forty-eight.

We were given a very special gift that year, one not purchased in any mall or from any online retailer. Most people don't know when a holiday will be the last for a loved one, and seldom do they have the opportunity to shop for a perfect gift for that special person. Shopping, especially for gifts, isn't about sales or bargains or grabbing something just to get something. Shopping for loved ones is a selfless endeavor that pays dividends in the form of priceless memories.

Terri Duncan

Comfy Pajamas

You aren't wealthy until you have something
money can't buy.

GARTH BROOKS

When my son, Thayne, was born, normal new-mom insecurities were compounded by being single, seventeen and having very little family. Even my few friends had vanished during my pregnancy. Most of the time, it was just Thayne and me. I was plagued by doubt, fearful that I would end up as a disappointment to my son, and even questioned whether I deserved to be a mother. We had very little money, lived in a small one-bedroom apartment, and although I knew that love was the most precious gift I could give my son, struggling to provide for him was a source of anxiety and depression.

Our lives became even more difficult when Thayne began having seizures. While I sat alone beside his large hospital crib for weeks at a time, I daydreamed about all the wonderful things I would buy for him if I was rich. Finally, he started getting better and was able to come home. I decided we would do a little shopping and get him some comfy new pajamas to celebrate. We spent hours in the department store, reveling in the sights and smells of life beyond a hospital room. We joked and laughed uncontrollably as we marched up and down the aisles, looking at everything from vacuum cleaners to toys. It was just the right distraction that we both desperately needed.

Our shopping adventure ended with one pair of eight-dollar pajamas, but that didn't matter. It wouldn't have mattered if we went home empty-handed. What mattered was the time we spent together, the memories we had made, and the new tradition we had started.

That night after he had fallen asleep in his new PJ's, I lay beside Thayne. I stared at his peaceful face, and I knew that even though there would always be hard times, I was good enough for this little man. We would be okay. I didn't need all the money in the world to make him happy. I just needed to be happy with him.

From that day on, I started putting a few dollars away to save for tougher times. When they came, Thayne and I would take our "tough-times cash" and head out shopping. Sometimes we spent it, sometimes not, but we always had fun. It wasn't long before I found myself making up silly reasons why we should head to the mall. Now that Thayne is eight, he makes up his own excuses.

In quiet times, instead of daydreaming about having an infinite supply of money, I now picture my son, fully grown, ready to start a family of his own, and always ready to shop with his old mom after a bad day.

Jodie Haley

Mistaken Identity

Answer that you are here—that life exists and identity, that the powerful play goes on, and you may contribute a verse.

WALT WHITMAN

My friend Lisa's baby was two weeks overdue, and the doctor advised her to start walking to perhaps bring on labor. I had planned a trip to the mall the next morning, so we decided to spend the day window-shopping.

In her last stages of pregnancy, Lisa had about outgrown most of her clothes . . . all except a bright floral maternity dress. The dress was about the only thing my extra-large friend could get into, and I had teased her about really needing to find something else as it was all she ever wore.

We window-shopped until she tired and decided to people-watch from the food court while I continued to shop. About a half hour later, as I approached the shop where we had agreed to meet, an excited customer came out of the store. "There's a woman in there giving birth . . . they just called the paramedics."

I knew it was Lisa and rushed to the store to be with her. She had been so excited about the baby—her first— and I wanted to be there to share her joy and give her comfort. Pushing my way through the group of people standing around a figure in a bright floral dress, I dropped to my knees next to her. Grabbing her hand, I told her to relax, that an ambulance was on its way, and I'd make sure Mark was called at work.

ROOM TO GROW

Maternity wear is a $1.5 billion part of the clothing market and has seen 36 percent growth since 2000. More babies? No, it's supply and demand. Pregnant women are demanding more choices in great styles, and maternity clothes are available from a wider variety of retailers.

"Who's Mark?" a strange voice asked. Finally, I glanced at her face—and into the eyes of a perfect stranger.

Embarrassed, I looked around and saw Lisa leaning against the door to a dressing room doubled over in laughter.

She gave birth to her first son early the following morning. The doctor said the belly laugh was as good as a ride over a bumpy road.

D. K. Abbott

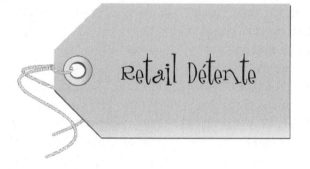

Retail Détente

Peace, like charity, begins at home.

FRANKLIN D. ROOSEVELT

I grew up in a neighborhood that was a stronghold of Catholicism. Nestled in this womb of the faithful was the Kaufman family, Eastern European Jews, who owned one of our two neighborhood grocery stores.

I loved the Kaufmans' store. The door squeaked when it opened, the wood floors creaked under the slightest bit of weight, and the smell of garlic pickles in a big, wooden barrel filled the air. All the shopkeepers in our neighborhood lived above their stores, and the Kaufmans' tiny kitchen was just beyond where Mr. Kaufman butchered fresh cuts of meat. Mrs. Kaufman tended the front, splitting her time between the cash register and stocking the shelves.

One day after school, my grandmother sent me to Kaufmans for one pound of ground beef. I sped down the block, carefully opened the squeaky door and inhaled the aromas of the old-fashioned grocery store. When Mr. Kaufman asked how he could help me, I repeated the order as politely and carefully as I could, "One pound of ground meat, please." Off Mr. Kaufman went to the refrigerator, the heavy door closing behind him. He returned with a tray of various pieces of meat and proceeded to push them through his grinder.

I watched the fresh meat go in as chunks and come out like spaghetti while casting a wary glance at the knives hanging from the blood-stained chopping block, scarred by thousands of strikes from the cleaver. Mr. Kaufman reached for the roll of butcher's paper, snapped off a piece and skillfully wrapped up my pound of meat. He took the black marker from behind his ear and wrote a price on the wrapper, handed me the package, and said thank you in his thick accent.

I returned home, placed the package on the counter and rushed back outside to play. I was soon interrupted by my grandmother yelling and gesturing from the end of the alley. As I approached, she waved the package of ground meat in the air and asked, "Theresa, what did you bring me?" Confused, I didn't know what to say, "What you wanted, Grandmom. I told Mr. Kaufman what you wanted, and that's what he gave me."

For some reason, this set her off even more. "Then you take this back to those Kaufmans. We don't eat horsemeat. You tell them you want your money back, and take that over to McGarigills and get me a pound of ground beef. I don't care what they charge. At least they're good Catholics and know what good Catholics eat. We're through shopping at Kaufmans. He's a shyster!"

She thrust the package into my hands and stomped off. All I could do was what I was told. I slunk back to Kaufmans, opened the squeaky door and quietly waited my turn at the butcher counter. When Mr. Kaufman looked up with a puzzled expression, I said my piece. "Mr. Kaufman, I'm sorry, but my grandmom says to tell you that we don't eat horsemeat and that we want our money back. She says you don't know what good Catholics eat and that I have to go to McGarigills from now on, even though they charge more, because you're a shyster." The words were catching in my throat as I spoke, hoping I got it right, just the way my grandmother told me to say it.

I would miss Kaufmans. McGarigills never smelled like garlic pickles, and their floors didn't creak, and the door opened smoothly. They had bag boys and boys who stocked the shelves. While I was lost in thought, I didn't realize that Mr. Kaufman had turned a deep shade of red and that Mrs. Kaufman had come running down the aisle. They spoke rather heatedly to each other in a language I didn't understand. Mrs. Kaufman snapped the package out of my hand and ushered me back to the front of the store. She opened the register and promptly counted out my refund. "You go now, and you don't come back. We sell good meat, not horsemeat, and we take care of our customers. We don't need troublemakers here."

I scooped the money off the counter and made my way toward the door. Customers and other kids were staring. The only sound in the place was that squeaky door. Sadly, I headed for McGarigills where I stood politely in line and waited for the butcher to ask me for my order. For the second time in a half hour, I ordered the pound of ground meat.

Home again. The kitchen smelled like a combination of Pall Malls, boiled potatoes, butter and Bushmills Irish Whiskey. (After all, it was after five.) I put the new package on the counter and watched as my grandmother opened the butcher paper, looked, smelled and poked at the meat. "What is going on around here?" she said. "Don't these butchers sell decent meat anymore? I'm going to give them a piece of my mind!" With that, she wiped her hands on the apron, untied it and threw it over the kitchen chair. She re-wrapped the package, tucked it under her arm and grabbed me by the hand. This 4'11" dynamo hiked down the alleys, crossed streets, dodged traffic, and muttered about butchers and horsemeat, all the while holding my hand with a grip that was cutting off my circulation.

At McGarrigills, my grandmother made a beeline to the butcher counter—which she could not see over—and pushed in front of the customer waiting in line. "You should be ashamed of yourself, calling yourself a butcher. What kind of ground beef is this?" The helpful customer, a few inches taller, passed the troublesome package of meat over the counter to the confused butcher, who calmly looked down at my grandmother, then at me.

Grandmom continued chastizing the butcher about service and quality as he opened the package and waited for her to finish. "Ma'am, if that little girl had ordered 'beef,' that's what I would have given her, but I distinctly remember her asking for 'one pound of ground meat.' I remember that quite clearly."

All of a sudden I felt every eye on me. Grandmom jerked my arm. "Theresa, what did you tell this fine gentleman I wanted?" I couldn't answer. "Theresa, what did you order? Did you ask for ground *meat* or ground *beef*?" Finding my voice, I stammered something like, "Isn't meat, beef?"

With that, my little Irish grandmother turned on the charm. "I am so, so very sorry, sir. Please forgive me. My granddaughter misunderstood. Please, let me have that back, and I'll be out of your way." The butcher smiled and replied, "No, you wanted ground beef, and that's what you'll have. Wait here— and maybe you can explain to your little girl that meat isn't always beef."

I listened carefully as my grandmother shared one of the great mysteries of life. "Theresa, some people can't afford to eat 100 percent ground beef, so in order to make ends meet, they order ground *meat*, and these nice butchers cut up some pork ends along with some beef and grind it all together. Now, we aren't poor (this came as news to me, since even at my age I knew we didn't have any money), and our family can afford to order beef. From now on, you be sure to tell these nice people you want ground *beef*, not *meat*. Do you understand?"

Suddenly, I did understand. The ground meat was an insult. My grandmother thought that our butchers were insinuating that she couldn't afford beef. It was as if the sky had opened up. On the way home from McGarigills I told Grandmom that I now understood perfectly, and it would never happen again. She squeezed my hand—a silent "apology accepted." As we walked, I wondered about the Kaufmans and tentatively asked, "Can I stop at Kaufmans and tell them I'm sorry? I really feel bad for calling them shysters when it was my mistake." For the second time that evening, I saw an adult turn beet red. "Theresa, you what? You said what?"

Confused (again), in my most innocent voice I said, "You told me to tell them good Catholics didn't eat horsemeat . . ." Before I could finish, we cut across the street and were headed straight for the corner—directly for that squeaky door of Kaufmans' grocery.

There are few times in my life that compare to stepping into that store, that evening, behind my tiny grandmother. I knew that my mistake had angered and hurt people, but as I stepped forward to apologize, Grandmom's arm held me back. With all the pride she could swallow, she cleared her throat, looked the Kaufmans in the eyes and spoke. "Please, Mr. and Mrs. Kaufman, my granddaughter and I want to apologize for our mistake. I sent Theresa here for one pound of ground beef, and she asked for ground meat—not knowing the difference. I also must apologize because what I said to Theresa, in a fit of anger over what I thought was your fault, were unkind, hurtful things that Theresa did not realize she shouldn't repeat."

Mr. and Mrs. Kaufman looked at each other, discussed something in that strange language and nodded. Mr. Kaufman asked us to wait a minute and returned with a package. On the wrapper, in big black marker was written "$0." He handed the package to Grandmom and said, "We accept your apology."

I quietly walked beside my grandmother toward home. Relieved and happy that I was still allowed to shop at Kaufmans, I was even more amazed that we ended up with two pounds of ground beef for the price of a pound of meat.

Theresa Peluso

Parting Gifts

It is easier to build strong children than to repair broken men.

FREDERICK DOUGLASS

For every thing, there is a season. A time to shop, and a time to buy. I like having new things as much as the next person. I just don't like cruising for parking spaces, browsing endless aisles of goods I don't want in search of the one thing I need, and standing in lines.

But now, my oldest child, Steve, has decided to flee the nest and get his own apartment. He is going to share rent with the son of my long-time friend, Brenda, and our boys are going to need a lot of basic necessities when they settle into their new place. So Brenda and I did what any good mother would do in this situation, besides weep and mourn the loss of her first-born—we went shopping.

Side by side, we rattled our carts down department store aisles, occasionally falling into single file when encountering another shopper.

"You get the mop. I'll get the broom."

"Do you think they'll need a toaster?"

"They'll definitely need one of these." (I tossed a plunger in my cart.)

"What color is their kitchen?"

"Do guys even care about color coordination?"

It was then I spotted the Batman blanket. There was the Caped Crusader himself, resplendent in steely blue and black polyester plush. The year that Steve turned five, Batman had posed on top of his birthday cake, ready for action. No other superhero would do. I remember searching several stores in the weeks before the big day, looking for matching paper plates, napkins and party invitations featuring

MUSTS OR MUST-HAVES?

Make a list of what you have and what you need to purchase. Then define what is essential and what would be "nice-to-have" before you shop. It will help you to stay focused and on budget.

the nocturnal crime fighter. For years afterward, Steve's weekly allowance often bought him another Batman comic book or action figure. Many fictional champions for justice came and went at our house, but Batman remained a constant.

Brenda joined me in the bedding aisle as I stood fingering the blanket.

"I know how you feel," she said. "I didn't think it would happen this soon."

Me either.

It wasn't long ago that I'd knelt on the floor in a department store like this one, cradling a newborn and attempting to reason with a toddler ("Just a few more minutes! We're almost done!"), while holding up size-six corduroys to my little boy's waist to see if they were long enough. They never were. He was growing so fast.

How many "Back-to-School" sales had I survived,

navigating between displays of three-ring binders and overloaded shopping carts of other harried parents, scavenging the bins for one last box of washable markers in basic colors?

Wasn't it yesterday that I dragged a sullen adolescent through the young men's department, suggesting he try on some nicely pressed khakis and polo shirts in lieu of baggy jeans and T-shirts with silly slogans?

About the time Steve abandoned his fear of being seen in public with the woman who bore him, I helped him shop for his first high-school dance. We picked out the perfect shirt and tie. He looked so handsome then, so grown up. Almost a man.

I didn't think it would happen this soon.

We raise our children to become self-sufficient. We do our best to guide them in developing skills to make sound judgments. If we're lucky, one day they are ready to leave home and be independent. Then we know we've done a good job. That doesn't make it any easier to watch them go.

Brenda and I wound our way toward the checkout lanes. "This was fun," she said, squeezing my arm.

"Just a minute," I said. "I need one more thing."

I steered my cart toward the book and magazine section and scanned the shelves. Yes! There it was. I made my choice quickly, tossing it on top of the bath towels and toaster, waste can and bed sheets—offerings of love and support for a grown son who would soon learn to fend for himself.

One more Batman comic book couldn't hurt.

Dianna Graveman

The Shopping Game

Whoever said money can't buy happiness simply didn't know where to go shopping.

Bo Derek

When I was a girl, I would settle into the cushions on the porch swing with the Sears Roebuck "Wish Book" propped on my knees. The hefty catalog would arrive in late summer, before school began, and the porch swing on our wraparound porch was a perfect place to escape the summer heat. My mother had fitted the broad seat of the white wooden swing with mounds of cushy pillows upholstered in flowered chintz, and I would lie there in the shade, my feet pushing the chains that suspended the swing from the ceiling, swaying back and forth. When the catalog arrived, I perched among the pillows and started at page one. The models were dressed in garnet red and gold, camel and forest green, posing with rakes against piles of leaves or walking along sunlit paths through the woods. Mentally trying on their outfits and studying their haircuts, I'd imagine what I would wear and what I would look like when I grew up. I loved choosing from the alternate colors, visualizing myself as an adult, wondering what kind of job and house I'd have.

Neither the children's nor the men's sections held any appeal for me, but at housewares I would furnish my imaginary home, contemplating kitchen appliances and bedroom sets, curtains and dining-room tables. After a while, I made up the shopping game. The rules were simple: I could pick one item on each page, left-hand and right-hand. If I didn't like anything on the left-hand page, I could "roll over" a choice to the right-hand page, and vice versa. However, if nothing appealed to me, I forfeited those choices, and moved on to the next two pages. I wasn't allowed to just pick something for picking's sake because that was "wasting my (pretend) money."

CATALOG SHOPPING

Sears, Roebuck and Co. began distributing mail-order catalogs in 1902.

When I recall those hours on the porch swing, swaying in the summer warmth and musing over the thin pages, I'm both vaguely ashamed of my adolescent greediness and gratified. Gratified, because for the only time in my life, I had the opportunity to choose my heart's desire without credit-card bills or delivery charges. Restricting myself to only one choice per page forced me to evaluate price and quality, and to trust my opinion. It was okay not to like something, and it was not okay to buy just for the sake of buying.

Those adolescent dreams of shopping for new outfits and a houseful of furniture never came true. When I did grow up and was struggling through graduate school on a tiny budget, the shopping game was my only form of spending recreation. Then I finally landed a job and couldn't spend money even after I'd earned it, not knowing how to break my frugal habits. Now, I pride myself on being a "minimalist" in these days of rank consumerism; I spend far more time combing thrift shops for clothes than I have ever spent shopping for sales at the mall. Such ingrained frugality has its drawbacks—being a miser is no fun! Even though I've paid off my student loans and carry no credit-card debt, I still can't bring myself to shop with the same abandon that I did on the porch swing. Where's the gratification in that?

The days of the wish books ended years ago. Now, we can shop on Yahoo and Froogle on Google, where millions of items are at our disposal from all over the world. We can sort through hundreds of choices in seconds, not hours, and not even have to make a trip to the mailbox to order. The search engines play the shopping game for me, aligning all my choices in one column and sorting them by price or color in one keystroke.

I miss the original shopping game—the summer afternoons sprawled out on the porch swing, shifting a heavy catalog on my knees, exploring the possibilities of adulthood while late-summer breezes riffled the pages. You still can't buy daydreams on the Internet, and for that I'll take the porch swing any day.

Kelly Austin

Heavenly Shoes

We are each of us angels with only one wing, and we can only fly by embracing one another.

LUCIANO DE CRESCENZO

We have all been there. Pay day has come and gone, and there's a little spare cash singeing a hole in your purse, just waiting to be spent. And what happens? You can find nothing—that's right, nothing—in the right color, style or size. The next time you have no money, that's when stores are filled with gorgeous garments and achingly attractive accessories. It's not fair.

After such a day in Glasgow, with rain threatening to drown even the most determined shopper, I gave up. I was footsore and weary, hungry, tired and worse—the cash burning a hole in my purse had now set fire to the lining and was threatening to flambé my entire handbag.

With a sigh of frustration, I sat down in the middle of a large department store and decided that I was going to buy something—anything—just to give me that rush of shopping satisfaction.

"Can I help you at all?"

A petite, blonde woman was standing before me wearing a helpful smile.

"I doubt it," I replied, a little on the grumpy side. "I have money to spend, and I can't find anything I want to spend it on. It's useless. I think I'll just go home."

She smiled the smile of someone who had been there. "Why don't you ask your shopping angels for help?" she suggested.

I thought I must have misheard her. "My shopping angels?" I inquired. She nodded in the affirmative. Now, don't get me wrong. I am a great believer in angels, and I have had many profound angelic encounters both large and small over the years for which I am truly grateful and thankful, but never before had I considered asking them for help when it came to sartorial suggestions. I've always thought they would be too busy. This sales assistant had really piqued my curiosity. I considered it for a moment. I asked my angels for help in many areas of my life already—I had my parking angels and angels who blessed the house—why not shopping angels?

"Okay," I said, "tell me how it works for you. I'm willing to give it a go."

She sat down beside me. "Well, you have to clear all that shopping negativity that you've accumulated today. Put it out of your mind. Close your eyes and take a deep breath. Focus on your breathing and relax. Keep that focus, but lightly, and ask your angels to come into your presence. Angels are all around us, but you have to ask for some assistance. You might get a feeling of warmth, or a breeze, or simply a sensation of peace. It's different for everyone. Let them know that you need their help in selecting just the right outfit if that's what you're meant to do today."

I felt a little self-conscious sitting in the middle of the shoe department, but I closed my eyes and breathed deeply for a few moments. Then I simply asked my shopping angels to come into my presence and help me out. After a minute or so, I opened my eyes and took a deep, relaxed breath. Maybe it was just the fact that I felt more rested, but my tiredness had lifted, and I had a renewed sense of vigor and energy. The salesgirl looked directly at me. "Now that you have your angels with you, take a fresh look and see what happens," she smiled. "And don't forget to thank them afterward."

With new enthusiasm, I left the store and wandered out into the street. *Okay, angels,* I said to myself, *I'd love some glamorous high heels that make my legs look endless but don't break the bank. Do you think we could sort that out?* I smiled inwardly. *Even if I don't get the shoes,* I thought, *this is fun!*

I wandered from shop window to shop window, but still nothing grabbed me. Perhaps I just wasn't meant to get shoes today. Without realizing it, my musings had taken me down a little street that I would not normally take. I was about to double-back when I spotted a window dressed with sparkly, high-heeled shoes.

Love is a many splendored thing and can, as we know, happen at first sight. One pair of shoes in the window was meant for me. They were just the kind of style I usually went for, the perfect color, heel—everything! Apart from the price, that is. They cost more than I would normally pay for shoes. I closed my eyes and took another deep breath, smiling inwardly at my angel. *Nothing ventured, nothing gained,* I thought. I felt a little internal nudge and decided to go in anyway and at least try them on. The bell over the door tinkled merrily as I walked in. A glamorous, mature woman appeared from behind a curtain. "Can I help you?"

"I'd like to try the pink heels in the window please, in a size four."

"Of course." She disappeared behind the curtain again

and appeared with a box. She lovingly unfolded layers of soft tissue paper to reveal the shoes nestling snugly inside. They were even more stunning close up.

"They're gorgeous," I breathed. Gently, I pulled them out of their tissue beds and examined them. Little jewels sparkled and danced along delicate ankle straps and gave way to the softest leather imaginable—veritable foot gloves! Sexy stilettos tapered from four inches to points of nothingness. Carefully, I pulled one on. Bliss. I felt as if I was walking on little cloud pillows. With the partner strapped on, I knew how it felt to be walking on air. Shoes from heaven. I gazed in rapture at my sparkling-clad feet in the mirror opposite. Shopper intoxication had set in. "I'll take them!" I exclaimed.

The assistant boxed them up for me and punched the code into the register. "It's always nice to serve customers who can appreciate craftsmanship," she said, smiling. The price flashed up on the display as my hand was halfway to my bankcard. I've always believed that honesty is the best policy, as they say, and now was no exception.

"I'm sorry, that's not the correct price," I exclaimed in surprise. The price on the screen was less than half the price that had been displayed in the window.

The assistant smiled at me. "They're on sale," she said, "just for today," and gave me a smile and a wink. A little stunned, I handed over my credit card and left the shop clutching my new purchase.

Remembering what the first shop assistant said, I silently offered up a little note of thanks to my angels, who, by the way, have since proven to be as interested as I am in current fashion trends on the earthly plane!

Judith Keenan

What My Mother Didn't Tell Me About Boxes

Thanks to my mother, not a single cardboard box has found its way back into society. We receive gifts in boxes from stores that went out of business twenty years ago.

ERMA BOMBECK

As I was growing up, I remember my mother hoarding boxes. My two sisters and I took great pleasure in teasing her about this addiction. Any box that came into our possession was tucked away in a closet or under a bed. I couldn't understand the value she put on a piece of cardboard, nor could I read the expression on her face. I now realize my mother knew a great deal more than I gave her credit for. My mother had already experienced the lesson I still had to learn.

My education began the day my friend Ed and I attempted to exchange a defective DustBuster for one that worked. As we walked into the store, we weren't the least bit concerned about our upcoming transaction. The store had quite a flexible return policy. Our attitudes became even more carefree when we saw there was no line at the customer service department. When we reached the counter, we cheerfully handed the broken DustBuster and the receipt over to Alice, the customer service representative.

Hoping to move the transaction along, I didn't wait to be asked why I was returning this item. I just forged ahead and said, "It doesn't bust my dust." At this time I was in a good mood and thought a bit of humor would be appropriate. I was so wrong. There were no questions asked to determine the cause of our unhappiness. The only question we heard was, "Do you have the box?"

With a perplexed look on my face and confusion in my voice, I said, "No."

Then we were told, "You can't return it without the box."

Ed and I just looked at each other dumbfounded. It never occurred to me to keep the box. When I bought it, I thought the thing would work. Who knew I would need the box? I told Alice I had the receipt, but she didn't care. I explained I didn't want my money back; I just wanted to make an exchange for something that worked. Alice still didn't care.

Shrugging her shoulders, we heard her consistent statement, "Can't do anything without the box." We had come to an impasse. I knew immediately Alice would not blink first, and I would lose the staring match that had ensued.

I then realized I was experiencing a situation for the first time that we all encounter more and more often. I've learned that what people say to me has a great deal more to do with them than me. Armed with this new insight, I simply asked, "Why is the box so important?"

With pleading in her voice, much like the tone she had earlier heard in mine, she said, "We can't get our refund

from the manufacturer if we don't send it back in the box."
There you have it. Receiving their reimbursement was the
issue, not my exchange. Now we were making progress.

Equipped with the knowledge of the problem, all we
needed was a solution. However, at that moment we were
literally at a standstill, and a line was forming behind us.
Realizing the problem was ours to solve, we
stepped aside to huddle for our team meeting. It didn't take us long to formulate
a strategy to solve our dilemma. I walked
over and got back in line while Ed
headed off to the vacuum section of
the store. He picked up a DustBuster
identical to the one we had. Then he
went to the checkout counter, paid
for it and walked back to the car.

Just as I walked up to the counter,
Ed returned with his arm extended
high in the air, his hand waving
wildly back and forth holding the much coveted box. As
he placed it on the counter, I told Alice, "I've changed my
mind. I want a refund, not an exchange." The expression
on her face reflected some puzzlement. Knowing it was
best not to ask any questions since this was all working
out in her favor, she started processing the paperwork. We
walked out of the store with a great feeling of success and
a lesson learned.

It seems to me since these boxes are more valuable to
the stores than the customers, they should be responsible
for the necessary storage. Here's what I propose. There
should be a box drop-off area between the checkout
counter and the exit door. The customer could take the
item out of the box, along with necessary directions and
warranty documents, leaving the box behind. Newly
purchased fragile items could go home in the boxes.

BREAKING IT DOWN

Ten cents of every shopping dollar is used to pay for packaging.

Customers could then return the boxes at their leisure.

However, I doubt that will ever happen, so I will continue to stash boxes in every available nook and cranny in my home, just as my mother did years ago. I now comprehend that boxes are a precious commodity and must be treasured.

The most startling revelation of this experience is that the theory proves true. Women do turn into their mothers. Do my children now tease me? Oh, yes! It doesn't bother me because my face is now a reflection of my mother's, while I think to myself, *Go ahead and laugh. Your day will come.*

Tena Thompson

Mom's Special
QVC Gift

In ordinary life we hardly realize that we receive a great deal more than we give, and that it is only with gratitude that life becomes rich.

DIETRICH BONHOEFFER

One early morning in December, I reached into my jewelry box for a necklace to wear and chose my beautiful, glistening, blue topaz that was a gift from my mother. Touching it took me back to the Christmas right after she died, the last time I would receive a gift from her.

Her gifts were always very thoughtful and special, with much love put into them. It was never about what she could spend on us or about giving us what we wanted. Instead, it was always about giving us something very special, something she thought we would love, and something she thought would reflect how much we meant to her. No matter how many gifts were under the tree, Mom's Christmas gift would always be the one we couldn't wait to open. We would all anticipate that irreplaceable special gift, knowing we would cherish it or

A BETTER MOUSETRAP

QVC discovers new products by hosting an annual "Product Search" at their West Chester, Pennsylvania, headquarters. They look for items that demonstrate well, appeal to a broad audience, solve a common problem and possess unique features and benefits.

wear it proudly for others to admire.

My mother couldn't shop the malls or go to any of her favorite downtown specialty shops because of her struggle with cancer and two hip replacements. Instead, she would sit for hours in front of the television watching QVC, her favorite shopping network. I particularly remember the Christmas shopping season just before she died with a heart full of love. Mother wanted to make sure she had a special gift for each of her children, her daughter and son-in-law, and each one of the grandchildren—all sixteen of them, counting great-grandkids.

That Christmas, even though her body was frail and weak from cancer, she struggled to stay alive for her family, spending long hours waiting for just the right gift to be featured. Mother was determined to make sure this Christmas would be extra special, as if she knew that she wouldn't be there to celebrate it with us. She passed away the Monday after Thanksgiving weekend.

There are still moments when I find myself sitting in front of the television watching QVC, thinking of my mother and how much she would love the item being pitched with incredible detail through persuasive words.

That cold December morning as I put on my blue topaz necklace, I felt the warmth of my mother's love and care for my family and me. I fondly remembered the effort she made to make sure my gift was personal and unique. After putting on my necklace and wiping the tears from my eyes, I again glanced down into my jewelry box and saw even more expressions of her love.

I was reminded that Christmas isn't about what we give, or how much we spend for the gift, but about giving out of love. It is about expressing a love from deep within, a love that reaches far beyond the actual gift. It is about finding that perfect gift that expresses how much that loved one truly means to you.

Peggy Reeves

A Special
Holiday Bargain

When you do the common things in an uncommon
way, you will command the attention of the world.

GEORGE WASHINGTON CARVER

The day after Christmas was a Monday morning, and I braved the traffic and crowds in search of clearance sales at our local mall. Three hours later, tired and laden down with two filled shopping bags, I plopped on a bench to rest.

A little girl about four years old skipped up to me, wearing a silly grin on her face. "Hello. My name is Angelise. What's yours?"

"Suzanne," I answered, smiling back. Her name suited her well. She looked like an angel with her long blonde curls and ivory complexion. Her cheeks wore a rosy glow.

"This is my Grandpop," she said. I glanced up to see a man standing near the bench. He had kind emerald-green eyes; a few small lines etched the corners of his smile.

He extended his hand. "I'm also known as Kyle."

"Nice to meet you, Kyle. She's adorable, and I bet she keeps you busy."

"Yes, that she does."

I watched Angelise as she skipped around in small circles, singing a nursery rhyme in a singsong voice. All of a sudden, Kyle garbled something. I turned and saw him clutch his chest and then fall backward onto the ceramic tiled floor. I hurried to his side.

"Kyle, Kyle." He didn't respond. Lifting his head, I watched his eyes roll back as he lost consciousness. "Help . . . someone!" I shouted. A heavyset man dropped to his knees next to Kyle and started administering CPR.

I rose and grabbed my purse from the bench, seeking the cell phone inside. Shoppers stopped to stare as I dialed 911.

Angelise began to whimper. She knelt by his side, laying her head on his thigh.

"Grandpop!" she cried.

I slipped my fingers through hers and gently guided her to the bench where I placed her on my lap.

She continued sobbing and saying, "Grandpop, please get up." I removed a tissue from my purse and dabbed the tears rolling down her cheeks.

Holding her close, I rocked back and forth, patting her small back. I whispered that everything would be okay. Inside, adrenaline and old memories charged through me at the too-familiar scene.

Within minutes, two paramedics arrived with a stretcher, dividing the throng of onlookers. The larger of the two men turned to me and asked, "Do you know what medication he's taking?" I guess he assumed I was Kyle's wife.

Shocked by how this appeared, I mumbled, "No, I'd just met him." At this point, I felt useless. I could be of no help. My heart thumped.

The heavyset man stepped forward and asked, "Is he going to make it?"

"I'm not sure. It looks bad," answered the shorter paramedic.

I held my breath; my husband's life was taken by an unexpected heart attack in our living room while I watched helplessly as the emergency team worked to save him. All those memories resurfaced. I closed my eyes and whispered a silent prayer, pleading with God. Tears stung my eyes.

Angelise sobbed harder. I hummed a soothing melody and held her tighter. Shoppers strolling by shook their heads in sympathy. They probably assumed I was her grandmother by the way we sat huddled together. Looks can be so deceiving.

Kyle sputtered a few coughing sounds, and then his eyes fluttered.

The paramedic said, "Stop, don't shock him again. He's coming around." A few minutes later, I detected rapid footsteps coming from behind me and heading in our direction. The brisk high heels slapped the ceramic floor as they circled us.

"Dad, Dad!" a woman's voice yelled. I saw a young blonde woman kneel next to him.

Angelise screamed, "Mommy!" She struggled to be free, so I let her slide to the floor and run into her mother's arms.

By then they had propped Kyle in a sitting position. He was cautioned to remain still until they brought the stretcher around. They informed his daughter that he would be taken to the emergency room at HCA Hospital to undergo some tests and see the physician on duty.

Angelise reached over and hugged his neck, saying, "I love you, Pop Pop." He managed a weak smile. Her mother restrained her so the paramedics could lift Kyle onto the stretcher and wheel him outdoors to the waiting ambulance. Before they left, he whispered something to his daughter. She turned to face me.

"Mommy," Angelise said, tugging at her mom's sleeve as they came toward me, "this is Suzanne. She reminds me of Grandma Jeanne."

"Thank you, Suzanne, for your quick thinking. You probably saved my dad's life. And thanks for watching over Angelise," she added.

I hugged her and Angelise. Telephone numbers were exchanged, and we said our good-byes. I picked up my shopping bags and went home, glad that Kyle had survived. God had answered my prayer.

Two days later, I visited Kyle in the hospital. He had had a mild heart attack, a warning sign. We promised to keep in touch.

Three months later, after he was given a clean bill of health, he left a message for me on my answering machine. He wanted to invite me to dinner so he could thank me for my quick thinking and caring for his granddaughter, Angelise. I hesitated at first, and then I decided to accept.

Needless to say, we became quite good friends. Sparks flew, and one year later we were married.

Someone once said you don't go looking for love, but that love finds you. Now I know it's true. I never bargained on finding love at the mall, but somehow love found me.

Suzanne Baginskie

The Birthday Surprise

I had been in Germany for three months, living with my husband, Michael, on the Army base in Babenhausen where he was stationed. I was homesick and desperate for a friend when we were invited to a cookout at the home of another soldier and his wife. Daniella, German-born, tall and blonde, was a gracious host and the first person who had been friendly to me since my arrival. I hadn't been off the base much, so when she said the magic words, "Let's go shopping!" I accepted without hesitation.

The Real (pronounced ree-al) reminded me of a Wal-Mart Supercenter as Daniella pushed the shopping cart that contained her fifteen-month-old son Sean, followed closely by her neighbor's six-year-old daughter Anna. I didn't understand a word that was spoken as people conversed all around us, and I felt a pressing need to learn a few German phrases quickly. Until then, little Anna, who was bilingual, cheerfully translated some of the conversations for me as we walked along.

While I was looking at some clothing with Daniella, I felt a tug on my arm. "She needs to get by us. She is saying 'pardon me' in German," little Anna explained. An employee of the Real was pushing a rack of clothing down the aisle in our direction.

"Oh, excuse me!" I said, and quickly jumped out of the way. Realizing that I had spoken in English, and not knowing if she understood me, I just smiled at her and hurried on. Perhaps Anna was available for tutoring!

We headed into the grocery section, and Daniella began checking her list. In the baking aisle she seemed undecided on which cake mix to choose and asked, "What kind of cake do you like?"

"Well, chocolate's my favorite," I answered, wondering how to say that in German. "With chocolate icing!" As if my preference was the deciding factor, she chose a box of chocolate cake mix and tossed it in the cart. While we shopped I looked at the pictures on the cake box and was able to decipher some of the ingredients. The directions on how to bake the cake, however, were another story entirely! Would I ever be able to have a simple conversation in this new language?

We finished up our shopping trip with a stop at the local grocery store. Shopping there was an enjoyable, new experience for me. There weren't any traditional aisles like grocery stores in the States. Goods were left in crates and boxes and placed in a couple of rows in the small store. Milk was sold in small, easily recycled cardboard containers because the German people recycled as much as possible. After picking up a few items, Daniella went outside to a garden where the flowers and plants were displayed and selected two green plants to complete her shopping.

"I need some plants for the apartment," I told her, "but I wasn't sure where to buy them. They don't have them on base."

"You can find plants lots of places," she said, "but this store has a very nice selection."

I knew Michael would get a kick out of the local flavor

and unique layout of the little store, and since I hadn't taken much money with me that day, I made a note of how to find it again. My birthday was the following week, and I hoped Michael and I could come back then. As it turned out, our husbands had field training for several days, and Michael would completely miss my birthday.

My feelings of being homesick and lonely became more intense as I mentally prepared myself for my first birthday alone in a strange country. Military families are a tight-knit community. We rely on and watch out for one another, and we share the joys, and sometimes the sadness, of having a member of the family on active duty. I knew I would come to depend on that camaraderie as I got to know more wives and my circle of friends grew, but for now I reminded myself to be thankful that Michael and I were together. This was not the last celebration or holiday that Michael may miss; there were likely to be many during his service.

The day of my birthday arrived, and I went about the routine of a normal day. My mood was somber until, to my surprise, Daniella appeared at my door. Apparently, the intelligence-gathering ability of our little community in Babenhausen is quite good. During the cookout, Michael had mentioned he would miss my birthday and that I had wanted to get some plants to liven up the apartment. Lo and behold, here was Daniella, laden with gifts—the plants she had purchased at the little grocery store and a homemade chocolate cake!

Staci Mauney

Reprinted by permission of Mark Parisi © 2006.

Back in the Day . . .

Married couples who love each other tell each other a thousand things without talking.

CHINESE PROVERB

My dad was a traveling salesman and on the road three weeks out of four. He'd come home for weekends, in time to save Mom from cabin fever and to drive us to the supermarket for our weekly shop. On Friday nights we kids would scarf our dinner down and plaster our faces to the front window waiting for Dad's headlights to appear up the street.

Mom would start early in the day to get ready. She'd put on silk stockings—the real kind—and straighten their seams with spit-slicked fingers. She'd slide bobby pins out of her jet black hair and comb kiss-curls into a fashionable fringe. I loved watching her—the careful way she applied bright red lipstick, the smear of color powdered across her cheeks, the way she used the rim of a teaspoon to curl her eyelashes. I couldn't wait to grow up and fancy myself like that.

Dad would arrive home with a week's worth of dust and laundry. He didn't seem as keen on the shopping adventure as the rest of us as we'd pile into the car like children bent on the circus. He and Mom would exchange glances and kisses, and we'd head off to the store. Dad would doze in the car, fedora propped on his nose.

In retrospect, we probably looked like a bunch of bumpkins even back in 1959. My brother and sister and I found the automatic doors leading in and out of the supermarket magical, and sometimes got several laps of the circle completed before Mom settled the baby into a buggy and collected us. We'd follow her like a column of reprimanded ducklings, keeping our hands to ourselves and our voices down—our enthusiasm harnessed to a shiver.

We'd be especially good if Gramma was in town for a visit. She'd arrive on the Greyhound, bluish French roll, sensible black pumps and a secret stash of money that she kept hidden in a little white bag pinned inside her brassiere. We could always count on Gramma to dig into the little bag before we'd go to the store. We'd buzz with the anticipation of chocolate Puff cookies or sponge toffee and were never disappointed.

In those days we mainly shopped for staples—puffed wheat, peanut butter, laundry detergent with free towels hidden in the powder. Perishable items were delivered directly to the house. The milkman brought dairy goods to our back door several days a week. The clink of bottles in the chute would cause a stir in the kitchen, and we'd rush to the porch with our last-minute requests. The milkman wore a metal coin belt around his waist and could make perfect change without looking down. A couple of times a week, the bread man would rumble down the street. Mom would walk to the curb with her order and cash in hand. Sometimes he'd dish out day-old donuts to grubby-faced children. The Watkins man sold spices door-to-door from a black suitcase. The Fuller Brush man peddled a variety of products from his black bag.

It was a friendly way to shop; Mom was on a first-name basis with most everyone. The cashiers at the store made small talk while they processed our groceries. They were interested in the weirdest stuff—what recipe Mom was whipping up for Sunday dinner or what the weather might be like for the weekend. They'd always ask the questions with a smile on their faces and a genuine interest in the answer. They handled the most personal items with enviable nonchalance. Boxes of feminine hygiene products were bagged before they reached the bag boy.

Dad had an uncanny knack of appearing at the cash register just in time to pay the bill. I guess he was peaking from under his fedora while we thought he slept. When we got home, he would carry the paper bags into the house four at a time. He'd head back to the car for the baby and the kid who was pretending to sleep. He nestled the baby safely on one arm and flung the mock sleeper over his other shoulder like a sack of potatoes. The sleeper invariably giggled all the way inside and always woke up just as Mom pulled off his or her shoes and tried to tuck the pretender into bed.

Thinking back on those days, I realize that our grocery shopping adventures were some of the highlights of my childhood. They were family time when family time was scarce. They were also the prelude to whatever the weekend held for Mom and Dad. For years I thought the silk stockings and dolling up my mother used to do was for the benefit of the people at the store—I know better now.

Elva Stoelers

The Gift

Too many people spend money they haven't earned,
to buy things they don't want, to impress people
they don't like.

WILL ROGERS

For months I had been saving and stashing as many
ones, quarters and dimes as I could. Back then, money
was tight and times were hard. With just three shopping
days left until Christmas, I spilled it all out onto my bed,
sorted and counted it. With a total of twenty-nine dollars
and seventy-five cents in my pocket, I grabbed my coat
and car keys and headed out.

My husband and two children were totally enthralled in
A Charlie Brown Christmas and a giant bowl of popcorn, so I
knew I had a good couple of hours before anyone really
missed me.

With my little pocket calculator in one hand and my
short list in the other, I pushed my shopping cart up and
down the aisles, hoping to find the perfect presents for a
seven-year-old daughter and five-year-old son. With a
little luck maybe I could pick up a little something for

some other family members, too.

The sounds of Christmas came from everywhere. The pre-decorated Christmas trees and the life-size, animated Santas all played different tunes yet blended beautifully with the music coming from the ceiling. I remember "Deck the Halls" played as I swung around into an aisle of cookware. There, just a few feet ahead of me, lay something on the floor. I reached down and picked up two neatly folded, very crisp twenty-dollar bills.

Then, within seconds, they appeared—the one miniature me, in an angel costume, just above me on my right, and the other miniature me, in a red devil suit, just above me on my left.

Of course, Little Red in a snotty kid's voice spoke first, "Finder's keepers, loser's weepers."

Then came the sound of Little Cherub's harp. Her tiny fingers strummed the tiny strings of the golden instrument she held in her arm. "I wonder who left it," she softly sang.

"Left it?" Little Red interrupted. "Some dumb fool was careless enough to lose it."

Well, I wasn't about to stand there all day listening to the two of them. "Be gone, both of you," I said, and headed to the service counter to turn in the money.

Taking my name and number, the nice woman assured me that if the money wasn't claimed within a certain amount of time, they would notify me, and it would then be mine to keep. And that was that. Happy with myself, I continued with my shopping.

By mid-afternoon, I had returned home. Of the six K-mart bags, I left four in the trunk and carried two into the house. As I walked through the door, my daughter came running to me. I handed her one bag and whispered, "Quick, put this in your room before your dad sees it."

She knew right away it was a Christmas present from her and her brother for Daddy. She returned with a big grin and sat with me at the table. As I showed her what was in the other bag, gifts for her grandparents, I told her about the money I had found and turned in.

"How come you turned it in, Mom?"

Wanting to teach her a lesson in life, I said, "I just felt it was the right thing to do."

She looked at me for the longest time.

I smiled and said, "God will reward me some day for being an honest person."

Finally, she spoke, "Well, maybe he has, Mommy."

After Christmas, curiousity got the better of me, and I called the store. Shortly after I turned the money in, it was reclaimed by a slightly frazzled, greatly relieved and very grateful fellow Christmas shopper.

Norah Griggs

KEEPING IT STRAIGHT
Tuck a list of birthdays, special occasions and people on your holiday gift list in your purse. When you find a good deal, check it off the list. This spreads spending over the year and helps you stay organized.

Sweet Shoppe

It is vital that people "count their blessings" to appreciate what they possess without having to undergo its actual loss.

ABRAHAM MASLOW

"Where are we going, Mommy?" Adrienne would ask. The answer was usually the same, "We're going shopping, honey."

My three kids and I spent most Saturday nights in the mall when they were young. Our finances were tight, and sometimes extra money was at a premium, but shopping was our escape. We could deal with our life during the week when we were busy, but come Saturday night we were face-to-face with reality.

Psychologists say there's an elevation of mood, a touch of serenity for some when they are buying or acquiring things. I wanted my children and I to have that feeling after my husband, their father, had recently died. It had been a long, lingering death that took its toll on the entire family. We needed to feel better, so we used shopping trips together as an outlet for our grief. That may sound strange to some, and even though we did more window-shopping than buying, it worked for us. With the bright lights and other people at the mall intent on their own needs and desires, we could fit right in. No one knew that we were grieving. We were just shoppers, like everyone else.

A SWEET IDEA

An eco-minded candy lover came up with an idea for handbags made from recycled candy wrappers. Not only are they cute, practical and ecologically friendly, but the manufacturer plants a tree for every bag purchased. www.ecoist.com

Our treat on each outing was a trip to a candy shop. Most often it was one where the kids could choose their favorite candy—gummy bears, Swedish fish or Good & Plenty. Occasionally, when I knew that their loss was affecting them more deeply, we'd go to the candy counter at the upscale department store where each of the kids would choose one lovely piece of gourmet chocolate. We would linger over the glass-fronted counter, looking at each beautifully made confection. The kids would make a different selection each time, but mine was always a dark, dark chocolate shell, filled with more dark, creamy chocolate. The aroma, texture and taste of the chocolate transported us. It always put us in a better mood, and as I discovered recently, I was making good memories for my children.

A bit of sugared candy or bite of chocolate wasn't much, but it satisfied a need. Our need to buy something? No. Our need to be together—our need for something sweet in our life.

Patricia Carroll Johnson

I keep my friends as misers do their treasures,
because, of all things granted us by wisdom, none
is greater or better than friendship.

PIETRO ARETINO

I cradled the green and gold sugar bowl in my hand.
$150. Did that include the lid? I was afraid to look.
Carefully, I set the bowl down on the display table in the
Fine China and Gifts department. I knew the rules.
Wedding gifts were supposed to be beautiful and perma-
nent. I looked at the other items on the list and sighed.
Crystal vases, silverware, engraved picture frames.
Nothing felt right. Erin would be walking down the aisle
in just two weeks, and I still hadn't found the perfect wed-
ding gift.

Walking around the department, I remembered how I
met my best friend. One spring day when I was about
seven or eight, Erin knocked on my family's door and
attempted to sell my mom some Girl Scout cookies. We
were friends instantly and not just because we were both
Girl Scouts. I impressed her by being able to read her

secret messages without the special decoder ring. She impressed me by owning a secret decoder ring.

Growing up in the same neighborhood, we put on plays for our parents, transforming towels into magic carpets, bullfighter capes and wedding veils. Voracious readers, we sometimes bent our heads over the same book for hours, limiting our conversation to "Ready to turn the page?" Other times, we'd play cards or board games, at first by the rules, and then coming up with our own elaborate variations. As teenagers, we cooked vegetarian meals while discussing the boys at school and their mysterious actions that week.

Examining a large silver tray, I thought about how Erin's life was going to change. I liked her fiancé, Dan; he seemed just right for her. I pictured the newlyweds laughing and washing dishes together in the kitchen of their new, still imaginary house. Setting the tray down, I suddenly realized why these fancy gifts felt wrong. For more than ten years, roughly half our lives at that point, Erin and I were part of each other's daily existence, sleeping over at each other's houses, eating meals together, camping and vacationing together. These wedding gifts felt like special-occasions-only objects that would remain in back cupboards, patiently waiting to be dusted and polished and admired. Erin and I didn't have a special-occasions-only friendship, so why should I feel compelled to buy a special-occasions-only wedding gift? Puzzles and games and drama. Those were the things that bound us in childhood. Why should it be any different now?

Leaving the world of Fine China and Gifts behind, I strode purposely over to housewares where I picked up some kitchen towels, a milk bottle, cutting board and other items. Back at my apartment, I spread out these ordinary objects and started writing a short play about Erin and Dan in their new life together.

ERIN and DAN are cooking dinner together in their new house.
ERIN: I'll start chopping the onion for the stir fry. Would you hand me (gift A)?
DAN: Here you go, sweetie. [DAN hands ERIN gift A.] How was school today? Are the kids enjoying that book you assigned? [DAN washes his hands and wipes them on gift B.]

And so it went. As I labeled and wrapped the gifts, I hoped that the couple would enjoy them together. Standing in line at the post office later that week, I began having second thoughts. Erin and I lived more than 1,000 miles apart now in our post-college lives. We didn't talk or write often, though when we did it seemed almost like old times. Still, maybe Erin had changed more than I realized. *Would she think that my wedding gift was silly? Would she be disappointed? Or would she understand how important our friendship was to me?*

Two weeks later at the wedding, I learned the answer. Standing in a beautiful California courtyard in the late afternoon sun, I chatted with the other guests before the ceremony. As I shook hands with Erin's former college roommates and other guests, almost everyone said the exact same thing when they heard my name.

"Oh, you sent the gift that made Erin cry!"

I didn't know how to respond to that. My best friend was getting married, and I was there to help her celebrate. I felt a little like crying myself.

Michelle Mach

Budget permitting, have some fun and get creative with those traditional anniversary gifts . . .

Anniversary	Tradition Says	Other than the Obvious, How About . . . ?
1	Paper	Adult board games; an oragami kit; something handmade in paper maché
2	Cotton	Cotton candy; customized T-shirts; a rabbit (for the animal lover)
3	Leather	Pair a vest with gloves and a (toy) Harley-Davidson
4	Silk/flowers	An assortment of seeds to plant; a beautiful silk scarf framed for wall art
5	Wood	A wood (the golf club); plant a tree in your loved one's name (*www.treegivers.com*) in your backyard
6	Iron	An iron (again, the golf club); a pair of horseshoes for good luck
7	Wool	Plan a trip to Taos, New Mexico, during their annual wool festival.
8	Bronze	Tanning lotion and tickets to a sunny getaway; a Bronze Cory for the fish lover
9	Pottery	A piece of Raku pottery, or a vacation including the Raku Museum in Kyoto, Japan
10	Tin	Spend a week in Nashville, Tennessee, during the annual Tin Pan South Songwriters Festival
11	Steel	*Steel Magnolias* (DVD); Danielle Steel novels; a Hawaiian Steel guitar for the musically inclined
12	Linen	Mini-vacation in New Orleans the first (or second) Saturday of August for White (or Dirty) Linen Night
13	Lace	A lace wedding veil for her to wear when renewing your vows
14	Ivory	Piano lessons (or a piano!); white roses; a trip to the Ivory Coast
15	Crystal	Billy Crystal *City Slickers* DVD accompanied by tickets to a dude ranch
20	China	Customized fortune cookies announcing something special (maybe a trip to the Great Wall of China!)
25	Silver	A piece of jewelry fashioned from silver coins from your wedding year
30	Pearl	A dream trip to Hawaii (Pearl Harbor); dinner at your favorite oyster bar
35	Coral	Snorkel a coral reef in the Florida Keys or Great Barrier Reef in Australia
40	Ruby	Red wine and ruby red roses
45	Sapphire	Vacation at Sapphire Valley Ski Resort in North Carolina or the Sapphire Coast in Australia
50	Gold	Golden Oldies CDs of your favorite music throughout the years
55	Emerald	Trip to the Emerald Isle (Ireland)
60	Diamond	Neil Diamond or Diamond Rio CD (after all, if you've been married sixty years, what more could you want?)

chapter 2

The Quest for a Bargain

I take him shopping with me.
I say, "Okay, Jesus, help
me find a bargain."

TAMMY FAYE BAKER

Electric Blue

People shop for a bathing suit with more care than they do a husband or wife. The rules are the same. Look for something you'll feel comfortable wearing. Allow for room to grow.

ERMA BOMBECK

L et's go to the beach this weekend!" Lynne said.

"Yeah, the weather is going to be perfect," added Colleen. "We'll bring the boyfriends along to carry the beach chairs and umbrellas," she giggled.

"I'm not sure," I said.

"Why not?" they asked in unison.

"I might be babysitting for the Edwards this weekend."

My friends had no idea I dreaded summer. While they wore teeny-weeny bikinis, looking sleek and tan, I had to wear an old-lady one-piece. I longed to be able to slip into a hot pink or lime green bikini with tiny strings that fastened around the neck.

But there was no way I would ever be able to wear a

bikini. A surgery at infancy left me with a horrid, jagged scar that ran from just under my right breast down to my navel. I felt like I had a deformity or a disability. I never told anyone how much it bothered me. In fact, most of my friends weren't even aware I had the scar. In the locker room before gym class, I was in my uniform before the other girls even got there. At sleepovers, I managed to get my pajamas on without being seen.

Shopping for bathing suits was torture. I could never find anything I liked, except for the time I came across one of those racy new one-pieces that had netting between the top and the bottom. I snatched it off the rack. It was almost as good as a bikini! I rushed into the fitting room, anxious to see how this beauty would look on me. I slipped into it and gazed into the mirror. My scar was clearly visible through the fine fabric! Disappointed, I slapped it back on the hanger and left the mall without a suit.

Every summer it was the same story. I'd watch my girl-friends head down to the water in their cool new bikinis. I wanted so much to be like them, but I was always the one who trailed behind as they pranced through the hot sand to find just the right spot on the beach, right where all the boys could see us. Only they'd never look at me— not in my hideous suit that looked like something my mom or one of her friends would wear. At least that's how it seemed to me.

With a discouraged spirit, I headed off to the mall in search of a bathing suit for this weekend's trip to the beach. If I went at all, I would probably wind up with some athletic-looking number in black or navy blue. That was my defense. I was on the swimming and diving teams. So when my friends would ask, "Sue, why don't you ever get a bikini?" my pat answer was, "I'm the athletic type, that's all."

Now, searching desperately through the predictable selection of one-pieces, I felt that same sinking feeling I got every summer. I gazed longingly at the display of bikinis that were so much sexier and fun. Maybe I'd just make up another excuse and skip the beach this weekend. I didn't know if I could stand watching them all slathering Coppertone on their flat abs as I sat there feeling like an oddball.

I yanked hanger after hanger, seeing nothing I liked. I combed rack after rack. There had to be something. *Please let me find a suit I can feel good in.*

But no, there was nothing but the same old, tired suits. Might as well wear my suit from last year. I was just about to leave the store when I noticed another rack off to the side, closer to the lingerie department. Funny, I hadn't seen it earlier. I flicked through the selection listlessly, when all of a sudden my heart started pounding. There it was! The suit! My suit! Not black and not old lady.

It was electric blue with a sexy, little zipper at the bust line, and the sides were open so I could reveal some skin. Oh, my gosh, this was incredible! I looked at the tag; it was in my size. With trembling hands, I took the hanger from the rack and headed to the dressing rooms. *Please let it fit. Please let my scar not show.*

MAKING A SPLASH

Swimsuits don't run true to size, so forget the tag size. Try it on! What you'll be doing in the suit should determine what type you buy. It needs to be comfortable and fit without pulling or stretching.

I put on the suit and faced the mirror. I held my breath and kept my eyes closed for several seconds, afraid to even hope it would look good. I tentatively opened one eye, then the other. It looked incredible! It fit as if it were custom-made for me. The zipper added just the right touch of sizzle, and the cut-outs on the side were not only sexy, they stopped well before my scar, so that even if I reached or stretched it didn't show.

I smiled. I made sultry kissy faces in the mirror. I posed as if I were on a photo shoot, and hammed it up good. I felt on top of the world. The suit was expensive, but I didn't care. I would happily pay any price. I blessed the designer as I shelled out the money at the cash register. I beamed at the girl behind the counter and grabbed the bag, clutching it to my chest.

That weekend, as I took off my beach wrap to reveal my new suit, my boyfriend let out a low whistle. I slathered Coppertone on my exposed sides.

"Awesome suit!" Colleen said.

"Guess you're not into the athletic look anymore, huh Sue?" Lynne asked.

"Nope, I'll save the athletic look for team practice from now on. This is the new Sue."

No more bringing up the rear for me. I pranced down to the water and left my friends to follow.

Susan A. Karas

The Power of Being Dishy

The truly important things in life—love, beauty, and one's own uniqueness—are constantly being overlooked.

PABLO CASALS

I was in a dress store making my first foray at mother-of-the-groom dresses. My son propelled me into this category by announcing he was getting married this year. I was delighted to hear the news. I love his fiancée and see a great future for them. My husband and I even get along well with her parents and the rest of her family.

With a late winter wedding in mind, I started to browse in the specialty shops for styles that would be pretty and appropriate for my fifty-six years and my new role. I had no intention of buying anything until three or four months down the road. After all, the bride-to-be hadn't yet bought her gown. Knowing that I wasn't buying freed me to try on whatever caught my eye.

All that was forgotten when I tried on "The Dress." Why this one called to me, at this time in my life, I'll never know. It was strapless, with a beaded bodice and a long, softly flowing skirt. I thought I looked good in it in the dressing room, but I have been known to pick out clothes that were less than flattering. I tend toward folksy styles with so much material that my thin, five-foot-two frame sometimes gets lost. When I came out to show the salesperson, however, I knew it was right. There were eight people in the shop, and eight pairs of eyes lit up. Nine, if you counted mine.

I had never worn a strapless dress before. I never thought I could carry it off. I was carrying this dress like I was born to wear it.

"That dress looks great on you," said one of the other customers. "You have the shoulders for it."

My trainer at the gym would be happy to hear it.

An older gentleman who was waiting sleepily in a chair while his wife tried on one dress after another was suddenly alert. He didn't say a word, but he didn't have to. I could tell I looked sexy. I felt sexy. His wife was trying on a more traditional-style dress and jacket, more like what I had expected to look at, and for a moment, I had a twinge of doubt. She was older by a good fifteen years, but we had the same amount of gray hair. Did I look foolish? She looked at me with an appraising look and smiled. I smiled shyly back in appreciation.

"This dress fits you like a glove," said the salesperson. "Usually we have to take in a few tucks here and there, but not this time."

I preened in front of the three-way mirror a little while longer before deciding to buy the dress. How could I not? One doesn't turn down Cinderella's gown. I walked out of the shop feeling like royalty.

At home I tried on the dress for my husband and got the same lit-up reaction.

"You look dishy," he said.

I laughed at the old-fashioned compliment and immediately became nervous. Was it okay for me to look dishy? Would it embarrass my son? Would it embarrass me? Was someone in her late fifties supposed to look that way? And why did it feel so good?

I didn't think of myself as dishy as a teenager. My hair was too straight, my body too skinny and flat. I remember wishing that I would be sexy, but when I developed curves, they seemed foreign so I covered them up. That did nothing to enhance my appeal. I was smart, but didn't see the desirability of that at the time. Later on, I worked at being professional and efficient as a girl maturing during the feminist revolution would.

> **DRESS CODE**
>
> *Formal* or *white-tie* means tailcoats for men and full-length evening dresses for women.
>
> *Semi-formal* usually means black tie for men (evening jacket and tie) and a dress for women.

And here I was, lapping up the admiring stares. I was glowing. But it was more about sensuality than sexuality. I didn't really care what was going through other people's heads when they saw me in the dress, though it was amusing to think that I might be prompting some lascivious thoughts. I just knew that I felt fluid and graceful. I wasn't trying to return to my youth, an impossibility after two children and thirty-seven years of marriage. It wasn't necessary anyway.

Dishy-ness is not a function of youth. I have a friend who is closer to seventy than fifty, who has people of various ages flocking around her with that light in their eyes. She recognized her sensuality all along while I played hide-and-seek for five decades before finding it.

To my surprise, I enjoyed being dishy. This new perception of myself was fun. There was energy here, a power I now understood. I started carrying myself differently. I walked taller and easier with the confidence of someone who has been a dish all of her life. The dress helped me claim the sensuality that I owned but never accepted. I knew I would look smashing. I was going to have a wonderful time at the wedding, too busy dancing to worry about my son, whose attention would be focused on his beautiful new wife anyway.

Ferida Wolff

Buy,
Buy Love

Dogs are not our whole life, but they make our lives whole.

ROGER CARAS

We'd been happily married for five years and living in Arizona for as long. We left two adult children and three grandchildren in New Jersey. Arnold taught high-school English, and I was writing my first book. We spent our free time exploring our new home state. Sometimes I did marathons at the keyboard, leaving him alone in the evenings. Once, he casually asked if I'd like to have a pet, adding, ". . . it could keep me company while you're writing and I'm watching TV all by myself." I got the hint.

We had passed the pet store many times during our exercise walks at the mall on Sunday mornings—that's where he got the idea. Then one day, like heat-seeking missiles zeroing in on their target, my speed-shopping eyes locked onto a puppy in the window. I felt a tug somewhere between my neck and my heart.

"What kind of dog is that?"

"An Italian Greyhound. Do you want to hold him?"

"No, no. I'd better not."

Thinking of myself as a wise consumer, I spent the rest of that day researching Italian Greyhounds on the Internet. "Look, Arnold, they've been bred to be companions! What do you think?"

"Sure."

"Let's find out a little more first."

By Thursday, we were experts on buying "Iggies." We learned to be aware of puppy mills and backyard breeders, so we didn't respond to newspaper ads—until we found out the local breeders had no puppies available.

"I'm just going to call to see what they say."

". . . What'd they say?"

"They have two puppies left, a boy and a girl. Someone just called about the boy. He thinks they'll both be gone by Saturday."

"Let's go!"

Arnold picked up the seal-colored, four-pound, wiggly, squirmy bundle of love-for-sale. They kissed and kissed. She was so excited, she pooped on his shirt! He didn't mind! Love cancelled out our consumer education.

"This is the one!"

"Do you want to take her now?"

"We don't have anything for her! We need to buy food, toys, a bed . . ."

"Okay, you can pick her up tomorrow morning."

Neither of us had been to a pet-store in over twenty years. We walked into one of those big pet-supply warehouses and gasped. Aisles and aisles of stuff, stacked all the way up to the ceiling! They even had shopping carts! Guided by our carefully prepared list of everything-you-need-to-bring-a-new-puppy-home, we shopped. It was like an episode of *Supermarket Sweep*. We whizzed up and down every aisle, stuffing things into our cart: food, treats, dishes, place mats, a bed, toys, a kennel, a crate, a gate, a collar, an ID tag, a leash, more toys.

At home, we rearranged our furniture and set up a doggy area in the kitchen. Then we set the alarm for 6 A.M.

On Saturday, December 20, 2003, we brought Cameo home in the finest crate, cushioned with the perfect washable, absorbent lining. The seller said, "We could have put her in a cardboard box for you." Unthinkable!

Four hours later, we took her to the vet for her first checkup. We bought special shampoo and special ear cleanser—only the finest would do.

Cameo didn't like vinyl or rubber toys, so she yanked on her little bed—four times her size—flipped it over in the family room and gnawed the foam out of it. We went shopping. We bought soft toys—and a new bed. While we were shopping, we bought another collar. Later, we bought pretty collars—in different colors for the different seasons. Then we bought holiday-themed collars.

We needed to take pictures of our puppy to share with friends and family—pictures we could post on Web sites. We went shopping. We bought a digital camera.

At four months old, Cameo went on a hunger strike. We bought every brand of dry food. She wouldn't eat. We bought every brand of wet food. She wouldn't eat. Then we bought gourmet dog food. Still not good enough. Finally, we went to the supermarket. We bought steak, chicken, turkey and ground beef. Once her food smelled and tasted like ours, she began eating again.

Cameo didn't like sleeping all alone in her crate. Like Goldilocks, she thought our bed was just right. But there wasn't enough room for the three of us, so we went shopping. We bought a king-size bed, king-size sheets, blankets and a bedspread.

It was winter, and her short fur didn't keep her warm enough. She needed jammies. We went shopping, but nothing fit. Italian Greyhounds are unevenly shaped—large chests on small, slender bodies. So we bought fabric to make custom jammies—and a sewing machine.

Cameo grew. We went shopping. Bigger crates, bigger dishes, bigger collars, bigger toys, more material for bigger jammies.

We took her everywhere. We'd put her in shopping carts, but her little paws kept falling through the openings. We went shopping. We bought a pad to line the bottoms of shopping carts.

When spring arrived, we took her to outdoor fairs, but there were no shopping carts. We went shopping. We bought a doggy stroller.

She loved to sunbathe, but she didn't like lying on the ground. We went shopping. A simple hammock wouldn't do—her elevated cot had to have sides for snuggling.

Before we took Cameo to New Jersey to meet the rest of the family, we went shopping. We bought an airline-approved carrying bag (none of our crates or strollers would do). We bought a plane ticket so she could ride in coach with us. We bought medicine to tranquilize her during the flight.

We only buy replacement items now—unless we see a great new, soft toy. The Beatles were wrong when they said you can't buy love; we know that now. But here's something we didn't know: Once you buy love, you may find yourself singing to an Everly Brothers tune:

Buy, buy love,
Buy, buy happiness,
I'm so penniless,
I think I'm-a gonna cry.

Marilyn Haight

Reprinted by permission of Mark Parisi © 2006.

Nothing at All

Too many people miss the silver lining because they're expecting gold.

MAURICE SETTER

I averted my eyes as he approached us. He wore a thin, white-cotton undershirt, baggy chinos riding low on his hips, and a bandana wrapped around his head. I'd seen his kind before, hanging out on street corners, smoking and harassing passersby. The way he swaggered down the supermarket aisle made me feel as if Mom and I had invaded gang territory.

I wished I'd let Mom stay in the car like she'd wanted. "Come with me," I'd urged. "The exercise will be good for you." She'd given me one of her looks, the same one I give to the aerobics instructor when she insists on ten more crunches. Mom had relented with a sigh.

We crept along, I taking one step for Mom's two, as she slowly pushed her walker, just like she'd been taught in therapy: push walker, left foot step, right foot step, push walker, left foot step, right foot step, each move deliberate and calculated.

I gently guided Mom to the edge of the aisle, keeping one eye on the tote bag that hung from the walker's crossbar, the other on the punk who was now throwing furtive glances our way. When he wandered to our side of the aisle, I stepped between my mother and him, feigning interest in a jumbo box of oat bran. Mom was oblivious to him, concentrating on each step, then stopping to scan the shelves.

"Where are the . . ." She looked at me, frowning as she tried to conjure the word from her stroke-afflicted brain.

SHELVING STRATEGY
A great deal of planning goes into where things are located in the supermarket. The most expensive brands are usually at eye level, so look for the best prices on the top and bottom shelves.

I usually helped her try to find the word, but this time I just filled in the gap. "Nuts."

"What?" Mom was deaf in her left ear.

"Nuts," I almost shouted.

The words came out slowly but just as loud as mine. "Where . . . are . . . the . . . nuts?" she said, as if reciting a speech lesson.

"I don't know, Mom. We'll just have to keep looking."

Mom stopped walking and sighed as if she'd just hiked a hundred miles, and maybe in her world, she had. "I'm tired."

I glanced at the punk; he was now slouching toward us.

"Uh, I can get them for you," he mumbled.

I eyed him warily, not sure I'd heard correctly. "Excuse me?"

"The nuts. They're over on the other side of the store." He looked at my mom. "I can get them for you." He grinned awkwardly, and then hiked up his pants. "What kind do you want?"

Mom smiled at this child-knight in untied high-tops,

who had rescued her from a trek across the market, "That's
. . . so . . . nice," she said.

The fluorescent lights seemed to be unusually bright; I
swallowed hard and blinked. I wanted to tell this young
man how much I appreciated his kindness; I wanted to tell
him how proud his mother must be; I wanted to apologize.

Instead, I just smiled and said, "Mixed nuts in the can,
lightly salted."

"Do you need anything else?"

"No," I said, fighting the urge to pull the bandana from
his head and tousle his hair. "Nothing, nothing at all."

Renee Holland Davidson

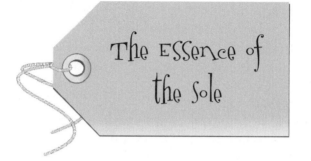

The Essence of the Sole

Why let life step all over you? Put on your biggest
smile and do a little shoe shopping.

JENNY SCOTT

Surrounded by stacks of shoes, I stood at the counter of
the quaint boutique, tapping my fuchsia-toed stockinged
foot. I was three thousand miles from home, yet only one
thought scampered through my mind: *I just have to have
them.* The woman returned empty-handed. My eyes
widened. "Our man only has 37½," she explained. "Shall I
bring those on out?"

"That should be fine," I reassured.

Waiting for her to return, I stared at the brown-suede
boot on the display shelf. Falling several inches below the
knee, it was delicately detailed with wrapped lace. Faux
fur trim subtly hid the inward zip closure. The interior was
softly lined, completely cushioned. Comfort and allure.

"Aye, here we are." She held out the beloved box, and I
didn't waste a moment tearing it open, pulling the stuffing
out of the toes, and sliding the boots onto my feet. I ostenta-
tiously gaited around the little shop, examining my footwear

in the floor mirrors. A bit big, but otherwise perfect. Before the woman finished saying, "Thanks a million," I sashayed out of the shop wearing my purchase and dumped my grubby, aged sneakers into a trash can on the streets of the Irish city.

It was my junior year of college, and I was studying abroad in the effervescent city of Galway, Ireland. As in any cultural metropolis, Galway offers a wealth of shops: bookstores, souvenir shops, Irish sweater/jersey depots, Irish department stores and mall complexes. Just like any girl would be, I was in seventh heaven. On my first day there, I was already imagining my new wardrobe of European styles and trends. On my second day there, I ventured into the city, wandering and exploring, mentally marking which shops to return to. On my third day there, I found the brown-suede boots.

In the days to come, in addition to making numerous other purchases, I traveled all over the country, wearing those brown-suede boots. I wore them climbing the Cliffs of Moher. I wore them on every Eireann bus that I hopped on and off of. I wore them hiking through midlands in the pouring, wintry rain, when I climbed to the top of Guinness Factory and when I visited my long-lost grandmother's grave.

Those brown-suede boots didn't just traverse Ireland. As I toured the Louvre, freefell through the Swiss Alps,

THE BOTTOM LINE
A VAT tax is included in the retail prices of most goods and services in Europe. It averages 16 to 20 percent, depending on the country. Some items, such as food, medicine, books and children's clothing, enjoy a reduced rate in certain countries.

strolled through the German marketplace, climbed to the top of St. Peter's Cupola and danced the night away, I wore those brown-suede boots. They were reliable, comfortable and ideal for any situation—secure for travel and physical activity, yet sophisticated enough for a day on the town.

Not only can I track every European place I've been to with those shoes, but I can trace the lessons I learned throughout my experience back to those brown-suede boots. I learned a deeper meaning of friendship than I've ever known when I brought Thanksgiving to my Irish friends. I was wearing the boots as I scurried around my house cleaning for company while cooking a turkey for the first time. I learned how utterly heartbreaking and unfair life can be when I was informed that one of my family members tragically died. I was wearing the boots when I received the life-shattering phone call from across the ocean. I learned the intense, overwhelming nature of love when I fell for an Irish lad. I was wearing the boots as we walked along the pier and stared into each other's dark eyes.

When I bought those brown-suede boots, I just had to have them. I loved their comfort; I loved their allure, so I tossed out my old treads and decided to fashion the new ones. However, I didn't know that those boots would be protecting my feet through all I saw, heard and felt during my overseas experience. I didn't know that as I felt my outlook on my life, my culture and myself changing, my brown-suede boots would remain constant. I didn't know those boots would be a part of my memories, memories that will last forever.

I still own those brown-suede boots. Sometimes I slip them on and whirl around my room, pretending I'm dancing through Europe. Sometimes I just stare at the sole, ripped from the wear and tear, and reminisce, awing myself with all I've seen, all I've felt, all I've done. I had no idea that my brown-suede boots would evoke so many emotions, memories and images.

You see, shoes are more than just a piece of footwear—they are a companion. At first, the friendship might be a little awkward, as you are breaking in the sole, but before long, the shoes become a part of you, going everywhere you do—whether just to the supermarket or across the world. And in the end, just like every shopper, every shoe holds a story, and every sole holds an essence.

Eileen Rafferty

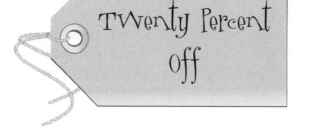

Great opportunities to help others seldom come, but small ones surround us every day.

SALLY KOCH

*C*limbing from my minivan, I clutched a coupon and patted myself on the back. In just a few minutes, I would be finished with my Christmas shopping a week early and save twenty percent on my last purchase! I slid the side door open, set my purse on the van floor, and unbuckled my 2½-year-old daughter, Abby, from her car seat. We were women on a mission.

Minivans with open sliding doors are like large, cavernous boxed canyons. They're easy to enter and exit when carrying a toddler—well, minivans are, anyway—but the formation can create unusual updrafts of wind. As I slid Abby from her car seat and stepped back from the van door, one of those gusts was born. It impudently yanked the coupon from my hand and sent it skittering under the van, around a neighboring car and across the parking lot. Ever the safety-conscious mother, I quickly slid the van door closed so that Abby wouldn't fall out and set off in pursuit. I couldn't lose twenty percent off!

My parking lot song-and-dance routine would have been the envy of Ginger Rogers and Fred Astaire. Dodging shopping carts, birds and oncoming cars with fancy footwork and a few choice words muttered under my breath, I caught up with the coupon, snatched it back from the wind and triumphantly returned to my vehicle, only to make a shocking discovery: I'd accidentally locked Abby inside!

THE ULTIMATE BARGAIN HUNTER

. . . knows when the local Target, K-Mart and Wal-Mart do their markdowns.

. . . heads straight for the endcaps for the deeply discounted items.

. . . has gifts already purchased and stored away, just in case.

. . . buys the kids clothes that won't fit them for a year.

"Abby, push the button!" I called, gesturing toward the passenger-door lock. She smiled, ate a week-old French fry that she'd found in a sticky cup holder and climbed over the back seat. "Abby! It's cold out here, and Mommy's coat is in the car. Please be a big girl and push the button!" Abby climbed into the driver's seat and pretended to drive.

My feet grew numb. (Who wears tennis shoes in December?) Several shoppers passed me by, some oblivious and others avoiding my gaze, before a friendly woman stopped to help. She offered me her coat and then went into a store to call a locksmith. *What a Good Samaritan*, I thought as I struggled to place her face.

When she returned, she said she'd be glad to keep me company while I waited, and, postponing her own shopping plans, she generously stayed until the van was open and Abby was in my arms. I thanked her again, returned her smile and then, horrified, I realized who my rescuer was: She was the bank loan officer who'd taken my mortgage application the week before! *I'll never get that loan,* I thought. *Banks surely don't lend money to irresponsible people who accidentally lock their children in their cars.*

Discouraged and twenty-five dollars poorer after paying the locksmith, I determined that to salvage the day, I should accomplish my mission and finish my Christmas shopping. With the twenty-percent-off coupon tucked safely in my purse, Abby and I mustered our dignity, threw back our shoulders, and walked into the store to find the sweater we'd originally come to buy. Then we looked at its price tag. It was on sale: twenty-five percent off!

Marti Kramer Suddarth

The Sweater

The eye sees only what the mind is prepared to comprehend.

ROBERTSON DAVIES

A sweater, that's all I was looking for, just one sweater. But after browsing through all my favorite shops and every department store in two towns, I was ready to give up. Nobody had anything remotely like what I was searching for, and I was getting desperate. It's not that I was being overly choosy. I simply knew what I wanted, and I refused to settle for anything less.

It had to be attractive, soft, lightweight and comfortable. Pockets would be nice, and I hoped to find something in off-white or ivory. Ideally, it would be roomy enough to fit over whatever I chose to wear, but not so bulky that it would be overwhelming. And it had to be dressy enough to wear to the funeral home.

My wonderful brother was terminally ill and in his characteristic, tenacious way, was defying the medical profession to the end. Now, it had been days since he'd recognized anyone, and he spent large chunks of his time in an unresponsive state. I knew that he could leave us at any moment. The last thing I felt like doing was more shopping, but I needed that sweater. I owed it to my brother to look as nice as possible when the time came.

One day, my niece joined me at the dining-room table for a snack. Neither of us felt much like eating, but it was comforting just to sit quietly together for a little while. She put her arm around my shoulders and gave me a hug. That was when I noticed what she was wearing: a soft, pretty sweater, as close to perfect as the one I yearned so desperately to find.

"Where did you get that?" I asked. "I've looked everywhere for something similar, and I'm just about ready to give up."

WOMEN'S WARDROBE BASICS

Black skirt, pants, dress, handbag and heels
A tailored, white cotton dress shirt
A pair of jeans
A pair of chinos or khakis
T-shirts in a variety of colors
A pair of tennis shoes
A pair of flats
An all-weather coat

Stroking the sleeve, she said she'd found it in a used-clothing store. The proverbial lightbulb flashed over my head. One of those stores was located not far from where my brother lived, and it was the only place I hadn't looked!

Later that afternoon, my husband, Allen, and I pulled into the parking lot and headed inside the store. It didn't take long to locate the section I needed. Sadly, I touched a gray knitted cardigan. Now that I was here, I didn't even feel like looking.

"How about this one?" Allen asked, showing me a pretty, but weighty-looking crocheted number. Shaking my head, I reached into the densely packed display and pulled out a sleeve that looked promising. It was the color I wanted, so I wrestled the whole thing out from the crowded rack.

The texture was just right, soft as a cloud, and snuggly. A row of pretty, pearly buttons marched down the front. Two pockets, tastefully placed, added to the attraction, and even better, it looked like it would fit. I slipped my arms into the sleeves and gathered it around me. "I think this might be the one," I said to Allen.

I stepped over to check my reflection in the dressing-room mirror. The sweater looked nice, and it fit perfectly. Still, I couldn't quite make up my mind. As I stared into the mirror, I patted my hands over the pockets and felt something small, rectangular and flexible tucked inside one of them. Puzzled, I reached in and pulled out a business card. I turned it over and gasped. Handwritten on the back was a name—mine.

It turned out that my sweater had been patiently waiting for me all that time, with my name stashed away in the pocket so I would recognize it when I found it. All I had to do was a little more shopping.

Anne Culbreath Watkins

A Girdle by Any other Name

Sometimes I can't figure designers out. It's as if they flunked human anatomy.

ERMA BOMBECK

It's nothing new. For hundreds of years, women have sucked in their sagging flab and squished it around to boost something up or flatten something down. As the years passed, I was witness to my own kind of continental drift. Slowly but surely, various body parts shifted southward, and my center mass took on new territories to the east and west. I discovered its full-blown effect while shopping for a dress for an afternoon wedding.

"May I show you something in a sheath?" a sales assistant offered. "Show," uh yeah, nice word choice. Everything showed: saddlebags, poufy tummy and, shall we say, less than perky derriere.

"Don't worry," she said, "we have these wonderful body shapers in Foundations."

"What are you talking about? Are you saying there are fitness trainers in the cosmetics department?" Then all of a sudden, it dawned on me, "You're talking about a girdle, aren't you?"

"We like to call them body shapers in this new millennium," her voice dripped with condescension.

As I rode up the escalator to lingerie, I rehearsed how I'd ask for the "body shaper." Swaggering up to the counter, I sized up the nubile twenty-somethings.

"Girls, I'm looking for a girdle. Call 'em whatever you like, but I need a girdle." Stripped bare in the dressing room, I examined myself from every angle in the three-paneled mirror. How is it possible that I look less lumpy naked than when I'm fully clothed? The salesgirl interrupted my thoughtful moment with a knock and an armload of the newest inventions to lift, separate, smooth and flatten.

"You can start with the tiniest brief and work your way up to the full-body shaper if you need more slimming," she chirped, then disappeared.

Feeling hopeful, I searched for the tiniest brief. "You must've forgotten the 'brief,'" I yelled out. "There's nothing in here that's small and lacking length." I grabbed the thing that was the size of a chair cushion and pulled it on. Aside from not being able to breathe, I realized this was a simple physics lesson. If you squish something here, it will pop out there. Yep, my stomach was definitely flatter, but now there was flab hanging over the top of the elastic, and a new roll had been squeezed out from the bottom, giving me upper thigh flab.

I crammed myself into the next full-legged brief. Why are they still calling these things "briefs"? This lifted my rear and squeezed my thighs smooth, but now my knees bulged. Finally, I tried the full-slip shaper complete with bra, but no matter how I adjusted the straps, the way it fit my shorter-than-five-foot frame made my silhouette resemble a tribal woman with oddly perky breasts popping out at my navel.

"Oh, you might want to try this," the salesgirl advised. "This one's not so tight, and it looks more like bike pants."

Perfect, I thought as I slipped them on. *If I'm in an accident, it'll look like I'm athletic.* Nothing bulged or hung out, and the bonus feature was that I could still breathe. I slid into my elastic-band pants and marched out to pay. As I stood in line, I felt the need to share this rite of passage, so I shouldered up to the woman buying the lacy D-cup bra and thong.

"You know," I said, "it's a lot more fun buying your first bra than it is your first girdle." Fondling her miniscule thong, she turned away—as if buying a girdle might be contagious. Okay, so thong-lady didn't share my moment, but it was no less epiphanous, because in that instant, I finally understood what older women have been talking about for years. They say that as a woman ages, she grows "more comfortable in her own skin." Trust me, it isn't philosophical—it's simply roomier.

Tsgoyna Tanzman

How Do You Size Up?

Int'l Size	0	1	2	3	4	5
Tops	XS	S	M	L	XL	XXL
Pants	2	4	6	8–10	12	14
Dresses	30–32	34–36	38–40	42–44	46–48	50–52

Horse Power-Shopping

My treasures do not clink,
They gleam in the sunlight
And neigh in the night.

ANCIENT BEDOUIN SAYING

When most people think of shopping, they think of clothes, furniture, household items or automobiles. When I think of shopping, I think of horses. I'm not sure if my horse addiction is genetic or acquired, but I've had many horses in my life. I ride and compete long distance, so when the four-year-old horse I was riding in 1994 was diagnosed with juvenile arthritis, I began shopping for a horse that was healthy enough to endure the rigors of long distance. In addition, I wanted a young horse that my grandchildren and riding students would be able to enjoy after he or she retired from competition.

Friends and relatives told me about several horses that I should investigate. The first horse I checked out was one my farrier was shoeing at the time. She was a five-year-old thoroughbred mare, ridden regularly by the owner and had never been raced, so she was injury-free. She was beautiful, but huge—at least sixteen hands and 1,300 pounds—much too big for a distance horse, or me at 5'3" for that matter. I didn't want to hurt the owner's feelings, so I tried her out. She was nice to ride and obedient, but very clumsy and lacking any spirit.

Next came a horse one of my friends told me was a "freebie." This was an Arab that had not yet been ridden. The owner had too many horses and needed to find a home for him. He was a little bay, about fourteen hands, very cute, but looked like he had never seen the farrier and was fat, which can be a precursor to serious health problems.

One of my sisters told me about a little mare, also a cutie, but when we visited the barn, I could see my sister really wanted this mare for herself. While I was waiting for my sister to come back from her ride, I felt eyes following me around the place. I wandered around the barn and discovered they belonged to the sorriest little gray stallion that I have ever seen. He was unkempt with a bloated belly, a long, knotted mane, a mangy coat, discharge oozing out of his eyes, and toes so long he couldn't walk properly. This little guy looked so unloved in contrast to the mare my sister was riding. His only beautiful features were his eyes, and they were pleading with me. When our eyes met, pinpricks of energy went up my spine.

Questioning the owner, I discovered he was the son of the mare sis was riding, four years old, and had never been ridden or schooled in any way. The stable workers were actually afraid of him and fed him by shoving food under the fence. I asked if I might take him around and "play with him." He seemed harmless to me and so undernourished that I doubted he would cause any trouble. I put a halter on him, took a lunge line and led him outside. He never took his eyes off me. It was actually spooky the way he kept staring at me, and I couldn't shake the feeling that I should know him.

I cued him to move around me in a circle, and to my (and the owner's) amazement, he did! He moved elegantly despite his long toes and unkempt condition. I coaxed him into a trot, and he just floated in a big, bouncy but slow-cadenced gait. He kept his head turned to look at me with those beautiful liquid eyes as he gracefully arched his neck, flagged his tail and moved over the ground in a fluid, elegant way.

I asked him to stop and change direction, and he did that as well. It was amazing he could move at all with an extra six to eight inches on his toes, and yet he had inde-scribable beauty, grace and pride.

My sister returned from her ride and we went home, but I couldn't get that sorry little horse out of my mind.

I went back the next day and made an offer I thought the owner would surely refuse, but he didn't. Knowing how much it was going to cost to get this little horse healthy and put meat on his bones (he was half the weight he should be), I thought I was taking a chance even with such a low offer. My new horse had never left the farm where he was born, so I anticipated problems loading him in the trailer, but to my surprise, he walked right in and rode quietly all the way home.

Although I had been shopping for a horse, seems he chose me. He turned out to be one of the nicest horses I have ever owned. The ugly duckling became a swan, breathtaking when he moved, intelligent and an enthusiastic learner. He never complained, never had a bad mood, nip or kick in him, and he excelled in everything I asked him to do. Our life together turned out to be too brief, but Smokey is unforget-table and will live on in my heart forever.

Vicki Austin

Stylishly Together, Forever

Old age isn't so bad when you consider the alternative.

MAURICE CHEVALIER

Now retired for many years, I was once a personal shopper in a major metropolitan city. One of my clients, Claire, was the daughter of immigrants who fell in love with a man that her family didn't approve of. Max was a bit older than Claire and from a different religious and ethnic background. Love could not be denied, and the couple married despite her family's objections. Striking out on their own, through a lifetime of hard work, they built a very profitable business. Having no children, Claire and Max wrapped themselves in the warmth of friends, employees and business relationships.

I thought I had seen and heard it all, but when the phone rang one late afternoon, I realized there was always more to learn about life and love. After a cheerful hello, Claire explained that Max, being an astute businessman, had suggested they take care of some of the many details that would need to be attended to in the event of their passing. This was many years ago, long before the idea of funeral planning was on anyone's checklist. He and Claire had several discussions over how they wished to be remembered and what their services would be like. Contrary to assumptions, talking about this wasn't sad or macabre; they found it actually brought both of them peace of mind and a feeling that they would be together forever, in this life and the next.

"You know Max and I aren't pretentious, and quite honestly I think this whole funeral business is nonsense, but so many people love Max, I know we have to have a beautiful service that gives everyone a chance to say their last good-byes when the time comes."

It was certainly true about Claire and Max. Nothing about their lifestyle would lead one to suspect that they were wealthy, other than the enormous financial and material donations they made to needy causes every year. In fact, my role as their personal shopper more often entailed finding something special and meaningful for others rather than anything for Claire or Max. There were literally thousands of people who had benefited from the couple's compassion and generosity. I shopped for home accessories for housewarmings for employees who Claire and Max helped with down payments on their first homes. Every year I had the pleasure of shopping for complete wardrobes for as many as five high-school seniors who were college-bound thanks to the scholarships funded by Claire and Max. Shunning publicity and wanting no one to know who was behind the kindnesses, I never divulged who my clients were—but somehow, people knew.

"Bea, my goodness there are so many choices and so many decisions to make with regard to one silly box," Claire was saying. "There are dozens of woods and beautiful bronzes or coppers. And the most sumptuous interiors . . .

it's all just so overwhelming." She paused to collect her thoughts for a moment and continued.

"Bea, Max and I would like you to pick out a couple of caskets for us that you think we'd enjoy spending eternity in." It took a second for Claire's words to settle in, and I couldn't help but laugh when they did. "That is, if you don't mind, of course. You always find just the right gift or that special dress when I need one, and Max lives in that gorgeous chair you found for his study. We just know we'll love what you choose for us, and to be quite honest, neither one of us wants to tackle it, and I certainly don't want to have to deal with it later!"

And so, I began my search for a couple of perfect caskets for the perfect couple. I'm happy to report I was successful, and when Max died a few years later, Claire made a point of telling me she was pleased with my selection. Sadly, Claire died not long after Max.

I joined hundreds of mourners to say farewell to a woman I respected and had come to love as a friend. Claire looked beautiful, and every detail of the memorial reflected her sense of style and grace—right down to the dress she chose to be buried in, one I had selected for her when she and Max celebrated their fiftieth wedding anniversary.

Bea Manheim
As told to Theresa Peluso

Oh, for a Bra That Fits

Nothing in the world can take the place of persistence.

CALVIN COOLIDGE

I have embarked on the most sacred of journeys . . . the search for a bra that fits. I have consulted all manner of bra-fitting "specialists," none of whom could agree on what size would best describe me, nor what style would best suit me. They did all agree that I should trust their judgment and pay small fortunes for the privilege of wearing their foundational undergarments.

I thought that this would be a fairly easy quest. There seems to be no end to the number of people who are happy to tell me what they think is best for me, especially if that is what they are paid to do. My first step on my journey was to visit a local department store that had served me well before and had at least two fitters on hand at all times. This department store is a little upscale, and I think their bra sizes run large so that the customer can pretend they are larger than they really are. Unfortunately, if this is not true, I really am bigger than I thought I was. This might be a good thing, if I was a teenager, or at least young enough that gravity was still my friend.

As if that isn't depressing enough, I have realized that as I have grown older (and heavier), my "lopsidedness" has grown more noticeable. Now we all know that one side is larger and one side is smaller, just like one ear is a little lower than the other ear, or one foot is bigger than the other. If you are lucky, these differences are small, and if not, there are things that can be done to help. A good haircut can make a world of difference for that droopy ear, and there are clubs for people who have different-sized feet. But what the heck can you do for that little boob? Stick a falsie in there? Well, yeah, that can work, but what if you are an in-between size? "I'll take two sets of pads, please, one in small and one in extra-vavoom!"

Anyway, I tried two different styles for a week and discovered annoying and irritating things about both of them. So I did what any normal woman would do . . . I went back and let them sell me some more. Three different styles this time. I didn't even make it a week on those.

Then I saw an ad for a "Bra Fit Event" at another department store. I was very excited because there would be fitters and sales, and I was sure my troubles were over. When I got to the store, there were plenty of customers, but only one check-out person and no fitters. When I inquired as to the fitters, the check-out person directed me to a display, where in tiny letters at the bottom of the poster were the words "By Appointment Only." With a heavy sigh and a sinking heart, I tried on more bras, but no luck.

I was into the second week of my quest and getting crankier by the minute. One afternoon, I walked into my boss's office and growled, "Can I vent for a minute?" Since this is a fairly common request from me, he gave me the go-ahead. "I hate bras!" I ground out between clenched teeth. To give him credit, my boss did not laugh out loud at my obvious dis-comfor. Rather, after he recov-ered his composure, he shared with me his wife's favorite place for such niceties. Even though this store, on the risqué side of respectable, was not one I was prone to frequent, I thought, *What do I have to lose?*

Well, to wrap this up nicely, I found my holy grail. The women at this last store listened to me, they looked at me, they measured and didn't laugh, and they found me a bra that fits. It doesn't poke or pinch or itch or bind. I think I am in love. I was so happy; I even let them talk me into applying for a store credit card.

I may have to contact the main office and see if they want an old woman to endorse their product. I

WHAT SIZE ARE YOU?
The number. While wearing a bra, measure just below your breasts around your rib cage and add 5. If the result is an odd number, you can go up or down a size, whichever is most comfortable.
The letter. Just measure around your chest below your shoulder blades and subtract your rib-cage measure-ment. The difference is your cup size; 0=AA, 1=A, 2=B, 3=C, 4=D, 5=DD

could work for bras. One look at my face and the public would know I was wearing a bra that fits. I am pretty sure I could get testimonials from my coworkers about the differ-ence it has made in their lives. Well, maybe not. But I sure am happy. And my husband is happy . . . and my kids . . . and my boss . . . and my friends . . . and, well, you get the picture. It's the next best thing to not wearing one at all.

Terry Lilley

If the world seems cold to you, kindle fires to warm it.

LUCY LARCOM

When my husband, Marc, and I first moved to Utah, we were unprepared for many things: home heating costs, longer commutes and the friendliness of strangers. What surprised us most, however, was the cold.

For seven years we'd made our home in Florida, where "winter" is a season accompanied only by frost for a mere two weeks in late December and early January. When our first Utah winter arrived with force in mid-October, we were stunned by the sudden temperature drop and howling winds. Quickly, the mountains visible from our apartment balcony disappeared beneath their winter garb, and the snowline gradually crept down toward our home in the valley.

Marc left for work daily before 6:30 A.M., and the cold during those early-morning commutes was growing bitter. We couldn't delay buying winter coats for another week. We tried anchor stores at the mall, but the coats they stocked were either inadequate fall jackets or far too overpriced for our meager budget. His public school teacher salary and my freelance writing income put tight restrictions on our spending, even for winter necessities.

Wrapped in layers one Saturday morning in late October, we ventured to one last store: the Deseret Industries thrift store in Provo. We were no strangers to bargain shopping, and with luck we'd find coats to quell our shivers.

"There!" I pointed to the left, toward a lone parking space at the far end of the lot.

Cars snaked across the asphalt, some toward the donations line, others toward the exit, and still more searching for parking spaces. This was far busier than any thrift store we'd ever visited. Marc carefully eased the car into the space, and we both flinched as we stepped out into the biting wind, not speaking until we'd jogged through the automatic doors.

"Wow." Marc said it all; the store was tremendous. Women's clothing to the right, men's to the left, housewares and furniture in the back, all carefully organized and sorted in the warehouse-like building. But no coats.

We walked through the main aisle, eyeing nearby racks for winter wear. Dresses? Nope. T-shirts? Not quite. Blouses? Silk isn't exactly warm. Active wear? The racks of sweatshirts were a bit closer. Finally, three rows deeper into the store, we found a rack of winter coats. Marc's was easy to find—a bulky, dark-green coat that had obviously seen better days, but the abundant pockets and detachable hood were great features. What's more, it was his size, with plenty of room for multiple layers underneath.

"How much?" I asked. Marc fumbled with the sleeve to find the printed price tag.

"Twenty," he replied.

"Not bad."

As we walked across the store toward the women's section, I noticed a disturbing sign above the cash registers: They didn't accept Discover, the only credit card we had. Pointing the sign out to Marc, I asked, "How much cash do you have?"

Pausing in a nearby aisle, he checked his wallet.

"Thirty-three," he replied. We'd gotten used to the convenience of using credit cards for the majority of our shopping, and payday was nearly three weeks away. Unfortunately, if the women's coats were similarly priced, I'd go home cold that afternoon.

Browsing through the racks of women's coats, our discouragement grew. This one was nice, but too expensive. Another was cheap enough, but not the right size. This is the reality of shopping at thrift stores: You never know what you'll find, and sometimes those great bargains don't materialize.

Turning to the last rack, I spotted the perfect coat: a rich cadet-blue suede with winter lining and a cozy hood lined with black fox fur. On impulse, I slipped the coat on before checking the price tag. It fit. Delaying the inevitable disappointment, I examined the sleeves and seams: spotless. The coat could have been new yesterday. Already I was warm in the luxurious coat.

"It looks good," Marc said, brushing off one of the shoulders.

"It does," commented a nearby patron, smiling at me as she riffled through a nearby rack.

"Thanks." I smiled back, clutching the hood closer to my cheeks to feel the velvety fur brush my skin.

"Now the big question: How much?" Marc asked.

With a sigh, I pulled off the coat and reached for the nearest sleeve, but couldn't find the tag. Marc checked the other sleeve, but still we couldn't find a price. Quickly, we examined the collar, zipper and other likely spots, to no avail.

"I'm sure it's expensive," I said, reading the care tag. "It's real fur and everything."

"Let's ask," Marc said, glancing around for an employee. Seeing no one, we headed toward the cashiers at the front of the store. Walking up to a young woman with a name tag, we asked her how much the coat was. We explained that we'd checked, but couldn't find a tag. She glanced at the sleeves, and then waved toward a passing supervisor.

"There's no price here," she explained, and waited for the supervisor's verdict.

As the supervisor double-checked the sleeves and frowned, we were certain the coat would be too expensive. After all, Marc's coat was obviously used and even frayed in places, but still cost twenty dollars. This one was newer, a better material, and trimmed with fur. The supervisor glanced at us, looked back at the coat and eyed us more closely. She shrugged.

"Five dollars."

"We'll take it!" I piped before she could change her mind. Quickly, we handed over both coats to the cashier. Forgoing a bag, we slipped our new coats on moments later and turned toward the door, easily braving the stinging wind without sacrificing our cozy warmth. Grinning, we ran across the parking lot, this time from sheer joy rather than a desperate attempt to escape the cold.

Melissa Mayntz

What we obtain too cheap, we esteem too lightly;
it is dearness only that gives everything its value.

THOMAS PAINE

Behind every great shopping female is a male just trying to keep his head above the pile of receipts in which
he sometimes feels himself drowning. A male just trying
to survive, to understand, to learn, and perhaps even hesi-
tantly, and clumsily, trying to join in. This speculation
became a reality one day when "my guy" proved just what
an amateur shopper he was, while showing just how
much potential he had!

I am a shopper by afternoon, evening and weekend,
but by day I am a middle-school language arts teacher.
At the last minute, before leaving for work one morning, I
remembered that I had promised my students that I
would bring an essay I had written when I was in middle
school. All of my essays are neatly stored in a very classy,
but cute, storage box, in my very well-decorated office
closet. I had bought this particular box on one of my
many shopping trips when I wasn't looking for anything

in particular, but ended up coming home with a lot of "in particulars." I knew I didn't have time to shuffle through all of the essays and still make it to work on time, so I just grabbed the entire designer box, complete with textured khaki fabric and black ribbon, and I took it with me to school.

The day progressed, the essay was read, the bell rang, and it was finally time to go home. As I walked into room 501—that of the said "guy," who also happened to be an educator—the teacher's aide looked at me and gasped with surprised delight. "Oh, did you get a present?" she inquired. I realized that she was pointing to my little treasure of a box.

"Oh, this is just a storage box from my closet," I explained. With a shocked look on her face, she glanced toward my fellow, who was standing on the other side of the room . . . my fellow who prided himself on being frugal. Though he had a cute little smirk of a grin on his face that he could not disguise, he was shaking his head in utter disappointment.

"How much did you pay for that box?" he inquired.

"Oh, it was cheap. I got it at T. J. Maxx, or Marshall's, or one of those places," I proudly replied.

"That is not what I asked," he stated as he tried to hold back what could only be described as a manly giggle. "How much was the box?"

"I don't know, like, maybe sixteen dollars for the set . . . there are two more boxes that go with it." I bubbled with enthusiasm about my ability to match and coordinate complete sets while rummaging through a store in search of bargains.

With quite a lack of appreciation for that which I considered to be a rare ability, he simply looked at his aide and casually commented, "Do you see what I am dealing with here? A girl who pays sixteen dollars for a box, and yet says financially we could make this work in the future?"

He playfully chuckled as he walked out the door exclaiming, "This is never going to work out."

A few weeks later, I took a day off to get caught up on some things at home. One of those things was to reorganize another closet of my apartment that had gotten a bit out of order. That morning, my shopper-in-training sent me an instant message to see how my day was going. I told him that I was about to head out in search of some organizational supplies to get my closet under control. His response became the source of quite a beautiful moment that day, and a hint that there is hope for even the most hopeless of shoppers.

"While you are at it," he said, "why don't you go shopping for some stuff to organize my closet?" He had just bought his first house and was not quite settled in.

"What do you need?" I inquired, as I found my way to the edge of my seat, a seat that I must mention was also a great deal acquired on a previous shopping trip.

"Just some bins or containers, maybe some sort of compartments."

"But what exact kind of containers are we talking here?" I asked, hoping that a little part of the shopper within me had finally rubbed off on Mr. Painfully McFrugal.

"Ahhh," he replied as the lightbulb went off in his head, a lightbulb that reminded me of the blue-light specials of days gone by, "I need some sixteen-dollar boxes to store my stuff."

The bells began to chime, the music began to play, and the cash registers began to click with joy. Ladies, hear me out. Don't give up hope. Grab the credit cards, and stick with those guys . . . they're learning! With a little help from the pros, even the most frugal man can survive!

Lea Ann Atherton

Shopping Daze With Mom

I have never known a really chic woman whose
appearance was not, in large part, an outward
reflection of her inner self.

MAINBOCHER

I know I am my mother's daughter when I let her loose
in a department store. Especially when the marquee
bears the words "discount outlet."

She gets this possessed look in her eyes, takes a deep
breath, inhales the chemical sizing on the new fabrics and
becomes focused to the point of filtering out everything
but the racks and hangers around her. When shopward-
bound, my dear old mom behaves as if she was dropped
in by helicopter and strategically placed to carry out a
military mission . . . SEEK and SECURE all BARGAINS!

At eighty-two-years young, despite loss of hearing, fail-
ing eyesight and a garden variety of health issues, my
mother has lost none of the bargain-hunting skill that she
fine-tuned as a young widow. Back then, in top form, she
made certain her three girls were always dressed well,
although our clothes didn't come from Bloomies or Lord &

Taylor. My mother hunted for bargains for
her brood at discount outlets like Korvettes,
Alexanders and occasionally Ginsburg's in
downtown Passaic, a New Jersey suburb.

Today, a scouting expedition with Mom
cannot begin until her blonde hair is perfectly coiffed and her nails manicured. Her
shoes must match her purse, which matches
her watch (one of dozens) that perfectly
complements her outfit. If jeans are the uniform
for the day, everything—I mean everything—is denim.

My eldest sister, the psychologist, fears that my mother
and I both share shopping as a substitute for therapy.
(Any more of us, and she'd be out of business!) After giving her assessment careful thought, I have come to the
conclusion that my sister is right, but that our shopping
therapy is only a problem at the end of the month when
the credit-card bills arrive. The upside is that it really does
feel like a quick fix that both soothes us and gives us
something we can enjoy together.

What my sister misses by living out of state is the bond
that "shopping therapy" creates between my mother and
me. Even on a day when Mom's not feeling well, I can usually coax her to brave the fluorescent lighting of a department store. Somehow, the thrill of the hunt supersedes
her discomfort, and she's game for another adventure.
When I see the light in her eyes and her enthusiasm, it
reminds me that each day we have together is special.

Wait . . . I hear the phone ringing. It's Mom's number on
the caller ID. Next target: Beall's Outlet. The mission: find
the perfect chartreuse T-shirt to match Mom's chartreuse
earrings, that go with her chartreuse shoes for her chartreuse print capris. Now, where are those gold espadrilles,
that match my favorite purse, that look fabulous with this
sundress?

Kim Weiss

The Gift Grinch

When the Godiva is gone, the gift of real love is having someone who'll go the distance with you.

OPRAH WINFREY

It was dark outside, snowy, windy and cold, two days before Christmas, and there we were schlepping up and down the aisles of Sam's Wholesale Club in Milwaukee. I was exhausted after a long day in my home office, but Andrew, my high-school freshman, and the only one of my four children still living at home, insisted we make the trip.

"Come on, Mom, you have to tell me what you want for Christmas. I really want to get you something nice, something you want. I don't know what you want. Give me some hints," he pleaded.

I harrumphed, noting my headache had intensified. Oh how I wished at that moment that I had a husband who could take Andrew shopping. I blurted out, "Andrew, why couldn't you have thought about this three weeks ago? Or three months ago? Why couldn't you have walked to the store near our house with one of your friends and picked out something that would be a surprise? Do you know how I hate being here two days before Christmas when I've got a thousand things on my mind with all the kids coming home tomorrow and meals to fix? Do you know how I hate having to pick out my own Christmas present?"

I felt hot tears piling up on the underside of my eyelids, but I blinked hard. I was not going to cry right there in the middle of the doggone store. I swallowed and continued my tirade.

"Are you going to wrap it up and expect me to act surprised when I open it in front of everyone?" My voice trailed off when I noticed the forlorn look on my son's face.

I took a deep breath as we rounded the book aisle and ambled over to the housewares section. I was starting to hate myself for being such a grinch.

"I'm sorry, Andrew. I'm just tired. You know what I'd really like?"

"What?" his voice sounded positively exuberant.

"A toaster oven."

"Great! Let's look at 'em," he said as he steered me over to the small appliances section.

Madam Scrooge surfaced again. "Oh, no. Look at those prices. You can't afford fifty dollars. I won't let you spend that much. There's no need. This is stupid, Andrew. I don't want to do this. Let's go home. You don't need to get me a Christmas present."

"Mom, please, I really want to get it for you. I've got the money. I've been saving for months, and I want to get you something nice that you'll use a lot. This is perfect."

"How about if I pay for half of it? Then it'll be a gift for both of us. You'll enjoy a toaster oven as much as I will."

"No! Mom, please, I want to buy it for you. Please let me do this." I stopped arguing and tried to put on a happy face as Andrew paid for his purchase with mostly fives and singles. As he carried the big box to the car, I noticed he was walking taller, happier.

At home I made myself a cup of lemon tea, went down to the family room, turned on the Christmas tree lights and flopped into my favorite rocker. *Why am I such a crab when it comes to gifts?* I wondered.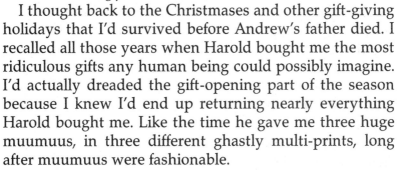

I thought back to the Christmases and other gift-giving holidays that I'd survived before Andrew's father died. I recalled all those years when Harold bought me the most ridiculous gifts any human being could possibly imagine. I'd actually dreaded the gift-opening part of the season because I knew I'd end up returning nearly everything Harold bought me. Like the time he gave me three huge muumuus, in three different ghastly multi-prints, long after muumuus were fashionable.

A few Christmases, Harold bought me so many gifts that when I returned them, I'd just put the money back into our checking account. He never caught on; at least, I don't think he did.

One Christmas, he bought the two of us matching sports jackets, maroon with yellow stripes, in an ugly shiny material. The next Valentine's Day, Harold came downstairs with his "I have a surprise for you" grin. Before I finished flipping the pancakes, he whisked me upstairs to see his latest declaration of love.

Six pink, plastic, life-size replicas of curved index fingers were screwed into the beautiful walnut paneling in our bedroom, every two feet along the wall. I looked at Harold's face to see if it was a joke. My heart raced as I started praying wildly to myself, *Oh, Lord, please let it be a joke! These plastic fingers do not go with my country antiques! Please, Lord, make this April Fool's Day and not Valentine's Day!* Harold's eyes were sparkling. "See, honey, you can hang your bathrobe on this one, your pajamas on that one, your bath towel over there, your clothes on these." All I could do was nod my head and hold back the tears.

One Christmas there were seventeen presents under the tree with my name on them, thirteen of them from Harold. That year he'd fallen victim to an ad that read, "Get thirteen surprise gifts for $2.98 if you order $50 worth of merchandise." Those thirteen surprise gifts that I had to "oohh" and "aahh" over ended up on my rummage sale table the next spring. In the meantime the children didn't understand why Mommy got so many more presents than they did, and my resentful gift phobia grew by leaps.

Another time, Harold bought me a wool skirt, blouse and sweater outfit from a very expensive store, but it was a style and color that made me feel thirty years older and twenty pounds heavier. I didn't have the heart to take it back, since it fit, but every time I wore it to please him, I felt like a flubbery version of an old schoolmarm.

I started to dread every gift-giving occasion because I knew Harold would either buy too many gifts that I didn't need and wouldn't use, or he'd spend too much money on something that wasn't my taste. Now here I was, fifteen years later, nearly fifty years old. The three older children were grown and on their own, and I was still acting skittish and mean-tempered about this gift-giving thing with Andrew.

I decided to see if I could find something in the world's best art-of-living book, the Bible, about the giving and receiving of gifts. I pulled out my concordance and looked up "gifts" in the index and discovered that gifts were mentioned or referred to in the Bible 129 times. So I started reading. Suddenly, those Christmas tree lights seemed brighter. It wasn't the gift itself that was the important part of the equation; it was the heart of the giver that made all the difference. Just then Andrew bounded down the family-room steps with his big box all wrapped. As he placed it under the tree, he smiled, "You don't have to act surprised, Mom. I'm just really glad you're going to like it. Hey, I think I'll even like it. I can make all kinds of things in a toaster oven, right?"

"Absolutely! Your favorite Italian bread with cheese on top, open-faced tuna and tomato sandwiches, even left-over pizza."

Andrew's face was as radiant as the Christmas angel's face on top of the tree.

Before the year of the toaster oven, I was always so wrapped up in what the gift was or whether or not I could use it, or if it fit properly, to pay much attention to the giver. But that Christmas, I got my head straight about the difference between the gift and the giver.

Now all gifts please me, whether they're pink, plastic finger hooks or something I have to pick out myself. What's important isn't whether or not I really like it or if it fits my lifestyle. What is important is that by the very act of giving, the giver has demonstrated that he or she loves me . . . and that is the best gift of all.

Patricia Lorenz

Requisite Shopping

The only thing that you can carry with you on your travels is your heart. So fill your heart with good things, and good things will follow you for the rest of your life.

SCOTT MURRAY

My husband and I were going to Maui on Saturday. Just the two of us. Without the kids. That was the good news. The bad news was me having to shop for a new bathing suit. I put the chore off for weeks, but with the departure date days away, it was time to go to the mall.

When I entered the boutique, my eyes roamed the walls, taking in life-size photographs of young models playing volleyball on the beach. As parents of four young children, my husband and I wouldn't be participating in those sorts of activities; we planned to put a priority on rest.

I assessed the salespeople carefully before I made a selection. One of them was chatting on the phone in a very loud voice, not someone I wanted to share my size with. The next girl, a blonde teenager, started toward me, so I buried my head in a rack of sunglasses. Eventually, I approached the oldest of the three, the one with a generous figure, with the hope that she might be more sympathetic than the other two skinny-minnies.

"Hi," I faked enthusiasm.

"How are you tonight?" She moved smoothly from behind the cash desk, hands clasped and resting on the front of her dark blouse.

"Great, well, except I really need to pick out a bathing suit for a holiday. Where should I look for styles in ... er ... my age category?" My voice sounded higher than usual.

The woman pointed to some racks near the entrance. "Let me show you the suits up front. The back half of the store is dedicated to junior sizes." I liked "junior sizes." It sounded more like undeveloped twelve-year-olds rather than slim sex kittens in their early twenties.

"What are you looking for?" she asked, her low voice working to calm my nerves.

The question surprised me; I had expected her to hand me a black one-piece and say, "This is the one we sell to all postnatal gals approaching forty; it'll hide everything."

Prior to my childbearing years, I was partial to two-pieces, which showed off the flat stomach I had then. I wouldn't mind wearing one again before I flopped over forty.

"A bikini. Yes, I'm buying a bikini."

"A bikini or a tankini?"

My confidence shook, I thought, *It has "tank" in it! What is she trying to tell me?*

"What is a 'tankini'?" I asked.

The woman stared up at me through long, dark bangs. "Okaaaay." She exhaled through pursed lips, sending the bangs flying. "Why not try both styles?" The hangers accumulated on her arm faster than the colors registered in my mind.

"Do you like stripes?"

"Yeah, sure. I guess."

She guided me to the changing rooms and hung her selections on the hooks inside. "Now," she said, "if it's all right with you, I would like to come back and take a look at you wearing the suits. It will allow me to give you better service. But only if you are comfortable with that."

Not wanting to be impolite, I agreed and pushed aside my pride.

The first suit was a "Marilyn" style top in soft pink partnered with a skimpy black bottom belted in pink and white stripes. I was shoving my full-panel panties into the sides of the bikini bottom when she knocked.

"How's it going in there?"

"Excellent, thanks. Your stock is very nice, great quality."

No response. I opened the door a crack to see if she had left, but there she stood patiently, with her friendly smile like I was the only customer in the store.

"I like that top, quite a bit. Would you like me to tie it tighter? Give you a bit more support?"

"Okay." I squeezed over to let her in to share my square of brown-grey carpet. I was beginning to like this woman. She made me feel as if the final purchase would really be my choice, a suit I'd feel good wearing. She wasn't pushy.

"Ahhhh, yes, that's the one! Definitely you! With some beautiful jewelry, you'll knock his socks off!"

In the mirror I witnessed the difference she had made with the ties at my neck and across my back.

"How's the bottom? You don't want it too baggy; it needs to be tight because it will stretch in the water."

I inspected the Lycra choking my white thighs.

She closed the door to let me try on another suit. The next top, striped in green, white, pink and black, exposed rolls under my armpits. The matching bottom was cut even lower across the front than the last one.

In my reflection, I studied the cellulite; it seemed to advance over new territory every year. I had a nice tan on my arms and legs, but it stopped six inches from the edges of the suit where my bone-white skin magnified the puckers—proof I had been hiding under T-shirts and capris all summer.

Who was I kidding? A vision of me, poolside in a bikini and a farmer's tan, filled my head. I recalled my commitment to lose weight for this trip. The tears started just as the saleswoman returned. She knocked softly.

I opened the door and whispered, "I think I'm losing my nerve; maybe bikinis aren't for me after all." I pinched one chubby armpit for evidence.

When our eyes met again, she told me firmly, "You CAN wear this. You're FINE."

FIGURE FIXES

If you have *short legs* and/or *chunky thighs*, medium-high cut legs and a V-cut bottom will help lengthen and slim. If you need to *slim your waistline*, go with a one-piece bathingsuit with detail or gathers on the sides. *Slumping shoulders* look straighter in a two-piece suit or a racer-back top.

I was the first to look away. "Thank you."

"Are you traveling with friends?" she asked.

"No, why?"

"So it's just the two of you?"

"Yeah."

"You said you have small children. I'll bet you haven't been away alone in a while."

I saw her point. I took a deep breath and resolved to treat myself at the bookstore after I chose a suit. There was one I had favored from the beginning. It was dark burgundy, not a flashy beach color, but it was nice next to my skin; it seemed a bit more dignified, understated.

When I saw myself in the bikini top and matching board skirt, I knew I had my new bathing suit. I hadn't chickened out with a one-piece, but the skirt provided enough lower coverage so that no one would have to look at all the chunky areas at the same time. Wearing it, I was beginning to feel pretty.

There was no need to wait for the saleswoman; I had made my choice. After dressing, I left the safety of the changing room with quick, light steps, excited about our vacation.

At the other end of the hallway, I spotted two women my mother's age showing off their selections to another salesperson. They were strutting playfully and giggling as they posed before the three-way mirror.

Self-esteem appeared to be spreading throughout the shop, and I saw that my helper wasn't the only one trained to instill confidence. The staff truly added value to my purchase, and what I picked up that night will last much longer than the swimsuit.

I smiled encouragement to my fellow shoppers and made my way to the register.

J. A. McDougall

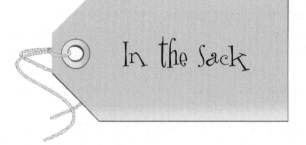

When in doubt, wear red.

BILL BLASS

"You want to go where, Grandma?"

"You heard me. Here. Right here." She pointed.

"Here? Are you sure?"

"Here." Grandma Vic was adamant.

With a sigh, Jenna shrugged the strap of her purse higher on her shoulder as she steered the wheelchair up the mall ramp and turned toward the store Grandma indicated. But she paused at the entrance.

"Grandma, you do understand what they sell here, don't you?"

"I'm neither blind nor stupid, dear. And contrary to what you might be thinking, I still have all my marbles. I know exactly what I'm doing." Victoria—Grandma Vic— took a deep, audible breath, cocked her silvered head even higher, and ordered, "Now, push me in."

Jenna shook her head in dismay. In all the years she'd cared for her grandparents, run their errands and taken them on excursions, nothing had prepared her for this demand. Nothing. It was downright embarrassing. Grandma Vic was asking too much of her this time. What would people think? What if they saw someone they knew? This was . . . awkward.

She sighed again, then wheeled her stubborn grandma through the front doors into Frederick's of Hollywood. Jenna stalled just inside the door, her own jaw dropped, and her arms hung limp at her sides as she took in the displays of intimate apparel. She hadn't been in Frederick's in a few years herself. A lot had changed. A lot. Everything was skimpier. More transparent. More daring. Why, some might even call it obscene! She should never have agreed to escort an elderly . . . suddenly, Grandma Vic impatiently self-propelled the wheelchair to a mannequin and studied the risqué lingerie.

"Hmmph. That's the newfangled underwear? Why, I've got Band-Aids that cover more," Grandma Vic tsked with an ornery grin into Jenna's stunned face. "I want to see it all—everything in the store."

"Grandma Vic . . ." Jenna was amazed to find a blush staining her own thirty-three-year-old cheeks.

"All of it, dear."

Row after sexy row, rack after sensuous rack, the two toured the store with Grandma delivering more spicy one-liners than a standup comic.

"You say it's called a 'thong'? How odd. We used to wear those on our feet!"

"They're 'bustiers'? They look as painful as my mother's corset. Of course, hers didn't come in leather . . . or leopard skin."

"Flavored lotions and edible undies? Why don't they just print up a menu?"

Jenna flinched. Customers grinned. Salesclerks eyed them doubtfully. At last, Jenna leaned into Grandma's face and looked her squarely in the eyes. "Now, are you ready to tell me what this is all about?"

"Jenna, you've always been so good to tend to our needs. Shopping, chauffeuring, even putting up the Christmas tree so we can celebrate the holidays. You're the only one in the family I could trust with this errand."

Grandma's chin sank a little further onto her ample bosom, and she sighed. After a thoughtful silence, she spoke low and falteringly into her lap.

"Our sixty-fifth wedding anniversary is just around the corner. I want to surprise your grampa. For just a few hours, I want to be young and whole again. Or, at least, look that way. For Grampa. For me."

Grandma glanced up with new determination. "I might be old and broken, but I'm not dead. I need a new nightie, something . . . suggestive, and I want to buy it here. At Frederick's."

Jenna bit her lip. Not in vexation. Not in embarrassment. Certainly not to stifle a giggle. She bit her lip to prevent it from trembling and hinting at the tears that threatened.

"Why, you old romantic!" She hugged Grandma. "I guess it's never too late to reinvent love."

Without hesitation, Jenna pushed the chromed wheelchair to a display of naughty nightwear and watched a pair of aged, corded hands lovingly caress diaphanous baby-dolls, sheer chemises and velvet camisoles.

"This one." Grandma's dove-gray eyes sparkled over the easy decision.

With a conspiratorial smile, the middle-aged salesclerk folded the full-length, spaghetti-strapped nightgown, rang up the sale and complimented them on their choice. As Jenna steered her out the door and through the mall,

Grandma Vic wore a smug look. And she made certain the sack from Frederick's of Hollywood—that cosseted her lacy, racy-red purchase—perched prominently on her lap.

When shopper after shopper turned to stare after her, she looked up at Jenna. "Let 'em guess!" she winked devilishly. "This Victoria's not keeping anything secret!"

Carol McAdoo Rehme

WHAT'S THE SECRET?

If you love to shop, look into becoming a "mystery shopper." Mystery shopping is a $600 million industry with over 1 million *Mystery Shoppers* in the United States alone.

These passionate shoppers are hired by market-research companies, retailers, restaurants, training organizations and hotels to give the company firsthand, objective feedback about the customer's experience.

Mystery shoppers help companies establish quality-control standards, improve customer service, evaluate merchandising strategies and achieve consistency in delivering services.

For more information, check with the Mystery Shopping Providers Association (MSPA) at *www.mysteryshop.org*.

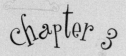

chapter 3

Shop Till You Drop

I have enough money to
last me the rest of my life,
unless I buy something.

JACKIE MASON

Bing Cherries: A True Story of Catholic Guilt

Truth waits for eyes unclouded by longing.

RAM DASS

My friend Michelle inherited two traits from her mother: She can't tell a lie, and she can't turn down a bargain when she is shopping. She aptly demonstrated both of these characteristics during a shopping excursion to Canada a few years ago.

While on a business trip in Seattle, Michelle and a co-worker rented a car and drove to Vancouver to spend the day sightseeing and shopping. Being the consummate shopper, the opportunity to partake in her favorite pastime in a "foreign country" thrilled my friend beyond words. It was a crisp, beautiful, fall day when they wandered into a spectacular open-air market. "Oh, look at these!" Michelle exclaimed as she came upon a fruit stand bursting with bright colors and delicious smells. Holding a container of dark red fruit, she gushed, "Bing cherries are my absolute favorite. We need to get these for the breakfast meeting tomorrow; they'll be fantastic. And what a good price—I've paid twice this much back in the States."

A few hours later, satisfied that they had found every bargain worth finding, the shopping duo stowed their treasures in the trunk of their rental car and headed back to Washington. As they approached the border check, large threatening signs appeared warning travelers that it was illegal to transport fruit between the countries. Michelle panicked instantly. "I didn't know it was illegal to buy fruit! What will we do? Will they arrest us? Will the car be searched? It's a rental car. What if they think there are other illegal items in the car and they trash it during the search? We'll never get the deposit back!" Her fear-fueled ramblings continued incessantly until her friend didn't know whether to keep laughing or smack her back to reality.

"Will you calm down already!" her coworker finally interjected with a laugh. "I've been to Canada lots of times. When they ask us what we bought, just tell them some T-shirts and souvenirs for our kids."

"I can't . . . you don't understand . . . I'm a horrible liar," Michelle confessed, waving her hands frantically in front of her face as she felt herself begin to perspire. "I'm Catholic for Pete's sake!"

"But you did buy T-shirts for your kids—so you're not really lying," her friend reasoned. But Michelle could not be swayed. Sensing her mounting anxiety, her friend added, "Okay, don't say anything. I'll do all the talking. Just sit there and be quiet. And for heaven's sake, quit looking so guilty!"

As they reached the checkpoint, a uniformed guard approached their vehicle, peered into the open car window and greeted them. "Good day, ladies, what brought you to Canada?"

"We were in Seattle on business and thought we'd do a little sightseeing and shopping while we were in the area," Michelle's coworker replied with a smile.

"That's fine, ma'am. Did you make any purchases?"

"Just some T-shirts and souvenirs for our kids."

Their whole exchange lasted about thirty seconds, but it seemed like long, excruciating minutes to Michelle whose mind was racing. *He knows,* she thought to herself. *He knows we're lying. I can smell the cherries from the trunk. If I can smell them, he can smell them. He'll arrest us just because we lied. I saw* Midnight Express; *I know what happens to people in foreign jails. Okay, it's just cherries, not drugs, and this isn't Turkey, but I can't take it.* Suddenly, she found herself screaming, "Cherries!! Cherries!! Cherries!!"

The guard, who had stepped away from the vehicle and was about to wave them through, leaned back down and said, "Excuse me, Ma'am? What did you say?"

Michelle, nearly sobbing now, replied, "Cherries. We have cherries in the trunk. It's my fault. I didn't know it was illegal . . . I would have never . . . ."

The guard smiled and said, "It's okay, ma'am. Let's just have a look in your trunk and see what you've got there."

Her coworker put the car in park and took the keys from the ignition to open the trunk, shooting Michelle a gaze in the process that said, "Which part of 'just sit there and be quiet' didn't you understand?" As the guard searched the trunk and pulled out the contraband, Michelle apologized again, looking down at the pavement, awaiting the rush of guards and handcuffs that she was sure would follow.

Suddenly, the guard started to laugh out loud. "Uh, ma'am, it's okay. You can get back into your car now. It seems these cherries here are from California," he explained, pointing to the markings on the bottom of the container. Placing them back in the trunk, he shut the lid and tipped his hat. "Good day to you, and thank you for visiting Canada."

As they drove away, Michelle glanced back toward the

border post. The guard who had just searched their car was talking to another guard, and he began laughing and slapping his leg as he pointed in the direction of their vehicle.

Years after her brush with Canadian law enforcement, Michelle can also laugh. Her love of bing cherries and shopping for bargains remains intact, and her Catholic guilt still makes her a horrible liar. Her mother is very proud.

Jodi L. Severson

The Best Shopping Ever

Don't spend two dollars to dry-clean a shirt. Donate it to the Salvation Army instead. They'll clean it and put it on a hanger. Next morning, buy it back for seventy-five cents.

BILLIAM CORONEL

When I drive through small towns and neighborhoods, I wonder if we Americans aren't the rummage/garage sale capitalists of the world. Fridays and Saturdays especially, it seems that there's a sale of some sort on every block in every town.

I've probably hosted fifteen or more garage sales myself in the past twenty years.

It's work. Hard work. Clean out the garage. Set up tables, most of them makeshift things made out of sawhorses and old doors. Unpack the boxes of junk, price everything, make signs, post them, put an ad in the local paper, then on sale day, lug half the stuff out onto the driveway close to the street so nobody driving past will miss the fact that you're having a rummage sale.

READER/CUSTOMER CARE SURVEY

REFG

We care about your opinions! Please take a moment to fill out our online Reader Survey at **http://survey.hcibooks.com.**

As a **"THANK YOU"** you will receive a **VALUABLE INSTANT COUPON** towards future book purchases as well as a **SPECIAL GIFT** available only online! Or, you may mail this card back to us and we will send you a copy of our exciting catalog with your valuable coupon inside.

(PLEASE PRINT IN ALL CAPS)

First Name _____ MI. _____ Last Name _____

Address _____ City _____

State _____ Zip _____ Email _____

1. Gender
- ☐ Female
- ☐ Male

2. Age
- ☐ 8 or younger
- ☐ 9-12
- ☐ 13-16
- ☐ 17-20
- ☐ 21-30
- ☐ 31+

3. Did you receive this book as a gift?
- ☐ Yes
- ☐ No

4. Annual Household Income
- ☐ under $25,000
- ☐ $25,000 - $34,999
- ☐ $35,000 - $49,999
- ☐ $50,000 - $74,999
- ☐ over $75,000

5. What are the ages of the children living in your house?
- ☐ 0 - 14
- ☐ 15+

6. Marital Status
- ☐ Single
- ☐ Married
- ☐ Divorced
- ☐ Widowed

7. How did you find out about the book?
(please choose one)
- ☐ Recommendation
- ☐ Store Display
- ☐ Online
- ☐ Catalog/Mailing
- ☐ Interview/Review

8. Where do you usually buy books?
(please choose one)
- ☐ Bookstore
- ☐ Online
- ☐ Book Club/Mail Order
- ☐ Price Club (Sam's Club, Costco's, etc.)
- ☐ Retail Store (Target, Wal-Mart, etc.)

9. What subject do you enjoy reading about the most?
(please choose one)
- ☐ Parenting/Family
- ☐ Relationships
- ☐ Recovery/Addictions
- ☐ Health/Nutrition
- ☐ Christianity
- ☐ Spirituality/Inspiration
- ☐ Business Self-help
- ☐ Women's Issues
- ☐ Sports

10. What attracts you most to a book?
(please choose one)
- ☐ Title
- ☐ Cover Design
- ☐ Author
- ☐ Content

TAPE IN MIDDLE; DO NOT STAPLE

Chicken Soup for the Soul®
3201 SW 15th Street
Deerfield Beach FL 33442-9875

FOLD HERE

Do you have your own Chicken Soup story
that you would like to send us?
Please submit at: **www.chickensoup.com**

Comments

Then comes the real work. Sitting there all day. Collecting money, worrying if somebody will steal your money box when you're not looking. Of course, your day starts in the wee hours when the doorbell rings at 6:30 A.M. and it's somebody who read your ad in the paper.

"Isn't your sale open yet?"

"No, not yet. It opens at 8:00," you sputter as you pry open your eyes.

"Oh, no! I'm on my way to work. Couldn't I please have a peek inside the garage? I won't take long."

After you push the garage-door button, you scramble to the bedroom, throw on some work clothes, pour water in the teapot and rush outside just in time to see the stranger walking toward her car empty-handed.

And so it goes. Some hours you have twenty people shoving each other around between the too-tight aisles amidst your trash and treasures. By midday you're so hot, tired and cranky from arguing prices with every customer who thinks haggling is a national pastime that you're ready to close up shop in favor of a hot bath.

That's how my past rummage sales went. But not anymore. I have developed a new method of having rummage sales. One that allows you to set up in twenty minutes or less. One that requires no advertising. One that doesn't even require you to be there. Cleanup is a snap because there probably won't be much left to clean up. What's my secret?

Easy. Simply make a huge sign that says everything is FREE. I kid you not. It's the answer to every rummage sale nightmare. The perfect solution to cleaning out your garage, closets, attic, basement and shed.

The day I had my everything's FREE rummage sale was a beautiful seventy-degree August day. As I dropped a bag of garbage in the trash can in the garage, I looked around and decided to get organized, which in reality meant I had

GARAGE SALE CHIC

. . . Make a planter out of that old sewing machine cabinet.

. . . Use old doors for tabletops and cabinets for end tables.

. . . Break up old dishes and create a mosaic table or countertop.

to get rid of a mountain of junk that had taken root on the ceiling-to-floor shelves that line one whole wall of my garage. Noting that most of it wasn't really worth much in terms of good American dollars, I decided on the spot to just give it all away.

Within five minutes, my teenage son had set up a huge sawhorse table for me next to the street. Then I just started handing him stuff to carry out, to set on the table and on the ground all around the table. Huge planters, old dirty throw rugs, garbage cans, plants, books, purses, shoes, shirts, baseball caps, even a huge, never-used crisper like they use in Florida to keep crackers and potato chips moisture-free. There was a well-worn mattress cover, an old torn comforter, bike fenders, a cracked butter dish, ancient plant food, plastic buckets, and more gadgets and gizmos than one person should be allowed to accumulate in a lifetime.

I found a huge piece of cardboard that I'd saved to put under the car to catch leaking oil and took a can of spray paint to it. Five minutes later, bright green sixteen-inch-tall letters proclaimed that one word, "FREE." But oh, what a wallop that one word packs.

While I was still bringing stuff out to the street, including a dozen, empty cardboard boxes (in case someone was moving and needed them), a gentleman pulled up in a van and started loading some of my castoffs into the back end.

"Just put my wife and daughters on a plane to Mexico," he said.

"She's gonna kill you for bringing all this junk home," I laughed.

The man beamed. "Oh no, this is good stuff."

I just shook my head and walked back in the house.

I went into my home office to begin my work for the day, but every forty-five minutes or so I'd look out the front door to see if any of my worse-than-junk collection was disappearing. By 2 P.M., two-thirds of it was gone.

The next day, while I was on Wisconsin's Lake Nagawicka having lunch on a houseboat with four friends, my "best-idea-ever" rummage sale was going full blast, with no help from me or anyone, except those customers who were enjoying their "all sales final" free shopping spree. When I got home, the only things left were one shoe that had no mate, two purses that Goodwill probably would have rejected, and a beat-up old metal garbage can with a hole in the bottom.

I figure most of those people who helped themselves to my junk must have needed those things. Or even if they just wanted them because it made them happy to get something for nothing, I know that the feelings that stirred within me were much more powerful and satisfying than anything anybody felt who took my stuff. Not only was it just plain delightful to give without any thought of getting anything in return, but with very little work my entire garage was cleaned out, and my collection of clutter and claptrap from inside the house was eliminated.

I enjoyed that rummage sale so much that I did it every year until I pared down my sixty years' worth of collections to the point where I was able to move to a small condo without suffering anaphylactic shock from trying to cram a gallon's worth of stuff into a quart jar.

Just think, if everybody had FREE rummage sales, parents of older children could share the baby clothes and toddler toys with young couples who really need the stuff. Older couples could get rid of their sixty and seventy years' worth of collections without a hassle. New home-owners could have the rakes and lawn equipment not needed by those moving to condos.

Second Corinthians 9:7–8 says it best: "Don't force any-one to give more than he really wants to, for cheerful givers are the ones God prizes. God is able to make it up to you by giving you everything you need and more, so that there will not only be enough for your own needs, but plenty left over to give joyfully to others."

Patricia Lorenz

Golfers bring caddies. Shoppers bring husbands.

UNKNOWN

Stepping closer, I read the sign painted on the side of a row of old buildings. "Every Friday from 8:00–4:00. Continual rummage sales. Used clothes and miscellaneous. CHEAP-CHEAP!" Curious, I read the words scrawled at the bottom of the sign. "Six sales in the morning, six sales in the afternoon."

Wow, I thought, *not just one, but twelve rummage sales.* It was the sixties, and we were struggling to raise four kids on a pastor's salary, so I squeezed and strangled our measly budget until I was exhausted. Here was a chance to save some money. I knew I was coming back on Friday.

That night, after a supper of hot dogs and macaroni and cheese, I announced my plans for Friday. "We aren't that bad off," Roy, my husband, remarked defensively as he scraped his dirty plate into the kitchen sink.

Hah! I thought, as I stomped down rickety stairs to dump the garbage. *You don't have to mend and stitch old, shabby garments that just want to lie down and die!* Friday morning, with two little ones and a sack lunch packed in our old baby carriage, I headed out. The two oldest forged ahead, propelled by the possibility of toy bargains, and by the time we arrived, the buildings were packed. The merchandise was as varied as the many different people buying. Everyone was digging for treasure in the bins lining the building's aisles. It was "dash" and "grab." No holds barred.

Hours later, the baby carriage was piled high with my loot. The old carriage, like a pirate ship full of treasures, sailed toward home with me in tow. I couldn't resist stopping every now and then to gloat over my booty. I imagined Roy's amazement at our good fortune.

At home, I spread my purchases on the couch: a red, plaid Kate Greenway dress covered with lace and bows for Lynn, our second-grader; a pair of black patent-leather shoes, like new, to go with the dress; a snow-white lace slip to complete the outfit. There was a darling jumper and dainty blouse for six-year-old Renee, and some cute play outfits for our two preschoolers. A church outfit for Jerry cost just twenty-five cents, and on Roy's worn recliner, I draped a beautiful, gray-striped Arrow shirt. I had spent a total of two dollars and fifty cents. Our tight budget gave a great sigh of relief!

When Roy came in from church visitation, I recited my great buys. "Just think of all the money I saved. The kids will look so nice in their 'rummage sale' clothes."

"Come with me next week," I urged him. "They have other things besides clothes for sale. You might see something you really need."

He rolled his eyes.

Thinking to soften him up a bit, I said, "I got you something, too." I handed him the gray-striped shirt. His eyes lit up.

"I guess you went by a decent store on your way home," he smirked.

"No," I smiled. "It came from the rummage sale."

Tossing the shirt aside, he sputtered, "If you think I'm going to wear that, you've got a screw loose!" This man who served God every day was letting his pride get the best of him.

The next Friday I was at the sale again and first in line. This was my rummage sale wheel of fortune! Soon my purchases were piled around the baby, and not much room was left. Then I spotted it: A brown clock radio sat atop a pile of pots and pans. Roy had been looking for a clock radio he could afford. This was just what he wanted. I picked it up before someone else snatched it.

After a long, hot stroll home, the kids tumbled into the house hungry and whining for a drink. Ignoring Roy, who was sprawled in his recliner, I hurried to fix the kids a snack. After lunch, I unloaded the buggy and deposited the bags on the living-room couch.

"Look on top of that first bag," I called from the kitchen. I could hear him rustling around, and then a dead silence. I peeked into the living room. Roy picked up the radio and began to fiddle with the dials.

"Probably doesn't even work," he muttered. A few minutes later, his curiosity won out, and he plugged it in. To his joy and amazement, it worked and had all kinds of neat extras. "Well, I guess it will do," he admitted grudgingly. "But I hope you didn't get ripped off."

I could hardly control my snickers now. "Oh, I probably did pay too much," I replied.

"How much?" he asked, half hoping he was right.

"Seventy-five cents," I replied humbly. "But I probably should have haggled for fifty cents."

His eyes bugged with disbelief. I decided to let him save face and ate my snack while he lovingly caressed his new toy!

A week later, Friday morning, Roy casually asked, "What

time do those sales open anyway?"

"What sales?" I asked innocently. "Oh, you mean those dirty, old, rummage sales? They have been open for hours . . . probably nothing left worth having."

"Well, if you're bound and determined to go today, I better take you in the car. Who knows what kind of "riffraff" hangs out there," he scoffed self-righteously. We parked in front of the first building, and Roy hunched down behind the steering wheel. Was he afraid that some "riffraff" from our church would see him?

"Are you coming in or not?" I asked, as I headed for the door.

"I might go in and see if they have any screwdrivers," he replied offhandedly. A few minutes later, I came out holding a whole set of screwdrivers aloft! I could see that the mighty preacher was weakening, but too proud to participate.

The next week I made my usual trek to the "mall" with kids and buggy before Roy was home from his office. About four-thirty, I heard the car pull up. Looking out the kitchen window, I saw Roy sneaking into the basement. *Wonder what he is up to?* I thought. Stealthily I opened the kitchen basement door and crept down the stairs and up behind him.

"Hi!" I shouted. He whipped around and dropped a box of ugly brown coffee cups.

"Aha! You've been to the rummage sale!" I accused.

He squirmed and blushed like a sinner at the mourning bench. "Well, well, ummm . . . you see . . . well yeah, I met this lady, and it was time to close, and she was tired, and she didn't want to take all the leftover stuff home, and . . ." he stuttered.

I looked beyond him to a huge pile of everything imaginable in the middle of the cement floor. "You didn't!" I groaned. "You didn't bring home a whole rummage sale!"

"Well, not exactly," Roy defended himself. "I actually brought home two rummage sales!"

The piles stayed there for months. Whenever we needed something, we dug through them. My girlfriends soon discovered our heap of has-beens and often trooped over with cups of coffee to spend an afternoon at the local archaeological dig.

Roy never again brought home another entire rummage sale—just many individual bargains!

Norma Favor

**MAKE THE
BEST OF IT**

To get the most out of a
shopping trip to the thrift
store, bring:

Patience
Time
Flexibility

Sidetracked at Silver Plume

We may run, walk, stumble, drive or fly, but let us never lose sight of the reason for the journey, or miss a chance to see a rainbow on the way.

GLORIA GAITHER

Rounding a hairpin curve, I spied a sign for Silver Plume and exited. It looked like time had stood still. A one-time mining community, all that remained were a few short blocks of sleepy Victorian houses rubbing shoulders on the narrow, unpaved roads. Quaint and quiet. A little too quiet, nearly a ghost town.

On the last leg home from my first uneventful, overnight speaking engagement, I conveniently disregarded my initial nervousness and was busy congratulating myself on my recent successes: discovering "life after kids," trading my "stay-at-home-mother" title for "working woman." Establishing a business in midlife. Even traveling without my husband for the first time.

Tense from the unaccustomed mountain driving, I stopped in front of a lone, weathered antique store. What better way to take a break, stretch my legs?

Inside was a sign: "More in basement. Enter at your own risk." A direct challenge to an avid antique buff! I ducked down the rough wooden stairs. They weren't kidding.

Loose planks of plywood blanketed the floor, sagging with each step I took. I peered into dim corners, peeked at chair frames tangled in skeletal heaps and prowled the maze of timeworn clutter. Working my way back upstairs, I paused in front of a copper-lined humidor.

I wonder how much it costs? And where IS that sales clerk?

I wandered to the back of the store and snooped around the corner, startled to discover a starkly modern kitchen, empty. At a lone door (the restroom?), I waited a decent amount of time for someone to exit and finally knocked. No answer.

That's odd. But I've dawdled long enough.

I headed to the front door and opened it. Only it didn't. Open, that is. What? It was true. The building was empty, the door was bolted, and I was locked inside. Alone.

Once more, I rattled the old door.

Do I laugh or do I cry? And what kind of place closes in the middle of the afternoon, anyway? Suspiciously, I looked around more closely. *Am I on "Candid Camera"?*

And I smiled—just in case.

I did another once-over of the store. I called out. I raced to the front door again and pried at the handle. Front door. Could there be a BACK door? Yes! More important, it was unlocked. But it opened onto a stairless fretwork sill with a sheer drop down the side of the mountain.

Okay. Stay calm.

After all, what better place to be locked in? There was a tidy row of antique books; I could read to my heart's content. There was a kitchen; I wouldn't starve. There was a bathroom; I wouldn't disgrace myself. Why, there was even a musty fainting couch and a worn, hand-stitched quilt; I could bed down for the night if it came to that.

Spend the night? This place is too spooky!

Pressing my face pancake-flat against the glass pane, I rolled my eyes to the linear left, slapping the window with both palms to get attention. Then I rolled my eyes as far as I could to the right. The graveled street was completely empty of life. And no amount of shaking, rattling, banging, yelling or rapping made the least bit of difference. But I tried them all again anyway. Especially the yelling. Nervous perspiration beaded my upper lip.

This was not funny, and I was certain I had quit smiling several hours earlier. If only I could call someone. Wait! A brand-new cell phone nestled inside my purse. Why didn't I think of that sooner? Punching in the familiar numbers, I phoned home. Nothing. The teeny monitor read: searching . . . . After all, Silver Plume was nestled in the cavernous Colorado Rockies.

This is a place of business. Shouldn't it have a phone? I hated to snoop, but . . . nope, none that I could find.

This is nuts! Picking up an antique iron cannonball, I speculated on its hefty weight as I contemplated the storefront. What was that old saying? Desperate times call for desperate measures. And I was beginning to feel pretty desperate. It would break my heart (which would mend) to ruin the ancient plate-glass window (which was probably irreplaceable), but panic was setting in.

Drawing my arm back, I squinted, judged the distance and took careful aim.

Then I opened my eyes wide. There, on the other side— the *outside*—of the bolted door, stood an equally wide-eyed proprietor. We stared at each other in shock.

I don't know what gave me away—wild, glazed look? pounding heart?—but that door was unlocked in record time. Amid profuse apologies and unintelligible explanations, she showered me with comforting hugs and hot tea. Lots of hot tea.

Yet, all I knew was the afternoon I had spent in that deserted store was the longest year of my . . . "What? What's that you say? I was only here ONE HOUR?"

Well, hmmm.

Anyway, I was cured. I drove the final miles with nary a stop. Why, each and every time the car veered toward a sign boasting "Antiques," I jerked it back on the road, gave it a piece of my mind and kept on pedaling. Straight-arrow home. Where I belonged. Huh, woman-of-the-world, indeed!

On the other hand . . . there was the cutest little walnut humidor at that Silver Plume Antique Shop. Somehow, I completely forgot to ask the price. I wonder if it's still there? It's probably worth a trip back.

Carol McAdoo Rehme

Buying America, Bit by Bit

Every time we leave home and go to another place, we open up the possibility of having something wonderful happen to us.

JOSEPH DISPENZA

Shopping for me at home in Scotland is the same as it is for anyone else anywhere in the world. Shopping for me when we vacation in the United States is an entirely different thing. It is not about getting a great bargain or following fashion. My U.S. shopping is my camcorder video, my photograph album, my cherished memories, all rolled into one. I obviously buy the same things as most tourists when in New York or Chicago. Where I come into my own is in my "small town and out-of-the-way" items. I pick up a pair of earrings, a pin, a T-shirt, a watch, and I hold them for a second, remembering exactly where I bought them. I often remember chats I had with the person who sold the items to me.

Putting on a silver, purple and red watch takes me back to Broken Arrow, Oklahoma. It is a burning hot day, not many people about, and we wander into a store selling lots of different gifts and things. As I buy my watch and a T-shirt, the man asks what brings us Scots to a quiet little town like Broken Arrow. "We saw the name on a map at home, and it just had a ring for us, so we decided to come here while we were in this area!"

There is my little black and green bracelet, covered in symbols to do with gardening that I bought in Wakita, Oklahoma, a tiny place, famous mainly because some of the movie *Twister* was made there. We went well off the beaten track to find Wakita and see the *Twister* museum. When we got there, it was closed, but the lady in a little gift shop tried to track down the caretaker who had the key. While she did this, we wandered around. It was still and hot, and the main street just disappeared out into the dry, flat prairie all around us. For people who live surrounded by mountains, lakes and trees, it was fascinating with a magic all of its own. When the lady had no luck with the caretaker, she found another key, opened up the museum and let us in herself. Absolutely nothing was too much trouble for her, and how could I leave a little town and people like that without something to bring them to mind?

My shopping is quite diverse. I have a pin I bought in The Badlands State Park, South Dakota, blue and silver with a buffalo on it. We followed an old dusty road, kicking up the dirt, *Dukes of Hazard*-style, as we drove. We couldn't see this road on our map, but we followed it anyhow. We came to the edge of The Badlands, and they were breathtaking, nothing like we expected. We thought it would be gray, bleak and depressing, but instead we thought it was awesome. We found the whole place so emotive, full of mystery and feelings, and huge! We followed our dirt track heading for what we hoped would be the Black Hills area and the town of Custer. That's when we came on the visitor's center. We went inside to learn about the area, and I bought my pin. Nothing that impressive could be left without a reminder!

I have a lovely handbag that looks as if it is made of marble that I bought in Galena, Illinois. The shop was called "Dreams," and I found the whole experience in that area linked to something out of a dream. Galena is the kind of town I would create if I had the ability, and within driving distance we found "The Field of Dreams" near Dyersville, Iowa, and the amazing "House on the Rock" in Wisconsin. I bought T-shirts and keepsakes at them all.

SHOPPING AROUND THE WORLD

Most stores are closed on Sunday in France, Germany, Italy and Spain. Italy makes an exception for stores in tourist areas, but many stores in Italy also close half a day during the week (usually Monday morning or Wednesday afternoon).

I have little trinkets from most of the forty states we have visited so far. Mostly, they are from small, unknown places. If I cannot find something with the town's name on it, like "Pikeville, Tennessee," then I buy a mug, a glass, anything at all that will remind me of the place and the people. When I go out on a Saturday evening, I am like a walking map of small-town America! This is the most wonderful shopping you can imagine. I have so many happy memories of people who told us about their lives and went out of their way to help us.

I can visualize Tortilla Flat, Arizona (a little glass and memories of delicious ice cream) to Nubble Light in Maine (a fridge magnet that looks like Wedgwood pottery and happy days shared with friends from Tewksbury, Massachusetts). My little wooden box, bought in Maggie Valley, North Carolina, during our very first vacation in the United States. A beer mat I picked up in a little diner in Glide, Oregon, while we took shelter from the rain. My shopping is priceless!

This year we are headed to Pennsylvania, Maryland and Delaware for the first time. I anticipate my shopping there with great delight, knowing that there will be more people and more memories for me to take home to Scotland and cherish.

Joyce Stark

Mom's Mail-Order Mistake

The moon belongs to everyone; the best things in life are free.

B. G. DeSylva

My mother can spot a good deal three miles away on a foggy day. I remember her coming home some days beaming like a child who'd just learned to ride a bike because she found a sweater for five dollars. Dad often commented that she bought things no one needed, and Mom always swore she'd find a use for it. If she didn't, she knew someone who would. But like any professional, Mom has made a few mistakes over the years honing her technique.

It was winter. Snow swirled around the windowpane, and a fire crackled merrily on the hearth. Mom perused the Sunday morning newspaper, cup of coffee in hand, as was her habit on such mornings. While surveying the ads, she came across something that had the words "free sample" emblazed in huge letters across the page. Perhaps she forgot to read the fine print, or perhaps my brother had picked up the cat by his tail just as Dad recounted his losing battle with the Christmas lights. But whatever the reason, she missed the details, and in this case, detail was everything.

My brother and I were enjoying the temporary freedom of Christmas break when the UPS man delivered a huge box on our doorstep. I was sprawled on the couch with a new book when I heard Dad shout down to Mom, who was in the basement, and ask what she ordered this time.

"I don't remember. Nothing big. It was a free giveaway," she replied, coming up the stairs with an armload of laundry. Dad looked exasperated and gestured at the huge box now sitting in the middle of the family room. Utterly perplexed, Mom tore open the container to see what it was.

"Hemorrhoid medicine!" Dad exclaimed. "You ordered a hundred tubes of hemorrhoid medicine? No one in this house has hemorrhoids!" The sides of his mustache twitched as he tried to keep the laugh inside.

"I thought it was just a free sample. I only ordered one tube," she whispered, running one hand through her hair. It was quite a sight to see my mother sprawled on the floor, utterly bewildered, and surrounded by one hundred tubes of hemorrhoid cream.

"But why?" Dad nearly cried.

"Because it was free," Mom answered as if this were the most logical thing she'd ever done. Dad looked at her like she'd spoken Greek. Then he laughed. His face reddened, and his eyes watered. He clutched the mantel for support and howled. For a moment, I thought he'd gone mad.

"What am I going to do with this?" Mom muttered. I suggested we give it to Grandpa, but Dad said he didn't need a hundred tubes. Mom stowed the box out of sight and would mutter about ridding herself of the embarrassment as she stirred dough for holiday cookies or wrapped gifts.

The answer came a week later when my parents had a

New Year's Eve party, and my father came up with a brilliant way to rid our family of Mom's mail-order mistake. When each guest left, he offered them a door prize—a free tube of hemorrhoid cream, complete with the story of how we'd acquired it.

Mom has yet to live down the hemorrhoid cream incident, but it hasn't dampened her shopping spirit. She's even expanded to auctions and online ordering. Though these days, she always reads the fine print.

Rachel Green

From Crop-Tops to Suit-Tops

Beware of all enterprises that require new clothes.

HENRY DAVID THOREAU

At sixteen years old, you could have seen me coming a mile down the road in fire-engine red Daisy Dukes hiked an eighth of an inch below my behind. That outfit would have been accentuated by a white Betty Boop crop-top that splashed the phrase "100 Percent Girl" across my chest. That is, you would have seen me coming if my father hadn't caught me trying to leave the house in "that get-up."

Ahhh, Dad. That gray-haired paternal figure whose hair became suspiciously grayer through my teen years. "You're not going to that MEAT market dressed like that!" he barked when I dared go to the mall with my girlfriends in one such outfit.

"But Daaaad, it's just a shirt," I protested, trying to defend what might as well have been dental floss wrapped around my burgeoning chest.

During these mall trips, my girlfriends and I prowled for the perfect buy, not to mention the perfect guy—Dad wasn't so clueless, after all—and if an article of clothing sparkled, showed off our belly buttons and infuriated our parents, it passed through to the checkout line.

Fast forward ten years, and while you won't catch me wearing pants with "Bootylicious" scribbled across the seat in silver glitter (sorry Beyoncé!), I have found myself at odds with the clothes of my past and my future. Take, for example, the business suit.

"Well, how do I look?" I breathed deeply as the dressing-room door creaked open for my mother to see. She smiled as I inspected myself in the three-way mirror under the harsh glare of the fluorescent lighting. A navy polyester skirt brushed my knees. A three-quarter-sleeved match-ing blazer and a burgundy, navy and white checkered silk top masked my petite body. I turned around to inspect my backside. *100 Percent B-O-R-I-N-G Betty Boop* sang through my subconscious.

"Well?"

My mother started to laugh. "I'm just not used to seeing you look like this," she said. "It looks great on you, just dif-ferent."

"Well, my job interview is tomorrow," I said. "And you do have coupons."

"And it's machine-washable," my mother quipped.

Today, when I slip on that navy drabber-than-drab power suit reserved for meetings with clients, I feel like the girl I once was who played dress-up in my grand-parents' basement with my cousins. My grandmother's old beaded gowns shimmied down my shoulders when I tried to walk, but in my imagination, they fit perfectly. Today, the business suits fit me well, but deep down, I know they don't fit me just right.

My transformation was clearly apparent this past Christmas when my well-intentioned mother-in-law gave me a red (she got the color right) conservative Sag Harbor suit complete with shoulder pads and elastic waistband in exactly my size. Holding it up, my husband burst out laughing, and my poor mother-in-law protested, "Well, Maria's a professional now. She NEEDS clothes like this!" Upfront, I apologize to my mother-in-law when I admit that the suit sold for twenty dollars on eBay.

Somehow showing off my body in extra tight crop-tops doesn't seem so much fun anymore. Perhaps that's because I've found self-expression through my words to be more powerful than any outrageous outfit could ever be. I don't think that clothes can miraculously transform a girl into a woman, but how comfortable she is in her own skin can.

I've also happily discovered that the fashion industry is savvy enough to swipe the sex out of sleaze and package it into trendy work attire that won't send a young professional into a total identity crisis (think Mom's hosiery and favorite navy pumps with the rounded toe for "added comfort").

Today, you can see me coming a mile away from the elevator at work because I'll be wearing fluorescent green capris, strappy black heels and a "smart" black power jacket. I never managed to figure out a way to bring Betty Boop to work, so she remains tucked away in the back of my closet. I'm confident I'll never wear her again, but I don't have the heart to toss her away completely.

Maria Pascucci

Just Perfect

URLs were the 800 numbers of the 1990s.

CHRIS CLARK

The Internet seems to be the greatest invention and the source of all evil at the same time. I know because I've walked into the den and my husband is clicking madly at all of the open windows on the computer desktop while standing up to block the monitor. Clearly, he wasn't checking his bank balance. My sons have a tendency to play online games in lieu of doing homework. My friends forward the same funny e-mails that have been recycled through cyberspace for the past five years, and my in-laws send such huge pictures of their schnauzer that they make my computer crash.

If it wasn't for my own bad habit, we'd be the only people on the block who weren't "connected." But as I said, I, too, am guilty. I don't tell a lot of people about it. It's not that I'm ashamed; I just like the mystery. You see, as an online shopper, when people ask me where I got my bright-pink purse with fluffy trim or my jeans covered in sequins and rhinestones, I never divulge the secret. I'll tell them it's the latest in New York or Milan, and if they happen to assume that I was in New York or Milan, who am I to say otherwise? The red lace bra, which peaked out only the slightest bit, had all of my girlfriends wondering if I also went to the Opera when I was in Paris. Wouldn't that be a dream life?

I didn't start out as an online shopper; I wasn't even a great shopper to begin with. There are just too many turnoffs: pushy teenagers who are trying to sound so knowledgeable while working for minimum wage; those tiny changing rooms with curtains that always open as you're bending over to squeeze into jeans that looked the right size; and the throngs of people who manage to find the best deals before you. Online, I skip the salespeople, the changing rooms and the crowds. It's just me, often in my sweats with a cup of coffee—which I would never recommend taking into the changing room—and a list of Web sites, or "stores," to check out.

While I am not posh enough to walk into a trendy Los Angeles boutique and hold my head up high, or rich enough to actually travel there come to think of it, the Internet doesn't discriminate. Thanks to cyber-shopping, Jennifer Aniston and I now shop at the same store, although I haven't exactly run into her yet. And while I mentally put together many outfits, I don't actually end up buying anything in places like that. Fortunately, I'm saved the embarrassment of telling the sales staff that I've changed my mind, or left my wallet at home, or don't think the color suits me. All I have to, do is type in another URL and hit go, and I'm whizzed down the block to the next boutique where Nicole Kidman shops, or right across the world to London or Tokyo, perhaps.

Most of the time, apart from that gorgeous silver belt buckle in the shape of a skull and crossbones, I try to stick to reasonably priced purchases, which means online auction sites. It's like a great, big thrift shop: You have to look hard, but you can find some treasures. Unfortunately, some of them are priced as if they were the lost treasure of the Knights Templar. However, my Lara Croft-styled boots (along with the gun holsters and tiny shorts), original, signed script from Indiana Jones (the second one), and the complete *Star Trek* collection on DVD were all great deals. I didn't actually end up dressing up as Lara Croft for Halloween last year as I intended, but the script is definitely an investment. I can turn around and resell that online for a profit. As for *Star Trek*, it turns out that my boys like *Star Wars*, but I'm sure they'll get into *Star Trek* sometime, and it's always good to have a few movies around for a rainy day, right?

At the moment, I'm expecting a little something for my husband. There's nothing like receiving a package in the mail, and this one is a little thank-you for putting up with me.

Esme Mills

"I'm going to the mall.
Tape the Home Shopping Network for me."

The past is malleable and flexible, changing as our recollection interprets and re-explains what has happened.

PETER BERGER

One day, while visiting the Bargain Basket, I watched a busy volunteer sort a donation that had recently arrived. "Look at these," she said, holding up a pair of red rhinestone earrings, dangling and shining in the morning sun. "I wonder who wore these, and what story they might have to tell?"

Visions of a young girl in a fancy red gown dancing at her senior prom came into my mind. Perhaps they were a gift from someone very special, or maybe the mother of the bride wore them at her daughter's wedding. Her question intrigued me as I began to look around the shop.

Among the children's books, I found a well-worn copy of *Good Night Moon*. The image of a mother rocking her baby and softly reading him to sleep came to mind. I thought of the many times I had done exactly the same thing, and then watched my own children follow suit years later.

What about these boxes of jigsaw puzzles? Who put them together? Maybe two young girlfriends on a rainy afternoon, sharing stories and storing memories for the future. I remembered a table by the door of the dorm when I was in nursing school that always had a puzzle in progress. After classes, or anytime we came and went, we stopped and put a few pieces in place—a true community effort.

I thumbed through the old records and came across Glen Miller's romantic *Moonlight Serenade*. It brought to mind a young couple dancing on a starlit night. Was that the song that was playing when the young man "popped the question"?

GET WHAT YOU PAY FOR
Jewelry & Gems, The Buying Guide by Matlins and Bonanno, is a trusted source for the savvy estate-jewelry buyer.

Did some college kid wake to the aroma of fresh-baked bread and brewed coffee from the breadmaker and coffee-pot sitting on that shelf? Beautiful glassware, now chipped and scratched with only three matching pieces remaining, were probably part of many fancy parties and family gatherings. What New Year did they ring in?

And how many frustrated parents cursed those twisted strands of lights, vowing that next year they would store the Christmas ornaments away properly as they declared, "This is the prettiest tree we have ever had!"

Bits and pieces of yarn and threads evoked the presence of a grandmother crocheting mittens and baby blankets for countless grandchildren. Was she like me, who barely finished one before there was another baby on the way?

On the "buy one, get one free" table are four beautiful, lace-edged slips and several feminine nighties, all brand-new and never worn. I recall my mother-in-law who saved her best lingerie and nightgowns in case she some-day had to go to the hospital. After her death, they all ended up at the thrift shop on a "buy one, get one free" table just like this one.

I wonder what story my possessions will tell and what images someone will conjure up as they hold my prized, red rhinestone earrings to the morning sunlight streaming through the shop window?

Roberta McGovern

Doing the Handbag Hustle

I don't design clothes; I design dreams.

RALPH LAUREN

The call came late on a Saturday afternoon. "I'll pick you up in fifteen minutes, and we'll go get Jill," my sister-in-law Donna said breathlessly. "Remember, cash or checks only; they don't take credit cards."

When the number of women carrying Dooney Burke, Louis Vuitton and Chloe clones exceeded the population of a developing country, Donna began trying to hook up with a hot, local purveyor of handbag knockoffs. Finally, when her connection called, the three of us dropped everything and headed for Boca Raton.

While Donna drove, Jill had her cell phone glued to her ear in the backseat, and I navigated. "You know, Nance, we're very lucky this woman called," Donna explained. "Everyone I've talked to is waiting to be invited to one of her private showings. She only sees so many customers a week, and I've heard she's got a great selection."

We cruised along dreaming of affordable leather clutches and alligator totes, catching up on work and family, when the directions got a little murky. "What did you mean here, Donna?" I asked. "It says, 'Wait for SUV in the parking lot.'"

"That's what the woman said," Donna confirmed. "Pull into the parking lot and wait for the SUV."

We parked in a spot, left the AC running (after all, we can't let them see us sweat) and waited.

"So, how are we supposed to know which SUV is 'our' SUV?" I ask, beginning to wonder if I should call my son to just let him in on my last-known whereabouts.

"Don't worry, Nance—they asked what kind of car I would be driving." Now I was really starting to wonder whether I actually needed my thirtieth purse.

A few minutes later, a loud slap on the trunk and rap on the roof scared the daylights out of us. Quickly regaining her composure, Donna lowered her window just enough to hear what the very large man on the other side had to say.

"You have appointment with Miriska?" he asked in a thick accent.

Donna smiled warmly, lowering the window further. "That's us! This is . . . ," but before she could properly introduce us, the man was rapping on the roof and slapping the trunk, saying, "Follow me."

"Geez, this is quite a production," Donna said, echoing my thoughts as Jill took another call. Feeling like aging Charlie's Angels, we pulled into the driveway of a trendy McMansion and parked next to a well-appointed Mercedes. As we made our way up the short walk to the front door, the thought of calling my son popped in and out of my head again.

Before Donna could ring the doorbell, Jill could take another call, or I could conjure up images of crime-scene tape, the double doors swung open and a voice boomed, "Hello, darlinks, please come in. I am Miriska."

With a flair for the dramatic, Miriska swooped us into

the foyer and announced, "Welcome to my home. Treasures await you."

We blinked a few times as our eyes adjusted to the dimly lit interior with cavernous ceilings. There before us was table after table after table of every imaginable color, shape and size of knockoff handbags, clutches and fine silk scarves—hundreds of them. Like birds of prey, we circled before making our move.

"Oooh, Nance, look. Isn't this beautiful?" Donna swooped in and picked up a deep-red, ostrich shoulder bag.

"This is so cute!" I exclaimed over a finely embroidered silk clutch.

"These prices are unbelievable!" Jill cooed, turning her cell phone to vibrate. "Look . . ."

We lost track of time, touching and styling something from every table until Miriska's voice echoed from beyond. "Well, darlinks, you have found beautiful treasures, no?"

"Yes!" "Yes!" "Yes!" The Three Musketeers responded in unison.

"Well, let me see what you have selected," Miriska instructed. I showed her one of my choices, a "Louie Vittoun" classic tote.

"Oh, yes! Beautiful. But you must have these also if you are to wear that bag well," offered Miriska, my accessories mentor, as she handed me a matching cell-phone cozy and lipstick holder.

"Yes, yes, I'll take them," I sputtered, as Miriska turned her attention to Donna and Jill.

Once satiated, I began to notice our surroundings. Curiously, nowhere in the five-thousand square feet of marble opulence did I see a single piece of furniture, not even around the zero-gravity pool. A buzz in my head started, and a little voice was whispering—my voice: *Yes, son, that was dear, old mom on the eleven o'clock news at the knock-off bust. Oh, by the way, does the camera really add ten pounds?*

"Hey! Nance!" Donna's voice interrupted. "Are you finished? Miriska has another appointment. Let's tally up."

"Cash or check, darlink?" Miriska asked, as I reached for the last time into my straw and leather bag from Macy's.

"Check, if that's okay," I reply.

"Oh, yes, darlink. Check is fine. I just need to see your driver's license," Miriska purred.

After the cloak-and-dagger routine, our ride home was uneventful. We chattered on about what a great deal we got and how stylish we would look next Sunday at the Pittsburgh club watching the Steelers.

A few days later, I got together with my son and daughter-in-law and showed off my new friend "Louie." Careful not to leave out any of the details, I regaled them with our exploits of the secret meet, the empty mansion, the Mercedes outside and the hundreds of handbags inside. When I got to the end of my story, I did my best impression of Miriska, "Oh, yes, darlink.

THE REAL THING

Here are some tips to spot knockoff Louis Vuitton handbags:

. . . If it's less than $300, more than likely it's a fake.

. . . If it's being sold online through an auction or ecommerce site (other than *eluxury.com*) as "brand new" it's probably a fake.

. . . If it's a new bag and the bag's handle is a different color leather than the piping, it's fake.

. . . If it didn't come with a dust cover or if the dust cover has rounded edges, it's fake. For more information on real LV bags, visit *www.mypoupette.com*.

Check is fine. I just need to see your driver's license."

It was at this point in delivering my dramatic replay that my daughter-in-law and son shared a look that gave me pause.

"Ah, Mom, you gave her a check and your driver's license number?" my daughter-in-law asked.

"Well, yes, she didn't take credit cards, and I didn't bring enough cash with me. If I had known what a selection . . ." Pause. There was that look again. "What? What's wrong?" I asked a bit more emphatically.

"Well, Mom, I think you might want to call the bank and close out your checking account," my son offered.

"And it might be a good idea to start getting a copy of your credit report every few months," my glum daughter-in-law suggested.

And then it dawned on me: Miriska, with her expensive car, her bodyguard, her mansion without furniture and her inventory of hundreds of knockoff handbags had everything she needed to become "Nancy Sullivan." But something told me to sit tight. For all of the trappings, Mariska struck me more as an ambitious entrepreneur than a thief. I decided to put my faith in a woman who seemed to appreciate the concept of owning a trendy handbag even more than I. And, despite the dire warnings of my kids that afternoon, I'm very pleased to tell you that Miriska turned out to be just what she appeared to be on the surface—the finest purveyor of knockoff handbags Boca's ever seen, and not an identity thief.

Now, if she'd only return with a house full of "Jimmy Choos" and "Prada," we'd be back in business.

Nancy Sullivan
As told to Theresa Peluso

Secondhand Lessons

Man's mind stretched to a new idea never goes back to its original dimensions.

OLIVER WENDELL HOLMES

When my children were young, we were very poor. I was a single mother working one full-time and two part-time jobs. The only gift I could give them spontaneously was my time, which was spent reading Dr. Seuss and singing songs in the kitchen while I made the dinner that the babysitter would feed them.

On holidays, all gifts came from Goodwill or the Salvation Army. I was always able to find cute, barely worn clothes and a few toys by visiting the secondhand stores in better neighborhoods. Social stigma aside, I liked shopping at secondhand stores. I could buy clothes my kids needed and still pay my bills.

I would carefully starch and iron the little T-shirts and wrap them in the scraps of paper the store used to wrap breakables. I spent a lot of time carefully removing garage-sale stickers from the toy boxes and taping up the frazzled edges. My kids wore those secondhand clothes to shreds, and if they outgrew them before they were destroyed, I would pack them up and take them back.

The toys I found were beloved. They still talk about the "Sit and Spin" and "He-Man Castle" that were already in sad shape when they got them. Those toys were popular years before they were born, so they were the only kids who had them. When their friends would come over, they would always rush to those two toys.

Years went by, and fortune was kinder. My ex-husband got a better job and was able to increase his child-support payments. My low income made it easier for me to get grants for college, enabling me to find better jobs, and I met a man who found it no burden to help raise my children.

Although I no longer needed to, I still shopped at second-hand stores until the day my eleven-year-old daughter, Wren, came home angry. She had noticed a little girl wearing a shirt that she had outgrown and I had donated. "You gave away my bug shirt to Goodwill, and there is a stinky third-grader wearing it!"

Her bug shirt had been a secondhand store find with a little hole in one sleeve. I had sewn a ladybug appliqué over the hole, and she had adored it.

"I got that shirt from a thrift store, and I don't see the problem. You are wearing jeans that a sixth-grader probably wore," I shot back without thinking.

There was silence in the room. Then a high-pitched "Ewwww . . . someone else wore these jeans before me? Ewwww . . . that's disgusting!"

She went straight to her room and took them off. She gave them to a friend the next day without mentioning a word of it to me. After that, she questioned every article of clothing she wore and refused to wear the secondhand ones. Nothing I could say would convince her that it was acceptable to reuse clothing, although she carefully rinsed and recycled every can and piece of plastic that left our kitchen "to save the polar bears."

My son dutifully wore his secondhand clothes with pride. He even went shopping with me. He found his favorite Japanese emblem shirts there, and there were always good electronic parts at our local Goodwill.

One day, Wren and I were volunteered to do a play at our community theater when a conflict arose among the actors, and half the cast was suddenly unavailable. One of the remaining cast members, Meredith, was a beautiful, talented girl who my daughter followed around like a puppy. "She wears the coolest clothes, she knows the coolest songs, and she's sooo pretty!" Wren would squeal.

MAKE IT COUNT

Make your donations wisely and support a good cause. About 84 percent of Goodwill's revenues go directly into employment and training programs for people with disabilities and other barriers to employment!

Meredith was a kind girl whose parents were also divorced. The three of us were making small talk in the dressing room when she noticed a skirt I was wearing and asked me where I had gotten it. "I paid $1.50 for this at the Salvation Army!" I bragged, temporarily forgetting that my daughter was listening—not for long as the look of horror on her face made the whole room visibly darker.

Meredith brightened it immediately. "These jeans were $1.00 at St. Vincent de Paul!"

"This jacket was $2.00 there!" I bounced back.

"Shoes, twenty-five cents at a yard sale!"

"Those are excellent shoes," my daughter piped in. "My

favorite shirt of all space and time came from a second-hand store."

I couldn't think of a word to say. I just beamed.

The next day, I took my daughter with me to a second-hand store, and she found a pair of green suede shoes. She wouldn't tell anyone where she got them, although several people asked.

When she got money for her birthday, she asked me to take her back. That child bought four pairs of pants, four shirts and three books for twenty dollars. Seems she's a natural thrift shopper and almost over her shame. Almost . . . she still won't tell anyone where she shops.

Dawn Howard-Hirsch

My Mother, the Stripper

If you've got it, wear it.

LOUIS MOUNTBATTEN

Mother and I were on our way back to our hotel from the MRI that confirmed her doctor's diagnosis of rheumatoid arthritis. At age eighty-two, she had been miserable and in pain during our week at the Mayo Clinic, enduring tests and doctor visits. Zooming down the freeway, I remembered there was a shopping center at the next exit. Hoping to cheer her up, I said, "I was going to suggest we shop for some new clothes, but I guess you're too tired now, aren't you?"

This was the first time she'd heard the word "shopping" in over a week, and without hesitating she responded, "Of course not! I'd love to!" I swerved into the exit lane just in time to head toward the new, upscale department store that was one of Mother's favorites.

I pulled as close as possible to the handicapped ramp and walked around to help Mother out. I left her standing there while I parked the car, chastising myself for not remembering the inalienable right of the handicapped shopper—her blue parking tag.

Walking toward the elevator, we admired the beautiful marble on the floor. It was unusually elegant for a department store. Mother walked with difficulty to the sale racks and found several jackets and skirts to try on. Since running a law office twenty years before, Mother wore only suits—even on her days off. The most casual item I could get her to wear was a denim skirt with a red blazer. We walked a very long distance to the dressing room where I helped her undress.

This trip to the Mayo Clinic had been our last hope that she could have less pain and be able to dress and walk without assistance. Carefully, I helped her undress, dress and re-dress, but none of the skirts fit. Discouraged, we put her skirt back on and left the dressing room.

Mother hobbled from rack to rack, replacing items we weren't buying. "The sales clerks will do that, Mother," I reminded, but she ignored me. I remembered all the times in my childhood when she had said, "If you always return something to its proper place, you won't ever have to wonder where it is!" and "A place for everything and everything in its place!"

As we approached the sales counter, we eyed some skirts we hadn't seen before. I looked at the long expanse of marble between us and the dressing room. "Are you going to try one on?" I asked.

"Of course!" Mother said. "But I'm not walking all the way over to that dressing room." Before it had registered what she was doing, she had unzipped her skirt and dropped it to the floor, right there between two racks of clothes!

"Help me get into this skirt, will you?" she snapped, as though I were the one doing something strange. Quickly, I helped her with the skirt, and she made her way to a nearby mirror. The skirt was not for her. She calmly let it drop, and I helped her step out of it. I got her into her own skirt as quickly as possible.

She purchased the jacket and blouse, and as we started back toward the elevator, we saw the sweaters—a colorful array of petite, mock turtlenecks with zippers in the back. Her favorite!

How did we not see these? I wondered as we went through the bright, sunny colors, trying to find her size and marveling at the good price. Fortunately for everyone, she didn't have to try these on, for she had enough sweaters of the same style that we knew which size would fit.

She was especially smitten with the lime-green one, and her choice in color told me Mother was going to adapt to her new difficulties with her usual flexibility and unflappability.

"Let's return that lavender blouse," she insisted. "That color is for an old woman!"

Lanita Bradley Boyd

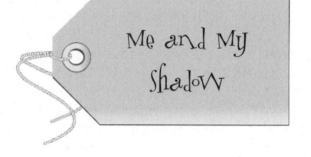

Me and My
Shadow

The years teach what the days never know.

RALPH WALDO EMERSON

It's the grocery store, not the boutique that tugs at my heartstrings and feeds my addiction. The sight of plump produce, the smell of fresh-baked muffins and the allure of the slick package attract me like a magnet.

This love affair with grocery stores began in my early childhood when I accompanied Yiayia (Greek for grandmother) on her daily outing. We stopped first at the produce section and nabbed a couple of grapes to get our juices flowing before we shopped in earnest. Just before we entered the checkout lane, we always swung by the candy counter for a couple of peppermint candies to go.

In between those two treats, Yiayia squeezed blood from a turnip as we wound our way through the maze of aisles. Each item landed in our shopping cart only after some mysterious mental gymnastics to determine that it offered the best value for our dollar. We nibbled our way through the store, stopping to chat with the women at each sample station. After we filled the cart with necessities, we always had enough money left to splurge on one special indulgence, some little something for our afternoon snack.

Yiayia carried a bundle of coupons from the newspaper and handled them like currency. What we lacked in coupon doubling and tripling back then, we made up for in Top Value Stamps and S&H Green Stamps.

SUPER-SIZE IT

A family of four can save $2,000 a year by choosing large sizes of cereal, juice, water and snacks instead of individual serving sizes.

On our way to the old blue and white Dodge, with a cute delivery boy in tow, the store manager would often stop us and ask, "Did you get your peppermint today?" Then he'd pull a couple more from his coat pocket, hand one to each of us and say, "Here, have one on me." That was then.

Today, we have those cozy, corner markets bursting with designer coffees and goodies adorned with luscious labels and the too-hot-to-touch price tags. Supermarkets stock savory homemade deli items, the ones that I've labored for hours to recreate at home for a fraction of the cost. The discount supermarkets combine the rib-tickling fun of rock-bottom prices with artsy store-brand labels.

Our neighborhood Harris Teeter tops my list of favorites. There's an old-fashioned allure about it, something about the place that makes me feel instantly at home, that takes me back to my childhood. It's not the double-coupon policy, though that certainly helps. It's not the frenetic annual triple-coupon feeding frenzy. It's not even Billie the butcher, who chases me down to say, "Put that pig back. Spiral ham goes on sale next week, and you'll get three for that price. Oh, and mum's the word," he adds with a wink. It can't be the delivery boys, because they exist only as a distant memory.

One evening, right before Christmas, the store manager walked me to my car, carrying my bags full of groceries— groceries for which Harris Teeter actually paid me two cents to take off their hands. I stopped to wish the Salvation Army Santa a Merry Christmas as I dropped a substantial offering into the black kettle, a donation made possible because of the lessons I had learned as I shadowed Yiayia through the grocery store. I suddenly felt Yiayia's presence, and I heard her whisper, *"Bravo, koritsi mou, bravo* (bravo, my little girl, bravo)!" I knew that she was smiling down on me, bursting with pride at the thought that she had taught me how to have my baklava and let others eat it, too.

M. J. Plaster

Momma's Girl

Nothing you do for children is ever wasted. They seem not to notice us, hovering, averting our eyes, and they seldom offer thanks, but what we do for them is never wasted.

GARRISON KEILLOR

I t's pure pleasure to shop when someone you know is expecting a baby, and if a mother-to-be knows her baby is a boy or a girl—good-bye yellow; hello pink or blue! Indulging your little one before he or she arrives is one of the pleasures of pregnancy. Okay, it's the only pleasure of pregnancy.

Walking around the baby section of a store, feeling the warmth and softness of the tiny clothes, cuddly stuffed animals, plush bedding, and then imagining how nurturing it would be for your child to have that same tactile experience . . . that's nourishment for the pregnant woman's soul.

But in my case, I wasn't actually pregnant. I didn't know my baby's gender with any certainty; I didn't know her age, her size or where she lived. That's the way it often is with international adoptions. Unfortunately, my shopping had to wait.

The best I could do was pray that we'd be matched with the baby we petitioned for from the China Center for Adoption Affairs: a healthy, female infant between zero and twelve months of age. I prayed she was well cared for and loved while waiting for her forever family. And I prayed for patience . . . it would be months before we received our referral, and I'd permit myself to shop.

Then one delightful morning in May 2005, the floodgates opened! Our social worker called us with joyous news: An eleven-month-old baby girl from the Jiangxi Province of China was waiting for us to bring her home. She had spent the past year of her life in the loving care of a single foster mother and hadn't spent one night in the orphanage. God answered our greatest prayers. We'd been matched with the perfect child we'd dreamed of. A single caregiver in a private home loved her for the first year of her life.

Finally, the wait was over. "Let the shopping begin!" I rejoiced that beautiful, fateful day. Well, those weren't exactly my first words . . . but that thought entered my head almost immediately.

I frantically looked up our baby's height and weight measurements on an online U.S. clothing size comparison chart I'd found, deciding six to nine months was my target. Recognizing that we'd be traveling to southern China in July (and that would be downright tropical), I had a plan. Buy conservatively for our trip, buy a few items for our immediate return, but save the real shopping for the days after I had held my child in my own arms and could pinpoint her actual size.

That first day out, I bought pretty pink onesies and non-slip socks. I bought delicate sundresses with matching sunhats. I bought bright-colored bathing suits and cozy pajamas and fancy barrettes and knitted cardigan sweaters. I was in love . . . with my daughter and the bags I was filling to the brim in her honor. This was the tangible sign I had wished for to prove that my dream was becoming a reality.

My other children, deprived of the shopping euphoria, wanted in. My oldest son picked out a soft, plush, white kitty cat with a bell in its belly that jingled pleasantly with every shake. My middle son picked out a pink, fleecy blanket with matching satin trim, one of those blanket-bear combinations.

Back at home and in her room, I hung my daughter's dresses in size order in her closet. I opened the packs of onesies and socks and laid them out neatly in her drawers. I made up her crib with her new pink sheets and a pastel crib bumper and placed the stuffed "friends" that my boys had picked out for their sister in the corners near where she'd lay her head down to sleep.

Before leaving my daughter's room that night, I smiled with satisfaction. Very soon I'd travel across the world to bring home the most precious gift since the birth of my sons: the beautiful baby girl that I'd longed for—and longed to shop for—all my life.

UP & COMING SHOPPERS
The largest shopping center in the world is in Beijing, China, with 7.3 million square feet of area. By comparison, the Mall of America in Bloomington, Minnesota, is the largest mall in the United States at 4.2 million square feet.

Karen Lynch

Caught Up in the Moment

Love the moment, and the energy of the moment
will spread beyond all boundaries.

SISTER CORITA KENT

Soon after we closed on the new home we had built, I
was sitting in the great room surveying my surroundings, totally overwhelmed with the thought of decorating
the place. Fortunately, an auction about forty minutes
away was known for its good buys on furniture, and my
husband, who like most men loves a good deal but not
dealing with salespeople, agreed to come with me.

One late Saturday afternoon, we arrived at the large warehouse just before the auction began. Several items were featured on the stage, and furniture lined the walls. We walked
around, taking time to study all the pieces and wondering
where the bidding would start, and how high the bidding
would go. We had never been to a live auction before, and
we had no idea what to expect, but there was something
about the character of the place that had us intrigued.

When the bidding started, the excitement drew us in to
the point of no return. We had finally found a way for both

of us to shop and actually enjoy the process together. Shopping wasn't how Tom liked to spend his time, but this had become a night of entertainment.

It wasn't long before we found ourselves bidding on a few small items: a wooden jewelry box and a framed picture. As we got into the late hours of the night, the auctioneers moved on to the higher-priced items.

Off to the side of the stage, I spotted a floral couch that had just the right colors and styling for my living room. Once we took a closer look, we agreed to bid on it.

"One hundred dollars! One-fifty! Two hundred! Two-fifty! Three hundred! Three-fifty! Four hundred, and sold! Sold to the couple sitting on the far-right side, four rows back, for four-hundred dollars!" exclaimed the auctioneer as he pounded his gavel for the final time.

In a matter of seconds, we had bought a new couch! This wasn't something we usually did on the spur of the moment, and I was contemplating the rash purchase when Tom leaned over and asked, "How are we going to get this couch home?"

Why was he asking me? I didn't know! We clearly lacked a way to transport the new purchase, and to our dismay the auction staff confirmed that purchases were cash and carry—we had to take it home with us that night. The only thing we could do was load the couch, upside down, onto the roof of our old white Honda Accord and tie it down with twine, which fortunately the men had plenty of.

For forty long, slow miles—in the dark—we drove back to our new home with that couch strapped to the top of our little Honda. We would be better prepared the next time!

Peggy Reeves

GOING, GOING, GONE

When attending an auction, it's easy to get caught up in a buying frenzy. Step back and look at potential purchases with a discerning eye. Take time before the bidding begins to evaluate items and do your research, especially if it's a significant investment or a large item that will be featured prominently in your home.

Invest in a guidebook to check values, markings or styles of antiques and vintage items. One of the best is *Kovels' Antiques & Collectibles Price List*. It's updated annually, and you can find them online at *www.kovels.com*.

Before you go to the auction, measure the space available and draw a quick floor plan and furniture layout of your rooms. If you see something interesting, you'll be able to determine whether you have the room and where it could go in your home. Bring a tape measure with you.

Living Within My Means

Life was a lot simpler when what we honored was father and mother rather than all major credit cards.

ROBERT ORBEN

If there is one thing I hate, it is living within my means. That school of thought that favors not spending more than you make almost seems un-American. It is not that I don't have enough to meet my basic needs—I do. I just don't have enough for everything else. There is a world of goods and services out there, just waiting for me to figure out how to pay for it all.

Some of those goods and services seem to be made just for me. They promise to fulfill my every dream, make me smarter, more beautiful, richer, healthier, you name it. I could be anything, do anything, go anywhere . . . if only I could figure out how to pay for it.

In the old days, when I was a single mom, I was the only person I had to answer to. Recovering from divorce, living on child support and student loans, it was easy enough for me to justify spending a little more than I should. It was easy because . . . well, because my kids needed this or that, or they really wanted it, or I really wanted it. Buy now, pay later, right? I figured life was too short to worry about when later was. I assumed I would never retire, that I would work until I was ninety. I always thought that someday I would start to live within my means. Just not today.

I wasn't completely irresponsible or mindless about money. I always kept up with payments, kept a good credit history, but the payments had no end, and there was no wiggle room left at the end of the month. We all need a little room to wiggle.

These days, money is not so tight. The kids are growing up; my career is shaping up; I refinanced my house at a great rate. It has been more than three years since I have used a credit card for anything other than hotel reservations. One by one, the balances are going to zero, and one by one, I am closing those accounts. I will keep one for emergencies and credit history, but one is all I need.

Still, there are days when I long for a little carefree spending. I yearn for the freedom to fling. I chafe against the restraints of common sense. Logic dictates that living within my means is the correct path; all the financial analysts say it is so. My right brain says I will really enjoy things a few years from now; just think of how much disposable income we will have. But my left brain is pouting. I want to dispose of that income now. I don't want to wait a few years. I want to win the lottery and be financially independent and never have to worry about my means again.

With a heavy sigh, I walk away from the latest major sale, turn my back on the latest inviting cruise package, ignore the offerings of an endless array of possibilities, and resign myself to being reasonable and responsible. Like a person trying to kick an addictive habit, just for today I will focus on living within my means. But I don't have to like it.

Terry Lilley

I Saw It First!

Elegance is not the prerogative of those who have just escaped from adolescence, but of those who have already taken possession of their future.

Coco Chanel

Some people come from a long line of respected doctors, lawyers or political figures, but when it comes to my family, I'm proud to say that I come from a generation of serial shoppers. It all began with Grandma Eva, a successful seamstress who sewed my mother's wedding gown, and Grandpa Yale, a hard-working tailor. My mother, Eileen, became a shopoholic by default, as she detested all the hand-me-down clothing she received from her two elder sisters. As for me, well . . . let's just say that the apple didn't fall far from the tree.

My mother and I share many similarities, from our addiction to dark chocolate to our intolerance for the smell of freshly peeled oranges, as well as our appearance—everyone comments that we look like sisters. But nothing compares to our passion for fashion . . . our raison d'être, if you will. As shallow as it may seem, shopping has always been our favorite pastime, the source of many laughs, and unfortunately, a few tears.

Most fashion fanatics I know shop solo to save time and avoid unwanted arguments with their best friend over who should score that limited-edition Chloé handbag spotted in a store window. For my mother and me, shopping together isn't a burden, but a blessing that enables us to bond. Because I moved away from my parents' home in Montreal years ago, my mother and I cherish our downtime together, which is inevitably spent (much to my father's dismay) shopping.

Sometimes, however, a competitive shopping streak develops between us, which eradicates traditional mother-daughter boundaries, resulting in an unhealthy love-hate relationship. One minute we're best buddies, and the next, rivals. Some of the unhappier shopping episodes began after college when I moved to the world's fashion mecca, New York City. I had just started a stressful editorial job at a well-known fashion publication when my parents came to visit from Montreal one weekend. We were to meet for a low-key brunch that Saturday at one of our favorite spots, followed by a Broadway play and, of course, some power shopping.

I couldn't wait to debut the new chocolate-brown pencil skirt and matching ruched jacket I had recently purchased at a trendy downtown boutique . . . that was until I arrived at the restaurant. Like a celebrity's red carpet nightmare, there was my mother coincidentally dressed in the exact same In Wear ensemble. Most normal women faced with the same dilemma would probably laugh hysterically about the incident and get on with their day. But since my mother and I aren't exactly "normal," the mood suddenly turned somber, and the situation took an unexpected turn for the worse.

As the hostess escorted my father and his shell-shocked doppelgänger dressers to the table, my mother was so embarrassed that she demanded I immediately head home and change into something else. Stunned and dismayed by her emphatic request, I wondered why my mother wasn't flattered that her fashion-obsessed daughter coincidentally bought the same outfit. I'd be thrilled to pieces if my own daughter embraced my inimitable sense of style. Somehow that logic was lost on Mom. Consequently, like a misbehaved child sent to bed without any supper, I begrudgingly went home to change.

Shortly after that disturbing clothing calamity, a similar pattern of competitive dressing spats began to develop. Since I was now in the workforce, I was constantly on the prowl for cool career clothes with a modern edge, and I found it easier (and cheaper) to shop back home in Canada's clothing capital, Montreal. Because I valued my mother's opinion and her winning wardrobe, she gleefully agreed to chaperone me to one of the chicest spots in the city and introduced me to Spy—a bustling, ground-level boutique that sells of-the-moment merchandise from international labels.

At Spy, it wasn't uncommon to find fashion-obsessed, mother-daughter duos like us rummaging through the racks in a frenzy, ogling and elbowing over the same stock. Unfortunately, that's exactly what happened. What started out as a nice bonding experience quickly morphed into a fighting match over who bought what first. Much like children calling out "dibs" to claim the front seat, I "ooh-ed and ahh-ed" over a particular Isabel de Pedro floral top, and my mom suddenly blurted out, "I bought that one, that one and that one," in a feeble attempt to mark her territory.

Although we've never been the same size and haven't lived in the same city for years, none of that seemed to matter to Mom. Miraculously, after some coaxing, I convinced her it was avant-garde and acceptable for us to buy similar items, since we paired things together based on what suited our unique sense of style, and what worked best with our body type. We also agreed to call each other in advance of any family functions to avoid any future clothing conundrums.

I must admit, to this day, whenever we go shopping together, it still feels like an Olympic sport, both of us jockeying for position to snag that must-have item before the other one spots it. Whoever scores the latest and greatest finds first gets the most points . . . or, in our case, credit card debt. But despite all the hysteria and tomfoolery we've been through, it's through this mutual love for shopping that my mother and I share such a special bond. If it weren't for our incessant buying (and returning), we wouldn't be nearly as close or crazy about each other. Like a father and son's connection through a shared love of baseball, shopping with Mom is the essential ingredient that enriches my life.

SHOPPING IN THE BIG APPLE

New York City sales tax is 8.65 percent, but is not added to clothing or footwear under $110. If you live out of state, have your purchases shipped directly home to avoid paying sales tax.

Only Mom has the chutzpah to call me on my cell and beg me to purchase the last available Theory skirt in her size at Bloomingdales, just before I'm about to catch a flight home. Only my mother can coerce me into spending a sunny Sunday afternoon with her to clean out her five walk-in closets and make room for the next seasonal shipment from Spy. And only my mother continues to buy me hoards of clothing when I'm feeling blue—as long as it's not already in one of her closets!

Dara Fleischer

The Mix Master

I will welcome happiness as it enlarges my heart; yet I will endure sadness for it opens my soul. I will acknowledge rewards for they are my due; yet I will welcome obstacles for they are my challenge.

OG MANDINO

Therapy of all kinds is a wondrous thing. I must admit I never thought about it much until I needed it desperately. What was left of my right arm labored hard those first grueling weeks to achieve skill with every prosthesis offered. I finally returned home with a dainty hook, a tough farm-and-ranch hook most men ran from, and a very fancy mio-electric hand. I called it my "go to meetin' arm."

My husband had traded in my old car for a new model with automatic everything so I could drive by myself. That first day out was a lark, and it felt good negotiating the curves down our long, woodsy mountain onto pavement. I intended to shop for just a few groceries, mainly the fixins for a velvety cake complete with gooey frosting.

I deserved it. I had lost thirty pounds, embraced a passion for cakes and had sorely missed my kitchen.

Apprehension brought on a few butterflies, but everyone at my favorite grocers made me feel at ease. Warm smiles and grateful hugs were unexpected from all those I'd been acquainted with for years. Upon much goading, I demonstrated how I could turn my new hand around and open and close the fingers, with fancy painted nails yet. I almost felt worthwhile again.

After tossing a few basics into my cart, I eagerly headed for the baking aisle. There before me stood shelves filled with brand-new delights. It was as if all manner of appetizing riches had been breeding in the night to tempt the following day's shoppers. Unfamiliar desserts of every size and flavor were displayed, row upon row. New cakes with more complicated steps, and fancy pans to bake them in, made me positively giddy. Not today, I decided. My mission should be something familiar, something easy. I selected a new French vanilla cake mix and dropped it in the cart while surveying the vast array of yummy-sounding frostings. With teeth clenched and a determined squint, my new mio-electric hand encircled a luscious-looking can of chocolate-fudge icing on the top shelf. Midway down, there resonated a loud pop, and the can began spewing showers of sweet ecstasy. The dark contents plopped off my hair and slid down my jacket onto new white shoes. The nooks and crannies of shelves in every direction were adorned in brownish-glazed splotches. Even the new coffee grinding machine behind me was slathered in chocolate chaos. *Oh, dear Lord, where's the nearest exit?* I mused while staring at the devastation and the daunting new hand that had not known its own strength.

A moment later a comforting arm was around my shoulder as the store manager offered words of encouragement. He apologized for snickering, but felt the incident was just too priceless not to give it a good chuckle. *Was this a prophecy of things to come?* I pondered as I threw my spotted jacket on a chair at home. While unloading my sack of groceries, I wondered what possessed me to act the smart aleck. I vowed then and there to concentrate on being a humble survivor instead of a harebrained showoff. Surely this fiasco would be a hot topic in the Safeway lunchroom for months to come. I cringed at the thought, but knew I must get a grip and begin to laugh at myself, for there stood the old Mixmaster my husband had hauled out that very morning.

The enticing photo on the box still taunted me with heavenly cake and frosting pangs. After turning on the oven, I stepped out to tap floured pans on the deck railing. Given short-term memory problems after so many surgeries, I paid particular attention to the high-altitude directions. With the mix, eggs, water and oil carefully measured and placed in the bowl, it was time to let 'er rip for the prescribed time. Rubber spatula poised, I flipped the switch and stood thunderstruck while beaters and bowl catapulted across the floor like a Brahma bull breaking from a rodeo pen.

The phone rang. It was my husband asking how I was doing, and how come I sounded like I was coming down with a cold? I told him that . . . sniff, sniff . . . cake mixes . . . sniff, sniff . . . and 1½-armed women don't mix. He said he would be home early. And he was—with a lovely cake from our grocer's bakery.

Kathe Campbell

[EDITORS' NOTE: *After ten years, there's very little Kathe can't do as she celebrates the fitting of her fourth new arm, leaving frostings, cake batter and hazardous spatulas in the dust.*]

chapter 4

Malls, Mail Order, and Mom & Pop Shops

May we never let the things we don't have spoil our enjoyment of the things we do have. As we value our happiness, let us not forget it, for one of the greatest lessons in life is learning to be happy without the things we cannot or should not have.

RICHARD L. EVANS

Jeans Please,
Hold the Whiskers

I wish I had invented blue jeans. They have expression, modesty, sex appeal, simplicity—all I hope
for in my clothes.

YVES SAINT LAURENT

My favorite three-year-old pair of Calvin Kleins was
fading and wearing thin. As much as I loved them, I
knew it was time to seek out a worthy replacement. I realized, as soon as I stepped foot in the mall's most popular
denim store, that I must have aged at least three decades
since the last time I bought jeans. Nearly everyone
employed there looked barely sixteen years old. One of
the fresh-faced teens approached and asked if I needed
help.

"Yes," I answered. "I'm looking for jeans."

"What kind of jeans?" she asked.

I was confused by the question. "Blue jeans," I replied,
and she stared back at me blankly, as if that wasn't
nearly enough information. She led me around the
perimeter of the store, pointing out the various types and
styles available.

"There's low-rise, button-fly, flare leg, boot cut, painter pants, peanut pants, low-rise easy flares, distressed and New Classic."

I was awestruck, like a denim-wearing deer in headlights. I had no idea jeans had become so complicated. The sizing and style numbers were only slightly less complicated than the U.S. tax code. It was a good thing there was a teenager there to explain it to me.

I let the salesgirl make a few selections for me and then wandered into the dressing room to put the first pair on, which was a struggle because there were four stiff buttons on the fly. I knew right away that a button-fly wasn't right for me. With a one-year-old child at home, I barely have time to go to the bathroom, let alone struggle with buttons on my fly. I needed a zipper—a fast one.

I discarded the button-fly jeans and found a pair with a zipper. I managed to shimmy into them and then turned to the mirror. Absolutely awful. These jeans looked to be in worse shape than the ancient Calvin Kleins I was trying to replace. They were faded on the thighs, with mysterious white marks in the place where my legs branch off my torso, as if bleach had been poured into the creases. I walked out of the dressing room and waved over the salesgirl.

"What is this?" I asked, pointing to the strange white lines.

"Oh, those are whiskers," she said.

"Whiskers?" I repeated.

"Yeah, whiskers," she confirmed, as if it was as common a term as, say, "bread."

"Are whiskers popular?" I asked. As she nodded yes, I got the distinct feeling that what she really wanted to do was roll her eyes and say, "Duh."

I looked past the whiskers to assess the fit. The legs of the jeans were flared in a way that reminded me of Bozo the Clown's pants. I studied my reflection in the mirror, trying to adjust to the flared-leg, whiskered look. After all, I did want to be in style. Then I checked the price tag, and that's what clinched it. I would not, could not, bring myself to pay more than eighty dollars for low-rise, flared-leg, distressed jeans with whiskers. I turned again to the clerk.

THE PEDIGREE

Jeans were invented in Genoa, Italy, perfected in France and redefined for America by Levi Strauss in the 19th century.

"Listen, what I really want is just normal jeans, you know? Plain old blue jeans with no flare leg or bleach spots or whiskers or buttons on the fly. Do you have anything like that?" She thought about it for a moment, shaking her head. I was beginning to think I'd have to wear my three-year-old Calvin Kleins until they literally disintegrated.

Finally, she came back with an answer. "I think there are only two jeans in the whole store that are like what you just described."

"Great, I'll try them," I said. So she led me to a far corner toward the back of the store, otherwise known as the "Un-hip Old Geezer" section. She dug out the two pairs of normal jeans, blew the dust off them and handed them over. I tried them on. They were a classic fit, zipper fly, and they were blue all over. Perfect. I rushed them to the register before some other desperate old geezer tried to snatch them from me.

With tragically un-hip jeans in the bag, I left Planet Puberty and returned home, where I will likely age at least four more decades before my next blue-jean shopping excursion.

Gwen Rockwood

Life on Mars for Venus

When women are depressed, they either eat or go shopping. Men invade another country. It's a whole different way of thinking.

ELAINE BOOSLER

We just moved into a new house, which, oddly enough, means that I spend an inordinate amount of time at Home Depot. One would think that a new house doesn't need home "improvements," yet I'm obsessed with improving our home, even though it was just built.

Admittedly, most of my need to quickly set up house is rooted in my military upbringing. With only two or three years to live in a home, I've always felt pressured to get settled fast so we can maximize our enjoyment before the next move. And for reasons unknown to me, getting settled—and remember, this is a newly constructed home—requires daily trips to the home improvement store.

But I can't pretend I don't like my trips to Home Depot because they've afforded me many lessons in the differences between men and women. Men walk into Home Depot with a purpose. They have serious, thoughtful looks on their faces as they wander aimlessly down the aisles pretending to know where they are going or what they're looking for. Sometimes men shopping at Home Depot even frown, but I think this is just to make us women believe that shopping for tools is hard on a guy and that they don't get any enjoyment out of it at all.

I, on the other hand, walk into Home Depot as I do every other store—with a bewildered look on my face and a well-intended shopping list crumpled in my left hand. It doesn't matter if I'm shopping for earrings at Target or for a caulking gun at Home Depot, when I hear the clickety-clack of shopping-cart wheels, my heart races and I am momentarily unaware of other things . . . such as my bank account balance.

This trance-like shopping state actually allows me to speak to and smile at other shoppers, which, if you'll notice, men at Home Depot never do. My friend Sonja and I met in one aisle and had a wonderful conversation about the difference between semi-gloss and satin paint finishes, while the men standing near us frowned at shiny green lawn mowers and tried to look really "busy."

Another difference between men and women at Home Depot is that men, for all the pained, serious looks on their faces, will always make shopping for hardware more difficult than it needs to be. While searching for a $^5/_{16}$-inch cross dowel nut (whatever that is), Dustin would have rather let our dog chew a hole through the deck than ask an employee in an orange apron for help.

"It doesn't have to be this difficult," I said to Dustin. "Just ask someone for help."

But no, Dustin would have none of it. Besides, that would take the fun out of it.

Meanwhile, a man and his wife standing next to us were having nearly the same conversation. They were shopping for a tool bench, and although the man was confused about which features came with which benches, he wouldn't take his wife's advice to ask for help. He was getting a lot more accomplished frowning at the display and rubbing his chin.

The man's wife looked on as he rapped the top of a wooden bench with his knuckles because obviously, at some point in his life, he had learned that testing the sturdiness of a piece of wood involves only knocking on it like a front door. I also watched with curiosity because I have never in my experience known a four-inch piece of solid wood to crumble beneath anyone's knuckles, and I doubted seriously that this was an effective way to evaluate a workbench.

After a while of this, and without Dustin noticing (which wasn't hard), I slipped away from aisle 10 to find help. When I returned with a man in an orange apron, Dustin's face looked panicked. Now he'd actually have to talk to a human being . . . in Home Depot!

So I was the one who asked the employee about cross dowel nuts, and when he said, "We don't have one that big because we're not a real hardware store, just a home improvement store," I thought Dustin's little heart would break.

But really, it makes sense, you know? I mean, why would a city filled with new homes need anything more than a store for home improvements?

Sarah Smiley

The Shopper's Guide to a Happy Marriage

If you adore her, you must adorn her. There lies the secret of a happy marriage.

ANNE FOGARTY

"*H*oney, I'm going shopping!"

My husband has heard those words far too often over the years. They cause him to panic, and perhaps leave him in a little physical pain. Yes, when I go shopping, there is no telling what I may come home with or in. I admit that over the years, my shopping expeditions have resulted in a few costly impulse buys, and some rather high charge account statements, but at the time of the purchases I did not feel that I was doing anything wrong.

My husband and I have always had an agreement that credit cards are for emergencies. In my eyes, clearance sales and one-of-a-kind merchandise qualify as emergencies. Therefore, I have never felt as if I have broken any sacred financial promises when I made purchases with the plastic. My husband, however, feels differently.

The fruits of my shopping trips have been plentiful.

Over the years, I have acquired some wonderful items, including designer attire (at super prices), several pieces of furniture (I just love the smell of new leather), precious animals (the poodles went over better than the Persian cat), and some stunning jewelry (that I can pass on to the children one day).

I may have gone a wee bit overboard when I purchased a house and a car without my husband's approval. I was not exactly shopping for either. In fact, the house was really my sister-in-law's fault. She is the ultimate professional shopper, and when she called to tell me about the two-story, brick traditional in a wonderful neighborhood that was a steal, who was I to argue with an expert?

She drove me through the neighborhood, and after we looked at every nook and cranny of the house, I could not have agreed more! Could I help it that my husband was at work and unavailable for comment? Every shopper knows that if you spot a bargain, then you had better purchase it on the spot or it may be gone when you come back. The risks were far too great! Anyway, my husband must have liked the house because his name eventually ended up on the contract as well.

When I purchased the car, I really meant to go to the grocery store. I had intended to shop for food. However, on the way to the local market, I ended up taking a slight detour through a car lot. That is when I saw it: a darling little green mini-SUV with a sunroof. One thing led to another and in a couple of hours, I was driving up the driveway in a terrific new automobile. It could not have been simpler! Once again, my husband's work schedule had impeded his ability to participate in the purchase. The only regret I had was that I had forgotten the groceries and had to order take-out for dinner. My husband, however, had numerous regrets about my little impulse buy, like the fact that I paid more than sticker price for the vehicle. Whoops! Shoppers can't be perfect with all purchases now, can they?

My husband and I will soon celebrate our twentieth anniversary, so my shopping trips have not been lethal to a perfectly healthy marriage. Over the years, however, I have grown and matured when it comes to shopping. For the sake of my marriage, I have attempted to alter some of my more costly shopping habits. I have also limited the sheer quantity of trips made to malls and shopping plazas. In addition, I insisted that my husband accompany me on the latest home and automobile purchases. I have discovered that compromise is not only the key to a happy marriage, but also the key to happy shopping experiences.

Terri Duncan

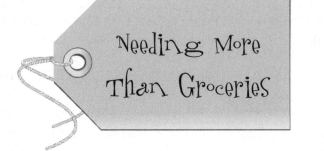

Needing More Than Groceries

Reality is the leading cause of stress among those in touch with it.

LILY TOMLIN

This was my first outing as a mother of two, and I'd prepared for it like a climber preparing to conquer Mount Everest. The diaper bag was loaded with colic medicine, breast pads, wipes, diapers in two sizes, little containers of Cheerios, anything and everything I thought I might need for an hour away with a newborn and a twenty-month-old. I tried to think of everything, cover all my bases. I was ready.

I strapped both girls in their car seats, took a deep breath and got behind the wheel for the first time in three weeks. *I can do this,* I thought. The first few minutes went well. Molly slept in her carrier nestled in the shopping cart. Not much room for groceries, but that couldn't be helped. As I lifted Haley up into the cart, I smelled a familiar odor. "Poo poo," she crooned proudly. No kidding. "There's a changing table in the ladies' room at the far end of the store," a clerk informed me. I headed that way.

As we walked, shopper after shopper stopped to admire Baby Molly, completely ignoring Haley. Haley squirmed and twisted around in the seat, trying to get their attention. When this didn't work, she grabbed a roll of paper towels off the shelf and dropped it on Molly's head. Molly wailed, and in my sleep-deprived state, I started crying, too.

Since I hadn't yet placed a single thing in the cart, this was not looking good. I scrambled to unstrap Molly from her carrier. Haley started crying, too. The second I picked up Molly, my breasts took it as their cue and started gushing. The breast pads packed neatly in the diaper bag did me no good. The front of my blouse was soaked in seconds.

Seeing me hold Molly, Haley started screaming, "I wanna get down! I wanna get down!" I felt like everyone was looking at me, and I thought of making a dash for the parking lot. *Maybe we can eat next week.* With my free hand, I lifted Haley out of the cart. As soon as her feet hit the floor, she took off running down the aisle and out of sight.

What a spectacle I must have been scrambling after her, a squalling baby in my arms, tears streaming down my face, my blouse soaked with breast milk. *I was wrong,* I thought. *I can't do this.* All I wanted to do was take my two babies home, crawl under the covers and never venture out again. I caught up with Haley two aisles away and sat down on the floor beside her exhausted—defeated.

Other shoppers passed. A mom with older kids half smiled. Another looked at me, then turned and walked the other way. I felt like I hadn't slept in months, and I thought, *Surely they remember what this is like.* I thought of my sisters who have four and five kids each. They make it look so easy. I bet they never fell to pieces on the floor of the dog-food aisle. I mustered what strength I had and got back to my feet. From somewhere in my cobwebby mind came an old trick of my mom's. I started singing, "We're almost finished. Then we're going home. Haley is a good girl." Haley stopped crying, more surprised than consoled. I coaxed her back to the cart, propped Molly on one shoulder and opened a box of raisins. I remembered something from my parenting books and started talking to Haley about what we'd do when we got home. She walked along beside the cart munching her raisins and listening— appeased for the moment. I considered whether to go on or just admit I was defeated and go home.

As I resumed the search for the restroom, still singing feebly, another shopper passed—a woman about ten years older than me, dressed in a stylish business suit and sporting a perfect manicure. I felt like a slug. She smiled as she passed and said, "Those are two lucky little girls." I can't tell you how her words bolstered me. They felt like a shot of vitamins and a good night's sleep all in one. *She's right*, I thought. *I'm doing the best I can. I am a good mother!* Just to know that someone understood how tired I was— maybe that's all I needed.

In six words she'd said so much. She'd given me permission to be human, to stop beating myself up when I couldn't be super mom. She may have known I didn't have a clue how to pull this off, but her words and her smile told me that she'd been where I was and survived. She knew I could do it, too. We were sisters in this sacred vocation called motherhood. I wasn't as alone as I thought I was.

I won't say the next two hours were easy. We made three trips to the restroom for diaper changes and one more to breastfeed Molly. The ice cream melted before we got to the checkout. Haley cried a few more times, and I pulled Mama's singing trick to calm us both. But I managed to buy most of what I set out for, and when we got home we all took a nice, long nap.

I wish I knew who that other shopper was. I wish I

could thank her for reaching out to a tired, overwhelmed, insecure new mom, for saying just the words I needed to hear, just when I needed to hear them. I'm shopping with four kids now, and I still have days when I wonder if I can put one foot in front of the other. But more often I find myself looking for another tired mom in the store, the doctor's office, the dry cleaner, who just needs to hear that she's not alone, that someone understands how tired and overwhelmed she feels. I always try to go out of my way to give her permission to be human.

Mimi Greenwood Knight

Look for the bright spot and move yourself toward it. There always is a bright spot. Learn to see it. Learn to value it, and you will learn to succeed.

RALPH MARSTON

I spied the handbag on a sale table. My closet was already packed with suitable options. I didn't need a new handbag, and I certainly didn't need a red one. The only handbag color I'd ever carried was black. But like a person possessed, I felt my spirit soar as I placed the soft leather strap over my shoulder and looked in the mirror. I was smiling. Not a big-grin-everyone-can-see smile, but an inner-knowing private kind.

Bringing it home, the handbag sat on the floor of my office wrapped in store packaging for days while I gathered my resolve. Finally, when I unwrapped it, an inner voice challenged my purchasing sanity with, "Why did you buy that thing? You'll never have the courage to use it."

Happily, that voice was wrong. And while buying a handbag is not usually a personal awakening, this one was. You see, that red handbag represents my bag of courage. My willingness to be "seen."

Most of my life I've been comfortable in supporting roles, an in-the-shadows person achieving from the sidelines, using others' voices as my own. Being shy, I never wanted to stand out, be in the spotlight or draw attention to myself. Well, maybe a few times. But generally, I thought of myself as an individual who needed validation from the crowd. Of course, that meant I would never, ever carry a red handbag.

But recently I decided to change that. I realized I've spent too much of my life wanting to fit in, wanting to please, wanting to be loved, wanting to be accepted, wanting to be what others wanted me to be, or what I thought they wanted me to be. Like a stranger living in my skin, I've tried on different selves during the years, waiting for some accomplishment or some person to give me permission to be me.

That will never happen. You see, I was waiting for the wrong person. It's my permission I need; my courage to let my light shine; my confidence to conquer fear that the "real me" won't be enough. But these days I've replaced those fears with a bigger one. With each passing birthday, I realize I could miss my chance. I'm afraid that at

THE PSYCHOLOGY OF COLOR

Red excites and stimulates us. One study claims gamblers make riskier bets when seated under a red light.

Wearing red boosts our energy levels and projects confidence and strength. It's the warmest color on the palette, the color of love and attention.

It alerts and warns; the color of stop signs and fire engines.

Advertisers get our attention with red tag sales and red sports cars.

So, when you're "seeing red," you're likely to spend your green.

the end of life I'll look back and realize this was my life and regret that, "I could have been me."

In the scheme of things, I've decided that's not a regret I'm willing to chance. It seems to me, being yourself is your life's responsibility, and your biggest contributions will come by being who you are. Dag Hammarskjöld said, "What you must dare is to be yourself." So, I've decided to take that dare, and my new red handbag is the symbol that it's the path I want to travel. Of course, I'll probably need red shoes to help me get there.

Nan Schindler Russell

A Picture's Worth a Thousand Words

Life is really simple, but men insist on making it complicated.

CONFUCIUS

I went shopping yesterday. Not so unusual. I went shopping the day before, too. And last week, and the week before that. But on each occasion, I came home empty-handed.

This time, I vowed, it would be different. This time I was determined not to return without my quarry. I took a deep breath, let it out slowly and opened the door to the electronics store.

Armed with advertisements, the latest issue of *Consumer Reports* and the advice of friends ringing in my ears, I marched past the large-screen televisions, strode through the audio department and circled around the computers.

There they were, arranged on three-tiered shelves. My resolve drained away as I gazed at rows and rows of small, shiny, digital cameras. Here we go again.

A salesperson materialized by my side. I wondered if he was old enough to have a driver's license or if his mother drove him to work. "Looking for a camera?" he asked as he followed my gaze.

"Uh, yes," I replied. "But I'm not sure. . . ."

"Well, this one here…" he picked up the camera nearest to him, "is on sale. Three-point-two mega pixels, three times optical and 3.2 times digital zoom, with USB connectivity. Great price." He handed me the camera as I fumbled with the *Consumer Reports* chart.

You can do this, I told myself. *You have a college degree. And a master's degree. You've managed hundreds of employees during your career, and you've been responsible for multimillion dollar budgets. You can do this.*

"Yes, but . . ." I glanced down at the chart and then back at him, "I was looking for something with higher mega—"

"Sure thing." He replaced the camera and reached for another. "This one is five-point-one mega pixels, three times optical and two times digital zoom."

Wait a minute. Mega pixels increased, but the zoom decreased. "Do you have something with a higher digital zoom?"

"The optical zoom is more important, but here's one you might like." He picked up a camera from the second row and handed it to me. "Four mega pixels, ten times optical, four times digital zoom. And it comes with a speedy image processor."

"A speedy image what?"

"A speedy image processor. That's just the company's way of saying that there's no shutter lag—you know, no shutter delay between when you press the button and when the picture is actually taken."

No, I didn't know, but I wasn't about to tell him that. "Of course," I said. "But this one has lower mega pixels. Don't you have something that has the speedy image processor and higher mega pixels?"

"Sure thing." He was still agreeable, but his tone was

beginning to lose its artificial cheeriness. "How about this one? Six-point-one mega pixels, three times optical, four times digital, sixteen megabyte internal memory. Just for this week it comes with a free 128-megabyte memory card."

"But no USB connectivity?"

This time, he simply pointed at another camera. "Here's a six mega pixel, with eight times optical and four times digital zoom. Sixteen megabyte internal memory and a secure digital media slot. And USB and video output."

I gingerly picked up the camera. "Only eight times optical zoom—not ten?"

He glanced over at another customer looking at the cameras, and then turned back to me. "Why don't you take your time looking at the models we have on display? There's a little card describing the features of each one. You can compare and decide which overall package is best for you."

I stared at the cameras as he walked away. A moment later, I heard him ask the other customer, "Looking for a camera?"

There was no point in continuing. I was ready to admit defeat. Too many choices for someone with too little knowledge.

But I remembered my commitment to not come home empty-handed, and on my way out of the store I bought a roll of 35mm film.

Ava Pennington

A Man's Heart Is in the Hardware

I am going in search of a great perhaps.

FRANÇOIS RABELAIS

Like most men, I have a pathological aversion toward shopping. This goes against our biological makeup as human beings, I suppose, as we are predisposed to be "hunter-gatherers." However, I somehow doubt that hunting for a bargain on drapes is the same thing as driving a herd of mammoths off a cliff. There is an exception to this rule, though.

Whether Home Depot, Lowe's or True Value, I love going to the hardware store. For it is there where I am at one with my "guyness," blissfully adrift amongst pressure-treated lumber, parquet flooring and stainless-steel widgets. I feel much more at home than at, say, Bed, Bath and Beyond.

It's impossible for me to emerge empty-handed from one of these do-it-yourself superstores. Sure, it may be an item I'll only use once or a "you never know" purchase like that 4x4 sheet of fiberglass-reinforced sheetrock, but I feel it's my solemn duty to contribute to the local economy ... and to the myth that I actually know what I'm doing.

While I'm not the Inspector Clouseau of Handymen, I'm not exactly Bob Vila, either.

Thankfully, these stores are fully staffed with the MacGyvers of home repair who are only too willing to cheerfully instruct me in the finer points of building a deck with a spork or why shag carpet on the toilet tank is the hottest thing since lava lamps. From these omniscient saviors of the tool room, I've learned that water conducts electricity, pipes freeze in the winter, it's not a good idea to "slide" a console TV down a flight of stairs, and it isn't real smart to burn plastic wood in the fireplace. My failures run the gamut from the time I destroyed the toilet rescuing a drowning Winnie the Pooh action figure (a Winnie the Pooh ACTION figure?), to when it took all of 2002 to install ceramic tile in my kitchen.

We have a nice little house in the country, not exactly a high-crime area. Even so, my wife thought it would be a swell idea to get a motion detector. After all, anything to prevent raccoons from stealing our empty pizza boxes or the gophers from hot-wiring the cars has my vote. Since any excuse to worship at the shrine of the fix-it shop is a good one, off I went in search of one of those modern marvels of home security.

Three hours later, I returned with a wood-burning set, an extension ladder, a rubber mallet, the "Family Pack" bungee cord set (what kind of "family" shops for bungee cords—the Mansons?), six cans of Fix-A-Flat, a gallon of Gorilla Glue and twenty rolls of electrical tape (they were on sale). Oh, yeah, and a motion detector.

Minutes later, the contents of the motion detector were spread out all over my kitchen table. I meticulously cross-checked each component with the master inventory: four two-inch metal screw thingies, check; three plastic wire-nut whoozits, check; one metal plate gizfotchy, check; one rubber gasket thingamajig, check; two lamp holders, uh oh . . . time to go back to the store.

Two hours later, I returned with the parts I needed. And some anti-freeze, Monkey Grip and something called "Crack Filler" (which I suppose has some sort of proctologic application).

Deciding it was too late to start, I flung everything into a cardboard box, placed it on my workbench and plopped down in front of the TV to watch *Ice Skating* with Celebrities.

Tomorrow was another day, after all.

The following week, I happened upon the motion detector box. *Ooops, I thought, forgot all about this. Better get this up before the squirrels violate my lawn flamingos.*

This time, I enlisted the aid of my son (who I rather uncreatively refer to as "The Boy") to finally install protection from woodland creatures.

After pulling my new extension ladder out of the garage, up I went to start wiring the motion detector. Minutes later, after getting up from the ground, I went downstairs to pull the outdoor lighting circuit breaker.

Several hours of twisting this, wiring that and filling the air with all sorts of Anglo-Saxon expressions of goodwill later, we finally managed to install the driveway motion detector.

Restoring power, I ran back and forth under its sensor (making chipmunk sounds for effect) and, after noticing the light coming on when called for, pronounced it a job well done.

Inspecting my work, "The Boy" stared at the underside of the brightly lit motion detector. Pointing upward, he said, "Hey, Dad, what's that written on the underside of the sensor?"

Deciding to eschew the ladder, I craned my neck skyward, squinted my eyes and saw some squiggles written on the plastic. "Oh, THAT!" I scoffed. "It's probably Chinese for 'Use only 60-watt bulbs' or something like that. Don't worry about it."

My testosterone at maximum level, confidently strid-
ing into the house, I thumped my chest and announced
to the womenfolk that I was, indeed, the "Conqueror of
Darkness."

"Here," my wife said as she flung a pork loin my way and
pointed at the grill, "now you can be the 'Lord of Fire.'"

The motion detector did its thing quite well for several
weeks. It could detect the movement of the smallest of
critters, energize its halogen lamps and instantly bring the
driveway to near-solar intensity. Our property became an
impregnable fortress, secure from wanton acts of nature.
And, if called upon, could be an emergency airfield.

Last week, though, we had the mother of all rainstorms.
Streams overflowed, gutters choked with sodden debris,
cars stalled in flooded intersections, and our neighbor
started packing in pairs of zebras and ducks into the bass
boat he built in his backyard.

Oh, yeah, and the motion detector stopped working.

Initially refusing to shut off, even during the day, the
motion detector was merely tricked by the gloom of the
storm. Or so I thought. But when the sun finally came out
and we needed sunglasses, the light still refused to turn
off. Seeing that, I thought that somehow the knot-head
designers of the thing hadn't taken torrential downpours
into account. Obviously, water had gotten into the whole
shooting match and shorted out the wires.

Of course, since I'm not exactly Marconi, the thought of
WHY something that was shorted would still WORK
never crossed my mind. Armed with an industrial-size
tube of silicant I bought on sale several years ago ("See?" I
sneered at my wife. "I TOLD you this would come in
handy one day!"), I once more ascended my ladder to
remedy the situation. (This time, though, I shut off the
power.)

After coating all possible openings with the waterproof goop, I descended the ladder, making sure I didn't go crashing into the garbage cans, forcing a visit to the local ER. After re-energizing the circuit, I returned to inspect my work. Ah, presto-chango, the lights had gone off!

Mentally exchanging high-fives with myself, I put everything away and proceeded to fix lunch (okay, cookies, Totinos and a Diet Coke). Once it gets dark, we'd just see how good a job I did!

Well, darkness came and went. And the motion detector worked as well as a clock made of cheese.

Perplexed, I returned to what was beginning to resemble the "scene of the crime." I figured that I'd have to take the whole thing off, dry it and re-install it. Balancing precariously on the ladder, I twisted the sensor off and grimaced as a stream of water cascaded into my armpit.

THAT figures, I thought. *Cheap piece of junk! What genius thought to put the controls on TOP of the sensor so rain could just roll in and fry the thing?*

I must admit that, in a moment of weakness, I was starting to lose faith in the wisdom of my "helpful hardware man."

As I was starting to mentally spend my refund after returning this hunk of junk, I noticed the words that "The Boy" had pointed out to me as I was congratulating myself weeks ago. Words that were printed on what I thought was the underside of the sensor. Words that, when turned the right way, clearly stated:

"THIS SIDE UP."

Time to go back to the store.

Kenneth Lynch

The Key to a Successful Shopping Adventure

The difference between perseverance and obstinacy is that one often comes from a strong will, and the other from a strong won't.

HENRY WARD BEECHER

Growing up, every other Friday in our home meant grocery day. Around noon, like clockwork, my mother would load all five of her children into our aquamarine Ford station wagon for the short trek to the grocery store owned by the company that employed my father. These trips would generally be considered mundane chores in the life of any other homemaker of the time, but somehow with my mother they always turned into an adventure.

In the midst of the usual fights over who got to push the cart, whose turn it was to pick the cereal and what type of lunchmeat we would have to live with for the next two weeks stood my competent mother. She kept a running tab of the purchases in her mind better than any calculator, despite the whines and demands of five, somewhat unruly children. She never made a list; she knew exactly what she needed to keep a family of this size fed for the next fourteen days until my father got paid again. She knew how long a jar of peanut butter would last, or how far she could stretch a bag of potatoes. With her coupons clutched in one hand, she methodically made her way through each aisle, and when she left the checkout line, she always managed to have enough change left over for each of us to get a piece of candy from the tempting gumball machines by the door.

"The key is organization," she would tell her friends. And my mother was the epitome of organization. She had everything under control, until she reached our trusty station wagon on that fateful summer day and went to unlock the door. Rooting through her purse and then her pants' pockets, she said to no one in particular, "Where are those darn keys?" Her frenzied search was interrupted when my sister shouted, "I found them, Mommy! They're right where you left them, inside the car!"

Yes, my mother, the Donna Reed of her generation had, in one careless act, turned into Lucille Ball by locking her keys in the car. As we stood in the blazing August sun, impatient to get home to our squirt-gun battles and newly purchased Popsicles, my mother pondered the situation. "Well, I'll just have to call your father. He has the spare set of keys," she reasoned.

Normally, this would not have been such a big deal. My father's office, up until a week earlier, had been located in the building right next to the supermarket. But he had been promoted, and his new office was now downtown, a twenty-minute drive away. Mom had no choice. The Popsicles were melting, and the heat was not doing the two gallons of milk she just bought any good.

I wasn't privy to my parents' phone conversation, but the look on my mother's face when she returned gave us every indication that my dad was not pleased to have to come to our rescue.

"Is Daddy coming?" I asked impatiently.

Lighting her second Viceroy cigarette since leaving the store, Mom exhaled loudly and said, "He has to leave a meeting, but he'll be here any minute."

"He has to leave a meeting!" shouted my brother, Bobby, the oldest and only male child in the group. "I bet Pop's steamed over that!" he added, as he blew a large, pink bubble in front of his face. My mother shot Bobby a look that caused the adolescent to burst his gum bubble with a loud pop.

SUPERMARKET SURVIVAL GUIDE

. . . Keep the kids busy at the supermarket. Their mission—find all the signs for "unadvertised special."

. . . Get to the supermarket early, before 9:00, to get marked-down items.

. . . Stock up on cheese, butter, milk and bread—they freeze well.

. . . Don't wait to run out of something. Stock up when you see a sale, especially items you use all the time.

He leaned against the car smacking his leg as he began to roar with laughter.

So there we stood waiting in the heat—five anxious children, two shopping carts full of perishable food, and one determined mother who was pacing back and forth in front of the car talking to herself as she chain-smoked her Viceroys.

Suddenly, my sister yelled out, "Mommy, Mommy, look! The back door is unlocked!" But before our cheers of "Hurray" could leave our lips, my mother opened the door in question, punched down the lock and slammed the door shut.

"What did you do that for?" asked Bobby, his young, male mind unable to see the logic in her actions. "It's hot out here, and we could have gone home."

Without hesitation, my mother took another long drag from her cigarette and replied through a haze of smoke, "Your father is driving all the way up here to get the keys out of the locked car, and that's just what he's going to find—a locked car!"

Whoever said blondes were dumb clearly had never met my mother. Although we were confused, we all vowed to keep the secret about the car keys that day, at least until we knew Dad would be able to see the humor in it all. I think it was around Christmas when he finally found out the truth. He pretended to be mad for a few minutes, and then we saw him laughing with Mom as they hugged under the mistletoe.

Jodi L. Severson

Middle-Age Orientation

Today, I feel like a sky-high pair of platforms in a closet full of flats.

JENNY SCOTT

I could feel it coming. The gray hairs had been sprouting for years, and now we even blended in a few blonde streaks as camouflage. The wrinkles were becoming far more defined, and the eyelids started drooping. Despite these symptoms, I wasn't quite ready to admit to being middle-aged.

When I was a child, I thought of fifty as middle-aged. That doesn't make too much sense, though, as not everyone lives to be 100. I also thought of fifty as being very old. Now that I am older and far wiser, I know that fifty is still relatively young. I do think my actions this morning, however, help to categorize me with the middle-agers.

I awoke with a sense of purpose that went far beyond making breakfast and driving kids to school. I showered, even applied makeup, and dressed a little better than usual. A bounce in my step and a song on my lips, I kissed my husband as he left for work and my children as I left them at the school's doorstep. Rushing to meet my best friend, I eagerly anticipated the fun we would have.

"Are you ready?" I asked anxiously.

She nodded.

"New shirt?" I asked. She, too, had dressed for the occasion.

Hopping in my car, we watched the clock. Would we arrive on time? We certainly didn't want to be late. We wanted to get our pick of parking spaces and be first in line for the excitement.

Celebrity sighting?

No.

A soap star visiting town?

No.

A Barry Manilow concert?

I can dream, can't I?

Our morning's events far surpassed all of these occasions. In fact, what we were about to do would be the most excitement we'd had in a long time. It was the most excitement our city had witnessed in months.

A Wal-Mart Supercenter was having its ribbon-cutting ceremony and grand opening!

The happy "Hi, Welcome to Wal-Mart" man greeted us at the shiny, new front door. From there we were given a shopping cart (also shiny and new) and a wealth of free gifts. We got mini energy bars and a powdered diet drink mix. We got samples of aspirin, vitamins and chewy pills for gas. They gave us plastic pill boxes and udder cream near the pharmacy, and magnets near the garden center.

It was like a birthday and Christmas rolled into one! A lady in the center aisle served us chopped-up pieces of Little Debbie snack cakes, and a man near her offered bathroom-size Dixie cups full of Coke.

A lady by the snack bar gave us pencils with the Wal-Mart smiley guy on them and long pads of paper for making lists of all the things we could buy there. Inside the snack bar, there were free honey-dipped donuts and delicious hot coffee. There was even a cake! (See, I told you it was like a birthday!)

After perusing the aisles and hoarding our cherished samples, we decided it was time to head for home. After all, we'd socialized, we'd gotten some gifts, and we'd eaten until our tummies could hold no more. We were truly lost in the throes of middle-age bliss.

How sad! We were once career-centered, goal-oriented women. We once thought of ourselves as intelligent and capable of plenty. And here we were, still shy of fifty (by a few years anyway!), enjoying a morning at a new Wal-Mart Supercenter!

Whatever will we do for fun when we're approaching sixty?

Yes, it's true. We've passed the official orientation of the middle-agers. Soon we'll be off to play Bingo and go on bus tours to the zoo. We'll sport our AARP membership tags proudly and enjoy our senior citizen discounts.

Hey, doesn't that mean we'll get a discount at Wal-Mart, too?

Kimberly Ripley

You grow up the day you have your first real
laugh—at yourself.

ETHEL BARRYMORE

I'm not much of a mall rat, truth told. While other
women veritably fly through the mall, handbags trailing
behind like wings on a Goddess of Speed hood ornament,
I trudge. At the mere sight of a mall kiosk, my feet turn to
cement. Don't even get me started on perilous escalators
and glowing double-sided directories. The mall is just not
my bag. My husband, who happens to have a few master's
level psychology courses under his belt, suggests that
somewhere deep in my psyche, negative childhood
memories taint my view of the mall.

"Think back to your childhood," he guides me, "back . . .
back . . . to 1976 . . ."

I'm seven years old, at our mall near St. Paul, Minnesota.
Outside, it's ten below; eighteen inches of snow cover the
ground. My mother and I, along with my younger sister
and brother, pull into the mall's parking lot in our 1974
Caprice Classic station wagon. Shivering, we shuffle through

the lot to the main entrance. "Remind me that we parked in the 'Penguin' lot, section D," my mother says.

The revolving doors spit us into the warm, dim innards of . . . the mall. Dutifully stomping the sticky snow off our boots, we peel off the absurd layers of winter clothing, and tuck mittens, scarves and hats into the arms of our coats.

"Mom, Mom!" I tug at the hem of her checked, flared miniskirt like a passenger tugging the handbrake on a trolley. "Mom, I have to go to the bathroom." But the trolley-mom doesn't even slow down.

"The nearest ladies' room is in Sears," Mom explains. She talks as fast as she walks. "Can you hold it, honey?" I nod. *Hold it till Sears. Hold it till Sears,* I repeat to myself. *How many miles away is Sears?* I wonder, struggling to keep up with Mom's frantic pace. "Here we are!" Mom sings to us kids. Sears, I hope. But the bold white scroll above the store's entrance reads Don . . . ald . . . son's.
Fancy letters. Fancy store. Not Kmartish at all, I think.

Donaldson's is the eighth wonder of the world. Inside Ladies' Cosmetics, a blonde model with shocking blue eye shadow and bouffant hair spritzes me with something like mosquito repellant and bathroom cleanser.

"Eau de Love?" she twitters. I begin to experience my first-ever headache, as if I executed thirty somersaults in a row. The store lights—so many fluorescent lights—heat up my headache like an egg in an incubator. The shiny see-yourself-in-them floor tiles squeak beneath my rubber boots as I drag through Ladies' Apparel. A fountain the size of my house trickles as we pass Ladies' Footwear. *Better not think about trickling water fountains right now,* I tell myself. *Hold it till Sears.* Redirecting my short span of attention, I am impressed by the mirrored ceiling panels that look down on Ladies' Accessories. I pause to gawk.

"Stay close, kids," Mom advises, pressing my hand tighter. "Ooooo . . . sequined handbags and ripe peach-scented body lotion!" squeals my six-year-old sister. My little brother lags far behind our chain gang. He, too, looks nauseated, as if he consumed a thirty-two-ounce Karmel Korn and a large cherry Slushy, then did somersaults with me.

"Here we are. Intimate Apparel," Mom says to herself. The rest of us have no idea what intimate apparel is, except maybe my sister. After casing the place, I decide that Intimate Apparel means really big women's under-wear. "Sit here for just a minute," my mom instructs my brother and me. Then she gets busy choosing something intimate. My brother and I collapse beneath a circular display rack loaded with women's briefs; we lean against its cool metal legs and sulk. "Ooooo! Look! Pretty little pink briefs! Cute!" I hear my sister's shrill voice from my perch in the confines of the underwear tree. Above, like ripe fruit on some exotic branch, hangs underwear. Big women's underwear. This underwear—uh, intimate apparel—looks just like shiny pastel helium balloons bobbing overhead at an Easter parade. Satiny pink. Powdery blue. And some color called "Nude."

Here the facts of the story become murky with the sediment of time. My mother insists this never happened. My sister says, "Yeah, you always had a big mouth." My poor brother refuses comment. But, I have uncanny clarity.

"Quick! Hide in here!" My brother yanks me deeper into the recesses of the underwear tree. "Some lady's coming!" The sound of the woman sliding hangers along the metal rod screeches above us like nails on a chalkboard.

"The call of an underwear bird," my brother whispers. The squeaking ceases. The woman's hand lingers over a pair of racy black bikinis—size M. At age seven, even I know that M means Medium, not "Maybe This Will Fit." I peek between a nude Playtex comfort brief and a red lace bikini to view the woman. *She is no M*, I decide. *She isn't even an L. She was one of those XXXL women.* Her prominent figure cast a shadow over us the size of my school bus. *Yep. XXXL*, I decide. I had seen an XXXL somewhere . . . over . . . there! A white cotton brief the size of the parachute we play with in gym class offers the only XXXL on this rack. *It'll have to do*, I think.

"Here, lady! Here! The XXXLs are over here!" I offer so helpfully, popping out of the intimate apparel rack. The enormous briefs wave in the air like a wayward weather balloon. "Excuuuuuse me?" the ample woman gasps. The woman's revulsion of my sales techniques frightens me, fragile child that I am, although I don't recognize my fear until it dribbles down my legs—a personal-sized water fountain trickles through my own . . . intimate apparel.

"Mommy, I couldn't wait till Sears," I cry.

Maybe that's why you probably won't run into me at the mall. Today, I prefer to shop in the comfort of my own home. Online shopping is where it's at for me. I love to hear the click of the keys under my fingers, feel the mouse under my palm and watch the "Check Out" icon light up during a purchase.

My husband says it's repressed mall anxiety; all I know is that the bathroom's closer here.

Cristy Trandahl

Three
Easy Payments

Before you try to keep up with the Joneses, be sure they're not trying to keep up with you.

ERMA BOMBECK

After a few minutes of channel flipping the other morning, I dialed up the 1-800 number flashing on my television screen and bought the exact same product that I bought two years ago and hated. It was a video that was sure to strengthen, tone and shape my body, bring vitality to my organs and relieve my stress. All I had to do was breathe, exhale forcefully with a POW, and my heretofore hidden, thin, serene self would appear. The first time around, I bought it with a friend, and doing it together only made us laugh. We thought it was silly. I think it stayed at her house. The other day, I bought it again.

Why, you might well ask, would someone buy a product that they hated the first time around? Well, I'll tell you: I bought it again because I saw it on an infomercial, and people loved it and testified that in no uncertain terms it worked for them, and I thought maybe this time, two years later, it would work for me. At that moment, I finally admitted to myself that I was addicted to infomercial shopping.

In the best, most compelling infomercials, Ron Popeil and Nancy Nelson electronically come into my living room and persuade me, with absolute conviction, backed by "ooohs" and "aaahhs" from the live studio audience, that not only will I love the product, but I won't be able to live a complete and fulfilled life without it. And I believe.

And why do I believe? I believe because infomercials are unpretentious, so heartfelt and so enthralling. They make you trust that everyone in the audience, and everyone who's ever tried the product, has somehow not only enjoyed and used the product, but has also somehow become a better person for it.

I also love wasting a gorgeous Saturday morning, since it feels positively sinful to lie on the couch in front of a first-rate food-dehydrating-machine demonstration or a fantastic rotisserie-oven show. It's amazing to watch great globs of fat spill from a swirling slab of beef and know, really know, that that meat is not going to clog my arteries. It's a joy to wipe the underside of my rusty car with a simple magic rag and expose a shiny new car beneath. It's thrilling to watch my skin suddenly look like a twenty-year-old's in split seconds.

I watch infomercials with the trained concentration of a professional knife thrower, and have, in fact, ordered several knives that slice and dice, and cut the legs off pianos, swipe through steel girders in seconds, and will no doubt be purchased, and pitched, by professional knife throwers.

I own it all: a mop that washes and dries the floor in a single action, a mitt that in one whoosh wipes up dog hair from any surface and, best of all, a Juiceman juicer. I juice tomatoes, bell peppers, parsley and carrots, and drink it with relish, hoping for health, but praying it will not make me look like the Juiceman, with his flying-buttress white eyebrows and hint-of-carrot colored skin.

I have a NordicTrack, a Thighmaster, an Abs Only machine, an Abdomenizer, and my latest delight, Bodyvibes isometric abdominal belt. Every time I relax those old stomach muscles, it tingles, and I tuck my tummy. I could have had a real facelift and tummy tuck for the money I've invested, but what fun would that be? I have a Stimulator, which is not what you think, but an electric acupressure thing that takes away arthritis pain. I have a never-ending supply of various skin creams: gels and toners, buffers and cleansers, all promising eternal youth from the neck up. I also have the most incredible vacuum-seal machine that keeps my food fresh, and if for some reason I wanted to plastic-wrap my blankets, I could suck an entire comforter into a huge airtight bag.

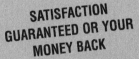

SATISFACTION GUARANTEED OR YOUR MONEY BACK

In 1984, infomercials were born when the FCC eliminated regulations on the commercial content of television. Edward Valenti and Barry Beecher, who developed the infomercial for the *Ginsu Knife*, are credited with the format's early development.

What don't I have? I don't have, and this is the best part, all the things I've returned! You can return everything, and you do get your money back. You've lost the shipping and handling charges, of course, but you've had the freedom of giving miracle products a try risk-free. Well, not totally risk-free, because I once took a bedtime pill made of shrimp shells that promised morning thinness, and I awoke with lumpy, bloated, shrimp-pink skin. I've returned fennel-smelling stuff that didn't make me thin no matter how long I sniffed. I've returned hair in a can (enough said).

On occasion, I have been in such an enthusiastic whirl that I have thrown away the original packaging and not been able to return the item. But astonishingly enough, infomercial products are multi-taskible! I have taken a travel-anywhere clothesline and used it as a dog leash. I've made my bicep-building straps work as bungee cords. And after cutting my hair short, I was still able to use my Richard Caruso Hair Styler for a steamy facial, and dream of the possibilities of future journalistic sleuthing and the need to steam open secret government documents.

More than anything, I wish there were some kind of fan-appreciation prize for infomercial shoppers like me. I wish I could win a trip to Los Angeles and a studio-audience pass to a real-live taping, where I'd have the chance to go up on stage and magically, in one fell swoop, wipe the hair from my upper lip, pressure-slim my waist, or quickly pre-pare my own personal turkey-jerky. And with the wild applause, I'd become Infomercial Queen for a Day!

Bonnie West

Life is just a blank slate. What matters most is
what you write on it.

CHRISTINE FRANKLAND

As I stand in the checkout line, arms laden with binders, notebooks, pens and an assortment of Crayola products, I realize that summer is coming to a close. The first day of school looms as heavy as an April rain cloud.

Behind me the blue light is flashing in the center aisle as the last of the colorful summer shorts and tank tops are marked down to ridiculous prices. I look around at weary parents, their debit cards in hand, as they try to calculate the damage this year's school supply list will have on their overtaxed budgets.

I make a mental tally of my own purchases, trying to picture the list that sits on the kitchen counter at home. The collection of supplies incorporates the requirements of three grades. Mixed together it looks more jumbled than my thoughts. *Was I supposed to buy a metric conversion calculator or a scientific one? A geometry set or a protractor? I can't remember if I need erasers or Wite-Out.*

I inch toward the cash register. Another blue-light special is announced: three-ring binder paper marked down from sixty-six cents a package to thirty-three cents, for ten minutes only in the center aisle. The dilemma: *Should I vacate my spot for a fifty-percent savings and risk another half an hour of listening to the crying baby in line at checkout three? Or cut my losses and run for it?* I decide to stay put. The line gets remarkably shorter as sale-crazed shoppers push past my basket toward the flashing blue light. The hum of voices grows dimmer as the monotonous beeping of the laser price checker continues its hypnotic rhythm.

My mind wanders back over the years, and I see myself standing beside my mother at the cash register of the corner dime store, my face flushed with excitement as the salesclerk rings in our purchases: three ten-cent notebooks, a pink elephant eraser, a box of eight colorful wax crayons, two HB pencils and my very own wooden pencil box. The wooden pencil box was the prized purchase, painfully chosen out of a pile of fifty.

BACK TO SCHOOL BASICS

June is "School Supplies Month."

Don't wait until August to stock up. Get shopping done early to minimize stress and get the best buys.

Mom waited patiently while I checked the "slide" of each lid and the "swing" of each compartment until I found the perfect box. I would take it home and carefully carve my name on its bottom.

The cashier begins to empty my basket, sliding each article across the laser checker and placing it haphazardly in a plastic bag. Another $43 is drained from my bank account. The bag of loot makes its way home and onto the dining-room table, joining previous purchases and waiting to be divided among my three students.

The children are enthusiastic about the start of another school year and the reuniting of friends. They organize and label their new supplies while making the all-too-familiar promises to keep their notebooks neat, and to keep up to date on their homework.

I distribute the notebooks and eye the yellow HB pencils—the one school supply that has remained timeless. I roll a pencil between my fingers and imagine the sensation of my teeth pushing through the paint and into the wood, flakes of yellow sticking to the end of my tongue and my lips. So goes the promise of a perfect year—the now-chewed pencil is the ideal tool for doodling in the margins of a brand-new notebook.

Elva Stoelers

The Little Horrors of Shopping

A woman's dress should be like a barbed-wire fence: serving its purpose without obstructing the view.

SOPHIA LOREN

I hate shopping for clothes, absolutely detest it. I much prefer hand-me-downs. That way, if it doesn't fit, I can donate it. If it doesn't look good, I can donate it. If my husband doesn't like it, I can donate it. If it shrinks, I can donate it. If it . . . well, you get the idea.

In 1996, when our youngest son was getting married, my future daughter-in-law had a color-coded plan for the church, buffet hall, her bridesmaids, groomsmen, and her mother and me. Since the kids were to be married in October, she had chosen deep autumn colors. Her father and my husband would sport brown suits. The bridesmaids were to wear burgundy gowns. The groomsmen's tuxedos were accessorized with burgundy paisley bow ties and vests, and the bride's mother and I were to wear green. How hard could that be? I was even looking forward to shopping for a dress. Weddings are so exciting.

So off I went with plenty of time to find the "perfect" dress. I found this lovely, soft green gown in my size with an empire waist. The "A" silhouette from the waistline to the floor would flatter my figure, and the gauzy flowing fabric would cover my arms. Its V-neckline and gold-tone belt buckle in the middle of the waist gave it an elegant touch. I took it into the dressing room, and what I saw took my breath away! It was a sight to behold, the likes of which I have never seen before in my life. I LOOKED LIKE A TREE! *How could it look so good on the model in the window? Okay, don't panic. Just take it off and put it back. Phew, that was scary. Don't care to ever see that again. Enough for today. Go home and recover.*

Next, I went to a well-known women's dress shop and found green pantsuits, green ball gowns, green business suits, even green house dresses. No dresses appropriate for weddings, especially my own son's wedding. Home again to recover.

A month or so after recovery, I went to another highly recommended ladies' specialty shop known for its wedding apparel. Here I found the other "perfect" green dress. It was a two-piece number. The top was a nicely shaped blouse with princess seams, no collar, just a softy scooped V-shaped neckline with gold buttons that adorned the front. The three-quarter sleeves were detailed with buttons to match those on the blouse. The blouse was hip length, dipped down in front, and in back and up at the hips for a nice slimming effect. A simple straight skirt completed the ensemble. I tried it on, and indeed it was beautiful. *Hey, I don't look half bad. I have a pair of shoes at home that will match perfectly. Wow, I am all set! Shopping isn't so hard after all.*

I carefully took my two-piece selection up to the counter where the woman started to ring it up. "You are very lucky today. This line is on sale, and we are taking fifty dollars off the price." It wasn't until that moment that I looked at the price tag, and I'm sure the look on my face would have choked a gator. It was $249.95 AFTER the discount. *What is it made of? The buttons must be real gold!* We farm for our living and never know if ends will meet, so we live within our means and carefully watch our budget. That takes the fun out of shopping for clothes. Wishing that I could evaporate into thin air, I meekly said, "I'm sorry, but this is a little out of my price range," and ever so carefully returned it to the rack. I slunk out of the store. Home again, but I didn't think I would recover from that experience.

I found myself the day before the wedding without a dress to wear. Now, the upside of that "never knowing if ends will meet" lifestyle is a resourceful character. I sew. I went to my local department store, found a Quick-Sew pattern for two dollars, material for five dollars, matching undergarments for ten dollars and the result was . . . priceless. I created a simple, one-piece, scoop-necked, sleek dress with long sleeves that fell just above the ankles. It matched my shoes perfectly. I put on a silver necklace chain, silver hanging earrings, applied some makeup and did my nails. I felt like a queen, no one knew any better, and, best of all, I didn't embarrass my new daughter-in-law!

Vicki Austin

Shopping My Way Out of the Blues

I always say shopping is cheaper than a psychiatrist.

TAMMY FAYE BAKKER

At eighteen, I was issued a license—that right of passage so important for a young person striving for independence and autonomy. I was even more excited to get my license since I always felt different from the other kids, and that I had something to prove. Now, the gap was closing (no pun intended), and I was just like all the other teenagers, one of the gang, the cool girl in school with a license.

Picking up my friends and driving to the mall quickly became a ritual. We shopped until we dropped and enjoyed every precious moment. We helped each other pick clothes, buying like crazy until our wallets were empty. The morning after a shopping spree would find us at one or the other's house, helping each other get into our new pants that we purposely bought two sizes smaller. One of us would get on the bed, and the other two would help pull up the pants. I can still hear Marie yelling at me to stop breathing and hold in my stomach!

No new purchase was sacred; we swapped our new clothes and could make three new outfits look like ten. As our closets grew, so did our friendships. We bonded, shopping being the experience that brought us closer. No matter how different we each were in personality, we all had a love for shopping in common.

At nineteen, life changed, as you would expect it should for a young woman about to become an adult. Only my change wasn't typical. While I was driving with my boyfriend (who is now my husband) on a winding, country road in New Jersey, I suddenly went into a seizure. My muscles tightened, my arms curved to the left, and my foot went all the way down on the gas pedal. Our future together flashed before us as the car headed straight toward a telephone pole. Fighting me for the wheel was worse than fighting a boxer or wrestler. I had no control, and while in the throes of the seizure, I had the strength of a couple of bouncers. Finally, my boyfriend got control over the car, steering it safely away from the pole and bringing it to a stop. By then, my seizure had passed, and a new era in my life began. An angel was watching over us and spared our lives that day, but my license was revoked, and my days at the mall became fewer and more difficult to arrange.

I never expected that not being able to shop whenever I desired some "retail therapy" would have such an impact on my life, but it did. I became a prisoner in my own home, no longer able to hop into the car and go to the mall, to Dunkin' Donuts for a cup of coffee or Blockbuster for a video. I was at the mercy of other people's schedules. Not one to ask for people's help, my isolation became chronic. I felt very alone. I was a strong, independent person, and I wanted to take care of myself. I wanted to be that successful woman working in New York, shopping her heart out after work, and then going to the bar to enjoy an evening martini with friends. But that ideal wasn't realistic; my dreams didn't seem to have a chance. My confidence was shaken, my self-esteem at an all-time low. How was I going to be a success? I had epilepsy. Where was my life going? What was my purpose? I was depressed, hiding from the world and feeling hopeless inside. Afraid to tell others how I felt, I was trapped.

Having the freedom to choose where, when and how you want to go somewhere is something we all take for granted. I didn't realize how my shopping helped me until it was out of reach. Going to the mall had allowed me to focus on all the pretty things, and my old wounds took a back seat to the pleasure of shopping. As time passed, I began to accept my disorder and the consequences it brought along with it. I learned to accept the limitations in my life. We all have them. We all need help sometime or another. I finally broke through the wall that had become my prison, and I began to heal when I sat my family and friends down, opened my heart, and let my feelings and emotions pour out. I shared the hurt I felt and explained how I did not want to feel pitied or be a burden. My family and friends reached out, and I let them in. Something happened, something magical that brought us each closer to one another.

There's no substitute for the fun I have with my girl-friends on a day at the mall. However, the wonders of technology have opened up the world, and I have become an avid Internet shopper. Shopping, in every form, will always be my escape. It is a pleasure that helps keep wounds healed and brings peace to my soul, much to the chagrin of my husband—but to the delight of my neigh-bors who speculate about what's going on between me and the UPS man.

Stacey Chillemi

A mother understands what a child does not say.

JEWISH PROVERB

The cold January drizzle landed on the highway as Patrick and I headed for the mall. He was two, I was thirty-four, but we were both itching to run free in a dry place filled with unfamiliar sights and smells.

We ran up the stairs at the main entrance, still under construction after a hundred years of remodeling (give or take). His little legs carried him through the glass doors, and we both breathed a sigh of happiness when we could remove our coat hoods. I had a few dollars in my purse, not exactly the makings of a shopping spree, but we were determined to make the most of our loot and quickly found our way to a food stand.

We bought a small package of hot pretzel sticks and a diet soda. Four dollars flew out of our spending account, but we weren't worried. We munched our salty snack and sipped our drink as we made our way into the belly of the mall. For a gray Wednesday afternoon, the place was surprisingly empty. Some shoppers whizzed by, but it was generally our world to explore as we saw fit. Patrick broke into a run, and I chased him, eliciting squeals and giggles from my three-foot-tall "date."

We finished our goodies and entered a clothing store, not really looking to buy. We meandered to a full-length mirror, and to the hip-hop sounds coming from speakers overhead, we wiggled, shimmied and grooved. Our dancing was hardly worthy of a scholarship to Juilliard, but it didn't matter to us. We finished our routine by making faces at our reflections, sticking out tongues and crossing eyes.

A game of hide-and-seek rounded out our adventure at that store, with Patrick weaving in and out of clothing displays. I always knew where he was—a telltale snuffle of laughter from behind fashionable "low-waisted" trousers was a dead giveaway. When I caught him, I swooped him into the air, and for a moment, time stopped.

We walked back to the midway and ran on the scuffed linoleum past store windows with blindly staring mannequins, "Clearance Sale!" signs and chocolate treats. Elton John's *Blessed* was playing. Inspired by the haunting, nostalgic melody, I hugged Patrick tight and swung him around once, twice, three times. Dizzy, I stopped. But I didn't let him go.

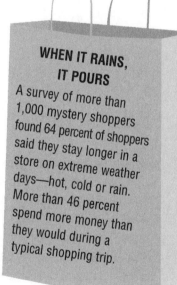

WHEN IT RAINS, IT POURS

A survey of more than 1,000 mystery shoppers found 64 percent of shoppers said they stay longer in a store on extreme weather days—hot, cold or rain. More than 46 percent spend more money than they would during a typical shopping trip.

At that instant, as I looked into his glee-filled, bright blue eyes with their long, dark lashes (courtesy of Daddy),

I was swept away with emotion. Love, longing, contentment, joy.

Without fanfare, Patrick broke our embrace and began to scamper down the mall's corridor, his sneakers squeaking on the floor. When I caught him, I plucked him up and onto my shoulders, and began to trot past the surprised kiosk vendors.

I was dressed in faded jeans. My hair was pulled back, and my face hadn't seen makeup for months. Sneakers were my footwear of choice. I was a disheveled mess, but I had one thing those other women didn't: a smile.

Patrick and I headed toward the bathrooms for a quick pit stop. On the way there, we noticed one of those quickie photo cubicles, something I hadn't seen in a few years. After our restroom break, we ventured into the picture booth. I slowly put in three dollar bills, and my little guy watched in awe as the machine "ate" the money.

Our photographs were candid, incredibly amateurish and wonderful. For our three bucks, we got two strips of shots, one copy for the refrigerator and one for Daddy's wallet. We topped off our mall visit with a trip to the nutrition store to weigh ourselves. Four quarters later, I found out I was still at my "fighting" weight, and Patrick hadn't gained since his last doctor visit. We hugged and celebrated nothing in particular and started back toward the mall entrance, which was soon to be our exit.

Patrick looked up at me and grinned.

It was then that I realized this had been one of the best shopping experiences of my life. We had spent about ten dollars during our excursion and had few material possessions to show for it. My wallet was nearly empty, and I had emptied my coat pockets of change, yet I knew I would remember this afternoon for the rest of my life. My heart overflowed as I scooped up Patrick and carried him out into the mist.

Angelique Caffrey

The Name Game

If we knew how to get the label on the outside, we'd all be in clover.

IRWIN GROSSMAN

There she goes, out the door toward the school bus in her Jordache jeans, Izod alligator shirt, Adidas shoes and London Fog jacket. There she goes . . . the neighbor's kid, not mine.

My daughter, unfortunately, is just as label-conscious, but fortunately, I'm not. Ah, here she comes now, running for the bus in her RS jeans. Never heard of that brand? RS stands for "Rummage Sale," a buck-fifty at a dandy, five-family sale down the block.

Her shirt is a genuine HMD (hand-me-down), graciously given to us by my younger sister who has great taste in clothes and never wears anything out.

Her shoes? A fine label, loved by mothers everywhere. They're "TRAX" . . . "Attention Kmart shoppers, today's blue-light special is located in the shoe department where our TRAX shoes are . . ."

That snappy, zippered jacket is an honest-to-goodness

"Seven-Miler." Two bucks at the Seven-Mile Fair, the biggest flea market north of the Illinois–Wisconsin border. It's a great place to shop for school clothes, hubcaps, chickens, fresh vegetables, pet rabbits, spray paint, old dishes and screwdriver sets. Once I even found a genuine pair of used Gloria Vanderbilt jeans there. Of course, I ripped the label off before I took them home to my daughter. I figured once she squeezed her little backside into a pair of designer label jeans, there'd be no going back to no-name land.

The designer label battle isn't over at our house by any means. The discussion will probably last until my last kid is out of college and completely on his own, paying his own bills, buying his own clothes.

When my children go shopping in today's label-crazed world, hopefully both girls and both boys will recall their growing-up years, and realize that there are other more important things to do with their money than pad the pockets of the owners of overpriced designer fashions. Hopefully, when they're grown and buying clothes for their own kids, they'll retain the same sense of prudent frugality that I, by necessity, taught them as children.

In the meantime, we aren't going the Levi's, Anne Klein, Nike route. Instead, we're going to this sale, that sale, everywhere a sale-sale. And instead of being a walking billboard for a rich clothing manufacturer, I'll hope that my children emerge with a sense of well-defined individuality, wearing fashions that they like and are comfortable, even if they're already broken in a little.

Patricia Lorenz

Why Is It That ... I Don't Just Buy Beige?

Eclectic means you can put anything together as long as it's expensive.

CHAUNCEY HOWE

These days I'm thinking that our military personnel and the average mother-of-the-groom have it all figured out: If you don't want to be shot at or, worse still, accused of upstaging the bride's side of the family, you ought to confine your purchases to subtle shades of beige. After all, the ability to blend in with the local landscape works for our guys and gals in uniform, and it keeps our family women from embarrassing themselves in a catfight at the altar.

And if I were clever enough to apply the same principle to my attempts at sneaking a new wardrobe into our house, our family budget talks wouldn't be as heated as our south-facing sunroom on a three-digit day.

I blame myself for the disharmony. For if every shirt, short, dress and skirt I owned could be disguised and stored within the kids' sandbox instead of flaunting its vibrant newness from my open closet door, things would be much more civilized around here.

I simply need to get over my attraction to color. Perhaps have the ole cones removed from my retinas. See life through a dog's eyes—nothing too drastic.

In all beige, all the time, I could smuggle in hundreds of different garments that would fly right in under the enemy's radar. Surely he wouldn't notice an array of cargo pants and flak jackets that I would wind up resigning myself to, especially since my color choices would range only from Sahara Sand to Mediterranean Olive. I might as well give up my favorite stores for the local Army Surplus while I'm at it. That would bring the added bonus of a closet full of industrial-strength fabrics that wouldn't even need to be dry-cleaned. Now we're talking true marital harmony!

In fairness to my shopping nemesis, I understand my beloved partner in life just can't comprehend the thrill a girl gets from debuting a new outfit. If only the brand spankin' new duds that leave me feeling radiant didn't leave him with an ire radiating throughout his coronary ventricles.

I fear that he may just be one ensemble away from planting a minefield that leads to his enemy's control center, otherwise known as my closet. The addition of one more hanger could just be the designated trigger to send the whole rod crashing down, moving us beyond our current "conflict" status and out into a declaration of war.

Fortunately, for the sake of domestic peace, a particularly volatile situation was defused a few weeks back when I met up with him at a performance at our daughter's school. It might be relevant to disclose (though certainly does little to garner support for yours truly) that the show took place only a few days after a little chat about fiscal restraint. His argument included something about massive layoffs at his company, plummeting stock values and no bonuses in sight. Yadda, yadda.

So when I replay the situation in my mind, I now see that doing my best impression of a spring flower in my new little island-printed skirt and its accompanying form-fitted red top might have been interpreted as an attempt to pick a fight. Yet there I sat, chatting with friends in a metal folding chair, feeling simultaneously bold, guilty and pretty darned cute while awaiting my hubby's arrival to the show.

Once he got there, I signaled him to the seat I had saved. Just after we exchanged hellos, the woman on my husband's left (much to my horror) leaned over to ask me if this "darling little number" was the one I had mentioned splurging on at Ann Taylor. My only defense was to give her a bug-eyed stare and state with all the conviction of a lying politician: "Why, yes. This is the outfit. But I'm sure you're mistaken . . . I found it on sale at Target!"

I never said the enemy was a dummy. That's why my remark made him laugh first and hardest. The children took the stage and gave me a chance to ponder the damage done. He did laugh . . . so how mad could he really be?

I'm still waiting to find out the extent of my man's wrath. Like any true enemy, he won't be announcing the exact time and place of his retaliation. Just in case there's still a possibility of a peaceful resolution, I am prepared to surrender my credit cards at a moment's notice.

But until I can persuade him to schedule a summit on neutral ground, I will continue to approach my closet with utmost caution.

Shana McLean Moore

That Takes
the cake

We have stopped for a moment to encounter each other. To meet, to love, to share. It is a precious moment, but it is transient. It is a little parenthesis in eternity.

DEEPAK CHOPRA, M.D.

Mrs. Barrett lived right across the street. She was a nice lady, kind of quiet. She kept to herself and didn't bother anyone, and no one really bothered her. Her husband had passed away a few years back. The rare times we talked when we went out to our mailboxes at the same time, I would ask her how she was doing.

"Oh, I'm fine," she'd reply.

"Really, Mrs. Barrett, is there anything I can do for you?" Her son stopped by once in a while, and I talked to him when he came out to get her mail. I knew that she was on a fixed budget, getting social-security checks and barely making ends meet. "Can I get you anything at the store?"

"Thank you so much, but I'm doing just fine," she would reply, smiling sweetly as she walked up her driveway.

Her house happened to be on the corner where the school bus stopped, and every morning at 8:10 the corner was abuzz with children. Some of them dragged their feet as they walked on her grass; some of them threw wrappers from breakfast granola bars in her flowerbeds. Some of the neighborhood moms walked their kids to the bus, dragging along little Fido or Fifi.

Mrs. Barrett wasn't bothered by any of that. She picked up the trash in her flowerbeds, watered her lawn to keep the grass growing nice and green, and picked up after Fido and Fifi—all without saying a word to anyone. I know, because I saw her.

I also happened to see her do something else, something that I thought was really beyond what ordinary people do.

We were in the grocery store's bakery aisle one day. She was pausing to look at the pies and cakes, and even lifted one up and then set it back down. There was another woman next to her, also looking at the cakes.

"I love coconut cake," the woman said out loud to Mrs. Barrett when she noticed the box in her hands.

"Oh, I do, too," Mrs. Barrett replied.

"But I just can't afford to get one today," the woman commented, then turned and walked away.

Mrs. Barrett watched as the woman left, then picked up a box of coconut cake and placed it in her shopping cart. *Oh, good,* I thought, *she's going to treat herself.*

After a few more minutes of shopping, I joined the long line to check out. I saw Mrs. Barrett, three people ahead of me, placing the items from her cart on the conveyor belt. There wasn't much there: a quart of milk, a small loaf of bread, an apple and some cheese. And that coconut cake.

"Good afternoon, Mrs. Barrett," the checkout girl said with a smile. "How are you today?"

"Oh, I'm fine, just fine."

"Well, look at this, a coconut cake. Are you having company?"

"Oh, no, dear. Please put that in a separate bag for me, would you?"

"You bet," the clerk replied.

After fishing out the dollar bills from her wallet and paying for her groceries, she wheeled her cart from the store. I had just finished paying for my few items and was walking to my car when I saw it.

Mrs. Barrett had a grocery bag in her hands, the one that held the coconut cake. I could tell because the bag was plastic, and I could see through it. She was walking as briskly as she could to a dark blue car parked halfway down the row. There she found the woman from the store—the woman who so much wanted a coconut cake, but couldn't afford it.

"Here, this is a present for you," she said as she handed over the cake.

"Oh, you shouldn't have! You are such a dear. Thank you!" the happy woman replied.

I knew Mrs. Barrett couldn't afford the cake, and I knew her budget would be stretched tight because of it. But she did it anyway, out of the goodness of her heart. I wonder who enjoyed the cake more, Mrs. Barrett or the woman she gave it to? I'll bet they both savored the memory of that cake for a long, long time. It was a lesson I wouldn't soon forget.

B. J. Taylor

TIMING YOUR BUYS

January is "white sale" month. Stores offer linens, towels and bedding at deep discounts.

In *February,* Presidents' Day sales make it "furniture" month, but Valentine's Day usually spurs an increase in the cost of flowers, especially roses.

March is the time to get ready for spring in the garden. Buy rakes, lawnmowers, fertilizer and other supplies. The Seed Saver's Exchange, *www.seedsavers.org,* specializes in rare and heirloom seeds.

April is when winter overstocks go on sale to make room for the new trends in spring apparel and accessories in the stores.

May's Memorial Day sales can save you lots of money on home and auto maintenance, building materials and hardware.

June is school supplies month. Stock up on what the kids will need for September and avoid the crowds later.

July is a good time to look for bargains on sportswear and sports equipment.

August is the time to check the summer overstock sales. Watch for sales on shoes and clothing for the kids going back to school and any last-minute school supplies.

September is a great time for sales on housewares.

October is a good month to buy a new car. Dealers usually get their current model year inventory in September and need to clear their lots of last year's models.

November is the kickoff to the holiday season of shopping and a great time to find deals on winter apparel and accessories.

December is the biggest single month for shopping, with toys, party-ware and gift items leading the list of "must-haves."

chapter 5

Seamless Customer Service

Customer service doesn't come
from a manual; it comes from the heart.
When you're taking care of the
customer, you can never do too much.
And there is NO wrong way—
if it comes from the heart.

DEBBIE ("MRS.") FIELDS

The Spirit of
the Season

The most vivid memories of Christmases past are usually not of gifts given or received, but of the spirit of love, the special warmth of Christmas worship, the cherished little habits of home.

LOIS RAND

It was my first Christmas in Los Angeles, and somewhere between the strangeness of the weather and the fact that I had never spent Christmas alone before, the holiday blues were setting in, in a big way. I spent my days behind a cosmetics counter, explaining the difference between various moisturizers and why night cream is so important. Just after Thanksgiving, we received a shipment of beautiful three-tiered silk moiré jewelry boxes our cosmetics company put out as a last-minute promotion. They had only sent three, and for a good reason. They retailed for about seventy-five dollars apiece, putting them far out of reach for most of our customers.

Having worked in retail for many years, I was used to merchandise coming and going, and rarely if ever wanted much, but the minute I saw the jewelry boxes, I wanted one desperately. I wanted it for a combination of reasons, the first being that it was absolutely beautiful. A deep, emerald green, it was full of the company's best products, meant to be used so that the box could later hold jewelry. Secondly, I was scrimping and saving every cent just to get by, and this was one of the most decadent, extra- vagant things I'd ever seen. I walked or took buses in a city in which everyone has a car, brought my own lunch every day rather than eat at the expensive mall food court, and clipped every imaginable coupon. The idea of not only owning, but buying something like this just seemed so unbelievably out of my reach. Finally, I was still very much a stranger in a strange land. Everything that year seemed challenging, and I suppose I needed something to just be easy and even, perhaps to make me feel as though this was truly Christmas time. The thought of just being able to buy the jewelry box seemed like a way to accom- plish both.

The jewelry boxes sat on the counter for two weeks and were admired and examined by almost every woman who came by, each one saying how much she'd like to have it. Although none actually purchased one, every time some- one looked as though she might, my heart always sank. The idea of someone walking away with one of my boxes was more than I could take.

The week before Christmas, a man of about fifty came up to the counter, clearly overwhelmed by the thought of having to pick something out.

"Can I help you?" I asked.

"I hope so," he said. "I need a couple of presents, and I don't know where to start. This stuff mystifies me."

"Well, what are you looking for?" I asked.

"I have absolutely no idea, and I'm in a little bit of a hurry. What would you want if someone were buying something for you?"

This question presented a moral dilemma for me. There was no question what I would want, but I didn't want to tell him. He might buy it, and then we would only have two left.

"Well, honestly, I would probably buy this." I walked him over to the box and proceeded to extol all its virtues, demonstrating every drawer, every hidden compartment, all the while hoping silently that he wouldn't buy it.

"I don't know," he said, looking at it pensively. "Seventy-five dollars seems like a lot."

I elaborated, explaining that any woman would be thrilled to have it.

"Well, all right. Can you wrap it for me?" he asked.

"No problem," I said, not sure if I had really wanted him to say yes.

When I came back to the counter from the stockroom, he said he wanted a second box. A little confused about why someone who was so ambivalent about buying one suddenly wanted two, I returned to the stockroom. When I returned, he said he wanted a third, wanted them all wrapped and would be back later with a credit card.

A GIRL'S BEST FRIEND

The price of a diamond depends on the *4 C's: cut, color, clarity* and *carats* (weight).

Color can be "graded" on a scale, but not every scale is identical. A "D" may be the best color for one scale, but not for another.

A diamond can be described as "flawless" only if it has no visible surface cracks or other imperfections that can be seen under 10-power magnification by a skilled diamond grader.

Forty minutes later, he came back to the counter.

"Did you get them wrapped?" he said, clearly ready to get his shopping finished.

"Yes, I did," I answered. "Would you like to put that on your charge?"

"Yes, but first, do you have gift cards?"

"Watch him," I whispered to my manager. "I'm starting to worry that he's going to take those boxes and run."

I returned with the cards, now getting a little angry, and more important, concerned that he had no intention of paying.

"Here," I said, handing him three cards and envelopes. "Why don't I ring this up for you?"

He handed me his credit card and took a seat at the counter, suddenly taking his time to fill out the cards.

To my surprise—and to a certain degree, my dismay— his card went through. My dream of having the jewelry box was over.

"Here you go," I said, handing him the sales slip to sign.

He signed it, and then took one of the gift cards and put it in an envelope.

"Just a minute," he said.

He took one of the wrapped boxes out of its bag, put it on the counter with the card and said, "Thanks for all your help. Have a great holiday," and walked away with the box still on the counter.

I was dumbfounded. Instinctively, I opened the card. It read: "Merry Christmas, Courtney. Love, Santa"

In the midst of all the Christmas chaos, in a town in which acquiring things is a blood sport, this man did something that stayed with me for the rest of my life: He gave me hope that even when things seem dark, someone will come along and make everything just a little easier.

C. L. Robinson

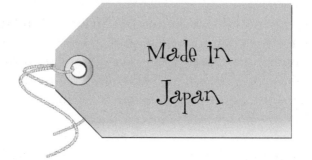

The love of one's country is a splendid thing. But why should love stop at the border?

PABLO CASALS

"Mom! I'm going to Japan!" exclaimed Lori, as she burst into the kitchen. "I'm the only one in my school selected to be an exchange student this summer."

When my teenager traveled to the other side of the world, she lived with the Omori family. During her stay, she bonded with the parents and their teenage daughter, Shoko. Although Lori was immersed in a different culture and didn't like Japanese food, she adapted with her sense of humor and drowned the food in catsup. She wrote letters about her adventures and the attention her blonde ponytail received when she visited a school. She promised to bring me a special gift.

At the end of Lori's stay, the Omori family struggled to say good-bye. They had tears in their eyes as they hugged their adopted American at the airport. The stoic Japanese father stared at Lori and stammered, "You—always my daughter."

When Lori arrived back in the States after several flight changes, we found her at three in the morning, dressed in a traditional kimono and sleeping off jetlag near a deserted baggage carousel.

The next day, she shared highlights of her stay in Japan and presented her family with gifts. Her older sister squealed over her pearl ring, her younger brother snuggled his stuffed animal, and her father munched on Japanese snacks. My eyes widened in delight when I received a gold necklace.

"I bought this small gold chain to cover the scar from your thyroid surgery," Lori explained. "I know the scar bothers you, even though you call it your 'second smile.' I bought it when the Omoris took me to a jewelry store owned by an old friend, and Shoko helped me pick it out. I measured it around my neck, and it should fit you perfectly."

After Lori secured the clasp, she stood aside and smiled at the necklace that concealed my scar. I treasured my daughter's gift and rarely took it off.

While on a trip to visit friends, I had trouble with the clasp coming undone. I removed my necklace and put it in my purse for safekeeping. I feared it could silently slip from my neck while we dined in a crowded restaurant. When I discovered the necklace had disappeared from my purse, I became frantic. I searched the house and the car, and inquired at the lost-and-found in the restaurant. I was devastated. Now, I had a visible scar on my throat and an invisible scar on my heart.

As fate would have it, my husband booked a trip to Japan one summer to celebrate our anniversary. I was thrilled, and thought about Shoko and the Omoris. Although many years had passed, and Lori and Shoko were married women with children, the two friends kept in touch and exchanged gifts. Lori sent Shoko the news her parents would be in Tokyo. Shoko replied that she and the Omoris would drive an hour's journey to greet us at our hotel.

Shoko was no longer the awkward schoolgirl standing next to Lori in pictures taken long ago. She was an attractive, gracious woman who greeted us warmly, as her parents bowed nearby. They exchanged a flurry of Japanese while gesturing that Lori looked like me.

"We take you our town where Lori stay," said Shoko softly. "She write you lose necklace and feel sad. You come, buy new one in same shop. Owner wait for you."

When we drove to the town where my daughter lived as a teenager, I was fascinated with the bustling streets and buildings crowded with tiny apartments. As I experienced Japan, I developed a new respect for my young daughter who had embraced this different culture.

Soon, the elderly owner was bowing and motioning for us to enter his jewelry store. He opened it during off-hours especially for us. Shoko spoke with him, then walked to a display of gold chains and carefully selected one.

"This one like necklace Lori buy. Try on."

The gold chain covered my scar perfectly and was identical to the one Lori purchased years ago. Suddenly, I had goose bumps as I realized this was a re-creation of Lori's shopping experience—with the same shop and owner, with the Omoris looking on, and with Shoko involved in the jewelry selection.

My new necklace healed the scar on my heart. It continues to remind me of my loving daughter and an incredible shopping adventure that was made in Japan.

Miriam Hill

Annie Is Number One With Me

Better by far that you should forget and smile,
than you should remember and be sad.

CHRISTINA ROSSETTI

Her cashier's station at the collectibles store faces the front door, and whenever someone enters, Annie flashes a huge smile and extends a cheerful greeting. "Welcome to our store, where every customer is Number One!"

"How can we each be Number One, Annie," I teased one day, "when there are so many of us?"

She just smiled again and called out over my shoulder to the next customer, "Welcome to our store. . . ."

Being an avid collector, I see Annie quite often. On one visit, with no customers at the checkout counter, she walked over and quietly stood beside me as I searched through the piles of items on the shelves, hoping to discover a soon-to-be-valued treasure.

"That is really beautiful," she said, admiring the piece in my hand. "There is another one over here that would look great with it," she continued, as she led me to a different aisle. I discovered that Annie had a real eye for beauty, and at that moment I secretly commissioned her as my personal shopper. That day, my shopping cart overflowed with more than I had intended to buy. Annie rang up my purchases and carefully wrapped the fragile items. As she worked, she leaned over the counter, her smile momentarily fading, and confided to me in a whisper, "My feet hurt so badly from standing so long. Please pray for me."

Making a mental note to pray for Annie's feet, I returned to the less-friendly world. My next visit to the store came a couple of weeks later. To my disappointment, there was no warm, friendly greeting. Without Annie around, with no second opinion to bolster my inner shopping voice, it became a humdrum shopping trip. As I left that day with just one purchase, I was puzzled. *What had happened to Annie? Was my personal shopper ill? Or perhaps, something even worse had occurred?*

GET IN THE MOOD

Eighty-five percent of shoppers surveyed said the mood and helpfulness of the sales associate impacts how much money they are willing to spend in the store.

Shopping day arrived again—something shoppo-maniacs look forward to with great anticipation—and my favorite store was crowded. To my delight, as I entered I heard Annie's familiar voice calling out, "Welcome to our store, where every customer is Number One." With spirits uplifted, I began searching for hidden treasures with renewed zeal.

Months rolled by, and Annie drifted in and out of the lives of her shopping clientele. Her unexplained absences from work were nothing mysterious, simply a matter of scheduling, but whenever she appeared behind the checkout counter, she offered positive messages and anecdotes to all who entered. On rainy days when customers grumbled about the weather, she would counter with, "I just love rain. I call it liquid sunshine." I pondered Annie's perpetually cheerful outlook on life, and began to put bits and pieces of our conversations together. The profile that emerged was one of a very special person.

At the tender age of three, Annie lost her balance while she was riding in the bed of a pickup truck loaded with freshly harvested corn. Her tiny body went over the side, and Annie landed in the path of the wheels. In just seconds, this healthy toddler's life was changed forever, her skull crushed by the wheels of the truck, and while she was blessed to survive, the accident left Annie with permanent disabilities.

What courage and character it took for Annie to undergo a lifetime of physical and emotional healing. Not only is she self-sufficient and independent today, Annie quietly advocates for persons with disabilities, serving on a number of committees, often in leadership roles. Now, when I walk into Annie's store, I see much more than a clerk behind a counter. I remain in awe of her winning smile and enthusiastic attitude, especially when her feet are aching. Knowing the challenges Annie has overcome in her life, now when I hear her heartfelt greeting, I silently respond with one of my own: "Annie, you're my Number One!"

Irma Newland

The Magic Carpet Ride

Half the world is composed of idiots, the other half of people clever enough to take indecent advantage of them.

WALTER KERR

Most shops had already closed, or were just about to, as I was searching for a carpet in Tehran's busy bazaars late in the evening. A silk carpet, displayed in one of the shop windows, caught my eye. It didn't have a price tag, but definitely looked expensive.

The shopkeeper, a middle-aged man, was just leaving. Nevertheless, when he saw me, he smiled and invited me inside.

"You want chai?" he asked me in broken English mixed with Persian. I politely refused, but he smiled and offered me a cup of chai anyway and a few dates.

I smiled back and started drinking the black tea, which tasted quite good. Hoping he understood English, I pointed at the carpet and asked him, "May I please see that?"

He offered me a few more dates and said something in Persian, which I barely understood. However, his warm smile made me feel nice and comfortable.

He removed the carpet and handed it over to me. It wasn't very big, maybe as big as a doormat. But it felt very silky; it was definitely handmade. "How much does it cost?" I asked him, speaking slowly, hoping he understood me.

"You like it?"

"Yes, it's very beautiful," I replied honestly, "but how much does it cost?"

He smiled and replied, "Nothing."

Guessing he didn't understand, I asked again, "Money? Rials or dollars? How much?"

BAZAAR BARGAINS

Prices usually go down the farther the shops are from a tourist area. Shop around—and let merchants know you are doing so—and the price may come down. Look like you know what you're doing—even if you don't! Shopkeepers are less likely to take advantage of a shopper who looks savvy.

"Nothing. You are my guest. It is free," he replied in broken English.

"Excuse me, free? No money?" I removed a hundred-dollar bill, showing it to him, still thinking he didn't understand what I was saying.

"No need. You are a guest in my country. I won't charge you for it."

Not knowing much about Iranian customs and traditions, I felt very awkward, but was sure that offering free handmade silken carpets to unknown foreigners was not an Iranian custom.

I picked up the calculator from near the cash counter and punched in 150, showing it to him. "$150? Okay?"

"No money. I do not want money for it." He started packing the carpet.

This guy had offered me tea, dates and kept his shop open, even though it was past closing time. All this, and he wanted to give me the carpet for free? I was expecting him to charge me much more; instead, he was telling me the carpet was gratis.

Very strange.

He finished packing the carpet and handed me the bag.

I looked at him, amazed. By now I had become accustomed to shopkeepers asking me for a higher price, and then I had to bargain ferociously to get a good deal. This guy was here to make money, wasn't he?

For a second, I felt like walking out with the free carpet, but then the guilt of doing so struck me. I removed $200 and kept it near the cash counter; my heart didn't allow me to take the carpet for free from this really nice man.

"Please, you have to take this. You kept the shop open especially for me. You were extremely warm, and I really loved the tea. I can't take this carpet without paying you. I would feel guilty if you didn't take the money," I said with a smile, desperately hoping that he took the $200.

He took the money. "Thank you. Do visit my shop again."

Feeling very satisfied, I smiled at him and left the shop, carrying the carpet with me.

After walking for a few minutes, a carpet in another shop window caught my eye. It was identical to the one I had just bought—the same size, the same color, the same design and the same material.

The only difference was that this one had a price tag; it said "Fixed Price—$50."

Yogesh Chabria

An Unexpected Purchase

Live so that when your children think of fairness,
caring and integrity, they think of you.

H. JACKSON BROWN, JR.

One of my favorite parts of vacation is shopping in
small-town squares or finding little out-of-the-way
stores and shops. I know that I'll always find something
fun, something unusual, something that fits one of my collections just perfectly. But one year, I found something
that I hadn't put on my shopping list.

We were on our first real vacation since our daughter
came along. We'd spent most of our time in the big city of
Austin, Texas, but had taken a day to slip away to a beautiful little area far from the city. After we'd done all the
touristy things of riding a little train through the wilder-
ness area and playing in the river, we found our way to
the beautiful town square full of shops and restaurants.

My daughter and I oohed and aahed over the handmade quilts and pieces of jewelry. We admired paintings
and pottery, clothes and antiques. While going through
the shops, I found a handmade candle that I couldn't

resist. We left the little shop with our new purchase, and wandered in and out of other stores for half an hour until we came to a café and stopped for lunch.

As we ate and relaxed, a young woman walked into the shop and looked around. She spotted us and hurried to our table. I was puzzled because we knew no one in this town. Then I recognized her as the clerk who had waited on us in the candle shop. She held out a dollar bill to me as if it were mine.

"What's this?" I asked, a little embarrassed that others were looking at us.

"I'm sorry, but I overcharged you for the candle," she explained. "I've been looking in all the shops trying to find you. I was afraid you had already left town, but since it is lunch time, I thought you might be here."

DOLLARS & SENSE

Congress adopted the dollar bill as the money unit for the United States in 1785. Today, the government prints nearly 17 million $1 bills every day!

I stared at the dollar. I hadn't realized I'd been overcharged, and even if I had remembered, I wouldn't have taken the time to look for that same shop again to get it back. Yet, it had been important enough for her to seek me out.

I was surprised by how much time she'd spent searching for us. Had she closed the shop or had to wait for someone to take her place while she searched?

"Thank you, but I never would have known about the slight overcharge," I told her.

She said, "Oh, but it doesn't matter the amount. The mistake was mine. I needed to find you." She smiled, and I knew that the honesty in her soul had been tested, and she was happy. She told us she hoped we would enjoy our time in her town. I told her that I already had.

When she left the restaurant, my daughter said, "That sure was an honest woman." I nodded. I hadn't put on my shopping list that day that I'd like my daughter to see an example of total honesty and someone who truly believes in customer service, but we'd received it all the same. I started to slip the dollar back into my purse, then added it to the tip we'd already put on the table.

Kathryn Lay

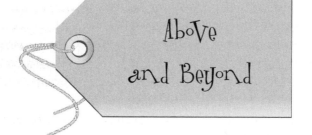

Above
and Beyond

The flower generation tore tradition to shreds, but in the 1980s some magic sewing machine has stitched it all up again.

LETITIA BALDRIGE

After we sold our home, having to wait ninety days until our new residence was ready, we temporarily relocated into my dearest friend's 1,600-square-foot Cape Cod–style house. Although a tight fit, my husband, two children and I managed.

Professional movers squeezed our furnishings and accessories into Pat's two-car garage. Our family had about fifty boxes of clothes and shoes that landed in her basement. Due to limited closet space, we left a meager selection of garments on hand. Since it was October, winter outerwear was the priority.

On December 20, my father, who had been suffering from emphysema for four years, was admitted to the hospital. Seven days later, he passed away with family members by his side. The day before the funeral, my husband and I realized that we didn't have any appropriate clothes for the solemn occasion. Pinched for time, we went through most of the boxes in the basement. Our treasure trove included a black dress for me (who cared if I donned accompanying loafers?); my son's navy-blue suit and dress shoes; my daughter's indigo dress and black Mary Janes; and my husband's only navy-blue pinstriped suit, dress shirt and wingtip shoes. We were ready to go, at least we thought.

Two hours before the wake, my husband took the jacket off the hanger, only to discover his matching pants missing!

"Oh! What am I supposed to do now?" he asked, troubled.

After deliberating through a litany of possible solutions, we decided that I would dash to the wake while he raced to a nearby department store that employed a tailor. When my husband, clad in jeans, white dress shirt and suit jacket, ran into the store, the men's department was swarming with consumers preparing for upcoming New Year's Eve celebrations. My husband, usually emotionless, was close to hyperventilating as he frantically searched for a matching pair of pants. Sensing his angst, a store clerk approached, asking, "Can I help you?"

"Please, I'm colorblind. Do these pants match my jacket?" he asked, holding up a pair of newfound pants.

"Ummm," the clerk said. Apparently forsaking rudeness, he chose not to tell my husband that his selection of a pair of chocolate-toned pants didn't coordinate with a blue jacket.

"Please," my husband whispered, this time swallowing a painful surge rising up his throat. "Please," he continued, "my father-in-law's wake is within an hour, and I have no pants to wear. My family's waiting for me! I can't be late!"

Without a minute to spare, the clerk stripped my husband's jacket from him, and in less than five minutes of shuffling through the rack, matched it with a nearly identical colored pair of pants. He then hooked my husband by the arm and rushed him across the store, cutting through a line of men awaiting the tailor-on-premises.

"Sorry, Tonio! You have to let this man try these on immediately. It is a matter of life and death, really!"

Somehow, probably because of my husband's distraught appearance and the clerk's relentless determination, without question the tailor raced my husband into his back room (no time to use the actual dressing room). Meanwhile, the store clerk explained the situation to the waiting customers.

FIT AND FEEL

Price isn't always the best gauge of quality. Good quality fabric keeps its shape and feels good to the touch. Loose threads and puckers are signs of poor quality in clothing. Just 1 to 2 percent spandex in clothing will help the piece retain its shape.

Moments later, my husband's pants bagged up over his wingtips. For the sake of time, the tailor immediately pinned them up instead of stitching them.

"Look," Tonio said, by now clued into the dilemma and ironing his handiwork, "the pins will hold the hem, and no one will see them. After the funeral, just drop the pants off, and I will stitch them up permanently."

Upon paying for his pants, my husband presented both the store clerk and tailor each with a twenty-dollar tip, which neither man would accept.

"Sometimes, the greatest deed needs no acknowledgment," the store clerk said, sounding like a great philosopher.

"Yeah," Tonio agreed. "Take that money and make a contribution in our name to your father-in-law's favorite charity."

Later, we did donate money in their names to my father's church, and we wrote a thank-you note to the department store's owners expressing our gratitude.

Because of their kindness, my husband arrived within minutes of the wake, and in relative calm we were able to put my dad to his final rest.

Stacy Lytwyn Maxwell

So little material raised so high to reveal so much that needs to be covered so badly.

CECIL BEATON

Well, spring is just around the corner. Time to clean the closets and face the music—see what fits and what doesn't. Time to introduce my South Beach Diet to my white capri pants! Okay, so I didn't quite meet my diet goals. I've accepted and adjusted. It's a be autiful day, and I'm going shopping.

The new hot colors—pink, turquoise and purple—jump right out at my winter-weary eyes, and my spirits begin to soar as I pile up the cart. Suits, tops and even bigger pants . . . who cares? If I buy lots of funky shoes, they will look right past the big pants, straight down to my feet and say, "Oh, look at those adorable little shoes!"

At the fitting-room door, I hear the usual pronouncement, "Only six at a time, ma'am." But if I take in one suit and five blouses to see which one looks best, I will be here for days. Frantically, I start sifting and sorting to see which ones I really like, and which ones I like just so-so, until my arms are falling off from exhaustion. Finally, I just grab a pile of six and go in.

I balance my large self on the tiny corner seat in the fitting room to catch my breath and calm my nerves. I get undressed and start trying things on. The lighting is ghastly, and the mirror is definitely not my friend. And it's much worse than I thought: Nothing fits! They should call this the "not fitting" room.

I try talking to myself. *You just started. Don't get discouraged. See if you have a piece of candy in your handbag for a little sugar boost.*

I get re-dressed, go out to the cart, get another six things, come back and try again. Awful! Back to the cart, into the dressing room, back to the cart, into the dressing room. I'm grumbling loudly to myself when I hear a cheerful voice outside my curtain saying, "Excuse me, can you give me your opinion on this bathing suit?"

I put my coat on over my underwear and step out. She is a very large woman in a very small bathing suit. I can tell by the way she waltzes back and forth in front of the mirror that she is really pleased with how she looks.

"Oh," I exclaim, "you look fabulous in that suit!"

"I think so, too," she says. "I was a little concerned about the pink, but I think it's a good color on me."

"Definitely!"

Exhausted, I get dressed. I need coffee and maybe a little something to go with the coffee. I push the cart to the checkout register and charge the whole load. I'll just take it all home and try it on tomorrow when I've lost another pound.

Avis Drucker

Big-city Kindness

Extend all the care, kindness and understanding you can muster, and do so with no thought of any reward. Your life will never be the same again.

OG MANDINO

After completing my studies in engineering, I decided to move to the city and hunt for a job. I came from a small town in the northeastern hills of India, and this would be my first trip to New Delhi. Before leaving to begin my new life and pursue my ambitions, I was given loads of advice by friends and relatives about the thieves and thugs who run rampant in a big city. I was advised to be careful about the shrewd vendors and taxi drivers who cheat innocent people. "They just smell who's new in town," a friend warned.

My train arrived at the New Delhi railway station, and before the passengers could even debark, an army of "coolies" in huge red kurtas (cotton pullover shirts) descended. They sported brass plates bearing a number on their arms and wore padded headgear. They rushed inside the train, as if to rescue the passengers from some disaster, eager to help them move their luggage.

Thankfully, I was carrying just one huge bag and could manage quite well on my own. I pushed my way through the hodgepodge of passengers, coolies and luggage, and the first thing that struck me was the crowd. There were hundreds of people scurrying in every direction around me.

I quickly came upon dozens of taxi walas (drivers), all offering genuine rates, or so they claimed. Some even suggested hotels at cheap rates, which rang in my ears as "cheat" rates. Remembering the advice that I got back home, I hastily moved away from the crowd of taxi walas and scanned the group, attempting to separate the "cheat" drivers from the good ones, hoping that by some fluke I could successfully identify them. I noticed a decent-looking, old driver standing beside his taxi who did not look like a nefarious type, and my sixth sense told me he was safe to approach. When he agreed to charge by the meter reading, I pushed my bag into the car. There I was, in this new city, all by myself!

The old guy was pretty friendly, talkative I would say. On the way to my cousin's apartment where I would be staying, he showed me the Film City and explained the significance of the magnificent Akshardham temple, which was then under construction. Locals hoped it would attract more tourists and preserve our cultural heritage. Being a self-confessed shopping freak, monuments of historical significance or sightseeing are not really my cup of tea. I asked him if there were some good places to shop, and he explained that Delhi was the hub for shopping, with markets unlike anywhere else in the country. He also told me he had two sons, who were useless, and a daughter my age who is married, but still bothers to care about her parents.

It was a smooth ride. My driver knew the area, door-to-door, and after reaching my cousin's home, he showed me the rate card and I paid him. I was impressed at the genuineness of this old chap, as most drivers don't even bother to carry a rate card.

As I gathered my bag, my driver informed me that he would be in the area the next morning to drop somebody and asked if I would be needing his services. My cousin was away on business, so I considered his offer. I thought it would be a good idea to begin getting my bearings and asked him to check with me after he dropped off his morning passenger.

Next morning around 11:30, the driver was at my door with a cheerful grin. "Madam, are you coming?" In no time, I was set to indulge in my favorite pastime. He suggested we go to the Palika Bazaar, famous for artifacts from Kashmir, especially Pashmina shawls of the finest quality. My personal taxi wala parked his taxi at the bazaar parking and informed me he would wait there.

The market was enormous. There were displays set up along the street and shops selling an amazing variety of items: potpourri, junk jewelry, antique items, cane furniture, bags, shoes, clothes. I didn't really need anything, but I couldn't stop myself from buying a pair of Kashmiri handmade slippers and two lovely night suits at half the price, as compared to my hometown. I then entered a shop specializing in the famous Pashmina shawls. After looking at dozens of them, I spotted one amazing piece in black with silver embroidery. It was gorgeous. You generally don't find Pashmina shawls in black so this was a unique piece, but the price was quite beyond my budget.

I moved on through the bazaar, unable to forget the beautiful black shawl. I made a mental calculation that if I didn't go shopping for the next two months, I could afford it—the trait of a genuine shopping freak. Without further

hesitation, I made my way back to the shop and purchased the shawl. I had spent almost four hours moving
up and down the streets of the bazaar, thoroughly enjoying my first day in New Delhi, but it was time to go home.
My legs ached, and I was literally starving! On my way
back to the taxi, the smells of food
being prepared by the cart vendors
made my mouth water. I
made one more quick stop
and picked up something to
eat.

My driver was sleeping
when I gently rapped on the
window. I offered him some
food, and I showed him my
purchases as we ate. I had
developed an attachment
for this nice old man who
had the same kind of innocence that I saw in my
grandpa. My good driver
thanked me for my kind-
ness, dropped me home
and wished me luck on my
job hunt.

STREET SMARTS

Street markets offer the
best prices, and haggling
is fun. The quality of merchandise is often less than
the shops, but you can get
great deals on knockoffs.
If a tour guide directs you
to shops that offer dis-
counts to people on your
tour, the shop is probably
giving the guide a kickback
for the referral.

I was content from my day of
shopping. I tried on the night suits and slippers, which were perfect, and then I looked for the shawl.
Checking the bags once . . . twice . . . it wasn't there! I
looked through all my purchases once more and all
around the house. My beautiful shawl was nowhere to be
found. I just couldn't believe it. Warm tears rolled down
my cheeks, and I was devastated. I would never find the
same piece again, let alone be able to afford it.

I mentally retraced my steps. I had moved the bags to

the front seat when the back seat got wet from a leaking water bottle, and I recalled the driver handing me the bags as I got out of the taxi. That was it! It was the driver . . . the cheat, the fraud! He must have liked the shawl and kept it for his daughter, or perhaps to sell and buy a small gold pendant for his wife. I treated him so well, and he had stolen from me!

All the feelings of good will that I had harbored for this kind old driver now turned to disgust, ruining my sense of independence and anticipation of life in New Delhi. I have never cursed anyone as badly as I cursed this cheating taxi driver. I spent the rest of the evening recalling our adventure, how smartly he had suggested Palika Bazaar and Pashmina shawls . . . it must have been his plan right from the beginning!

It was half-past midnight, and I was sitting with a book, hardly reading it and surfing channels on TV, when the doorbell rang. I looked through the eyehole . . . the old driver! "I'm sorry for disturbing you so late, but I knew you would be very anxious, madam. I will be going out of the city this morning, so I must return this tonight." In his hand was my beautiful shawl. After he reached home, he had noticed the bag, and he came all the way back to return it. I was speechless as the old man stood there, the same innocent smile on his face, completely unaware of all the disparaging thoughts I had for him earlier.

For many years since, I have lived and shopped in my adopted home of New Delhi. I am always careful, and a bit skeptical, but never doubtful of the dignity and innocence of people, thanks to the lesson I learned from my kind taxi wala on my first shopping excursion in the big city.

Deepana Mallik

Say, "Please"

Six essential qualities that are the key to success: sincerity, personal integrity, humility, courtesy, wisdom, charity.

DR. WILLIAM MENNINGER

Many years ago, to supplement my income as a young married man, I worked part-time at a supermarket in the meat department. One Saturday afternoon, an hour before closing, a very large man approached the counter, reached over and banged the bell, scaring the heck out of my coworker, Jim, who had his back turned to the counter.

Jim greeted the man with a polite, "Yes, sir, can I help you?"

Bell Ringer responded, "I want a fourteen-pound turkey."

The supermarket had advertised fourteen-pound turkeys (and less) for fourteen-cents a pound and had sold out by one o'clock. We still had larger birds, but they carried the normal price of twenty-three cents per pound.

"I'm sorry, sir. We're all sold out of the fourteen-pounders," Jim replied courteously.

This didn't sit well with our customer, who raised his voice to demand, "I want a fourteen-pound turkey."

This puzzling exchange continued back and forth until Billy, the meat manager, came through the swinging doors to see what all the ruckus was about. Bell Ringer yelled at Jim once again, "I told you I want a fourteen-pound turkey!"

Bill immediately addressed the out-of-control customer. "Look, sir, we sold out of that weight turkey, but I'll tell you what: We will give you a sixteen-pound bird for the same price." Expecting to have happily resolved this strange conflict, Bill was completely taken aback when Bell Ringer went ballistic.

"I want a fourteen-pound turkey! You people advertised it, and I want it!"

By this time, the altercation had attracted the attention of Mr. Walker, the store manager, who politely inquired, "What's the problem here?"

"I want to purchase a fourteen-pound turkey!" our irate customer explained.

"I came in to buy a fourteen-pound turkey that your company advertised, and I want a fourteen-pound turkey! I do not want a sixteen-pound turkey!"

Now, you don't become the manager of a customer-service-oriented supermarket without being able to think on your feet. Mr. Walker turned to Jim, who had been conscientiously cleaning the grinder since reinforcements had arrived, and said, "Jim, jump in your car and go get this man a fourteen-pound turkey."

Taken by surprise, Jimmy said, "No way will I get him anything. I tried to reason with him, but he has gone nuts."

We all waited, holding our breath listening for the pin to hit the floor. Mr. Walker held his ground. "Jim, take off your apron, go to another store and pick up a fourteen-pound turkey for this customer."

Jim glanced at the now smug-looking customer and then to Mr. Walker. He reached up and tore the apron from around his neck. Throwing it on the counter, he said, "I quit!" and walked out. Mr. Walker looked over at me, then to old Bill.

"Bill, go into my office and call all over until you find this man his bird." Turning to Bell Ringer, Mr. Walker said, "We will deliver your turkey to your house in a couple of hours. Please accept it as a gift from our store."

Eventually, Bill found a bird just over fifteen pounds on the north side of the city. Mr. Walker rewrapped it, marked it fourteen-pounds and delivered it to the demanding customer, free of charge as promised.

For weeks, without satisfaction, I scanned the newspaper, hoping to find a large man had choked on a turkey bone.

Another Saturday morning, as business was picking up there was a flourish of activity at the store entrance. Through the double doors strode Bell Ringer, followed by a couple of well-dressed men in business suits and a photographer. As customers and employees watched with furtive glances, Mr. Walker emerged from his office and engaged in a short

GOOD BUSINESS

It costs five times more to acquire a new customer than to retain an existing one.

Let angry customers *vent*. Don't interrupt.

Tell your customers what you *can* do for them, not what you can't.

Listen to what your customer is saying. Don't make an angry customer repeat himself.

Be sure your tone of voice reflects *sincerity* in solving the customer's problem.

Make the *extra* effort with the angry customer and ask if there's anything more you can do for him.

conversation with one of the men. He returned to his office, and the store PA system crackled to life, "All employees and customers, please come to the front of the store."

Bell Ringer wasn't an irate customer after all, but one of the chain's mystery shoppers. He and the well-dressed executives were here to honor Mr. Walker and our store with the highest customer-satisfaction award presented to any store in the chain.

At different times in my career, lots of customers treated me to similar abuse, and I had to take a position just like Mr. Walker. My livelihood and the success of my business kept me polite and accommodating when faced with the most irrational of customers, but I have Mr. Walker to thank for the lesson in keeping the customer happy that I've never forgotten.

William Geen

The Heartbeat of Africa

Modern man is frantically trying to earn enough to buy things he's too busy to enjoy.

FRANK CLARK

When Americans travel to Africa, we see the sights, go on the safaris, take too many photographs and—if we're lucky—mingle with the indigenous people. But, really, why go all the way to Africa if you aren't going to bring home souvenirs and artifacts?

The guidebooks tell you, you must bargain with the vendors; never accept the first price. So you learn how to haggle. You quibble and you dicker over a few dollars. It isn't that you can't afford that first price—of course, you can, but those fellows in the tie-dyed dashikis make it such high drama that it isn't long before you fall into the rhythm.

While I lived in Africa, I enjoyed doing business with these colorful characters. I purchased intricately carved beads from Peace Corps Babba who said he had once been to Kansas, and a Fulani wedding blanket from a young man who told me his name was John Travolta.

When I became a missionary teacher in Ghana and needed household items, my students wouldn't allow me to visit the marketplace alone. They told me the vendors would always charge too much. "Mama Susie," Kwesi said, "you must let me go with you. I will find you the best prices." And he did. Fifty cents each for two Williams-Sonoma kitchen towels, dusty but still in their original wrappings. Kwesi insisted on sniffing the bath towels before I bought them. "I can tell if they have been used," he said. "What else do you need?" I consulted my list: paring knives, a toilet brush, a plastic bucket, small drinking glasses, coffee mugs and a set of bath mats. Kwesi knew where to find everything in this market that was the size of four football fields. When Kwesi accompanied me, I noticed there was no playful bantering over the transactions, and I knew Kwesi had indeed negotiated the best price.

On the way back to our village, my purchases stowed in the back seat of our extended-cab Ford pickup, I remembered that I needed bananas. "Just drive over here," said Kwesi, motioning to the side of the road where a pretty young woman sat at a wooden table laden with mangoes, papaya, pineapples, bananas and a pile of thin, shimmering fish. "How many bananas do you need?" Kwesi asked.

"Five. No—seven."

He leaned out the car window and motioned to the girl to bring the bananas. She hoisted a huge bunch of bananas onto her shoulder and grabbed a machete. She charged me for seven, but gave me nine.

After that, I always bought my bananas from the car window on my weekly trips to town. And I never haggled over the price. On Friday afternoons, the pineapple girl came to our campus. She would walk gracefully from house to house in her neat white blouse, wraparound skirt and flip-flops. She balanced an impossibly huge collection of ripe pineapples in the shallow metal pan on her head and carried a sharp cutlass in her hand. When I saw her coming, I'd fetch a clean bowl from my kitchen, scoop up a handful of change, and meet her in the front yard. Each pineapple cost about seventy-five cents. For twenty-five cents more she would hold the pineapple in the palm of her left hand, administer a few swift strokes with her cutlass, and place in my bowl peeled sections of the sweet, juicy fruit.

After living in Africa for a while, I discovered that I had stopped shopping as an American tourist. And it wasn't just the fifty-percent reduction in my income. Somehow, bargaining with vendors had lost its appeal once I met those young women who sold me fruit. I had seen other women sitting in market stalls or by the roadside, hoping for a sale that would feed their families for one more day. I had seen where they lived, had visited with them in their homes.

I got to know the women who made the dolls and the tote bags and the pretty African dresses. The ones who set up their hand-powered sewing machines on rickety tables in their mud huts. They sewed in the morning, after their children had left for school. They sewed with sleeping infants swaddled on their backs. They sewed when the perspiration glistened on their foreheads. They squinted and sewed by kerosene lamplight after their families had retired for the night. They sewed for soap and tea and cooking pots. They sewed to buy shoes and pay for school fees. They sewed when their husbands couldn't find work. They sewed so their children could attend university. They sewed, so their daughters wouldn't have to.

I bought their dolls and their tote bags and their pretty African dresses. I bought their images on paintings and postcards, on watercolors and carvings. I knew that, one day, it would be important for me to remember these women.

They surround me now in North Carolina, these graceful ladies of Africa, the heart and soul of a continent. On the wall above my bed, two women in fluttering dresses of mauve and violet hold hands and dance while their friends clap and stomp their feet. On the bathroom countertop, a woman in pastel yellow wades into the river, bends down and scrubs the neck of her naked toddler. A slim, stately woman in indigo, carved from the finest hardwood, raises her pestle on my dining-room table, ready to pound grain for her family's supper. The watercolored women on the wall of my breakfast nook chatter amongst themselves. I join them for morning coffee, and I remember those strong women of Africa.

Susan Bauer

That's a Wrap

Determine that the thing can and shall be done, and then we shall find the way.

ABRAHAM LINCOLN

"Excuse me? You need what?"

My daughter's brows lifted as she placed a finger near her lips, nodded slightly toward the checkout counter and whispered, "Mom, listen."

The salesclerk rephrased her question to the twenty-something customer standing there. "I'm not certain what you mean, sir. What are you asking?"

"I'm asking you to wrap this gift for me," he answered with more than a little impatience.

"But we don't gift wrap, sir."

"What do you mean? The sign on your window says in big letters, 'Sale on Gift Wrapping and Cards,'" he huffed.

Katrina and I shared a giggle behind a store display. The Current Outlet was one of our favorite shopping destinations with its extensive selection of paper goods. We scoured the store for bargains—stationery, stickers, envelopes, ribbons and geegaws—and never left disappointed. Simply drifting through the aisles, fingering note cards and bookmarks and colored envelopes, whetted our writing and crafting appetites. With her degree in art, my daughter took pleasure in discovering bits and pieces among Current's inventory that she could re-purpose into an array of projects.

But the conversation now had our full attention. We eavesdropped openly.

The clerk tried to explain, "We sell gift wrapping."

"And that's what I want to buy," the man insisted. "Gift wrapping. I'm on my way to my boss's surprise birthday party." He plopped a fishing tackle box on the counter and pushed it toward her. "So, if you'll just quickly wrap this. I'm late already."

"But we don't gift wrap," she objected. "And, anyway, you found this here?" She pointed doubtfully at the box.

"Nah. I bought it at the bait shop awhile ago."

By now, the clerk's face had flushed to a deep crimson. "Let me get this straight, sir. You bought the gift at another place of business, and now you're asking me to wrap it— at this place of business," her voice rose an octave, "for free?"

"Well, no, I expect to pay for it. The sale price that your sign says. And wrap it really nice to impress him."

While the stunned saleswoman gathered her wits, Katrina walked to the register and introduced herself. She didn't even bother to hide her wide grin. "Sir, there's paper, ribbon, tape—everything you need one aisle over. Pick something out, and I'll wrap the gift for you—if we can borrow scissors and part of the counter here?" Still speechless, the clerk nodded her agreement.

"Okay." He looked at his watch.

Since he seemed overwhelmed at the array of choices and worried aloud at the lateness of the hour, Katrina made the appropriate selections. The clerk rang up the items, shaking her head and mumbling all the while.

Meanwhile, at the other end of the counter, Katrina created a gift-wrapped masterpiece, complete with artistic embellishments, Martha Stewart-style.

More than satisfied with the results, the gentleman thanked her.

"This looks great, really great," he gushed, "just what I wanted." Still clueless, he said with sincere regret, "I only wish I'd thought to bring in my Mother's Day gift, too."

Carol McAdoo Rehme

TOP TEN MARKETS
FOR RECREATIONAL SHOPPING

Market	Percentage*
Hong Kong	.93%
Indonesia	.93%
Singapore	.90%
South Korea	.89%
Philippines	.88%
Malaysia	.88%
Thailand	.86%
United Arab Emirates	.84%
China	.84%
Taiwan	.83%

* Combined percentage of respondents who shop for "something to do" twice a week or more, once a week, once a month, or less than once a month.

U.S. consumers are the world's most likely to say they "loathe" shopping for clothes (14%), and 70 percent of Americans see grocery shopping as a necessary chore. Americans, despite their reputation as indebted shopaholics, fall below the global average for recreational shopping, with only 68 percent shopping when they don't really need anything.

European consumers were least likely to be recreational shoppers, and nine of the top ten countries for "never" shopping unless it's necessary are in Europe.

ACNielsen, *The World's Biggest Shopaholics? Surprise, It's Not Americans*, 15 June 2006, New York, NY, USA. Excerpted with permission.

More Chicken Soup?

We would love to hear your reactions to the stories in this book. Please let us know what your favorite stories were and how they affected you.

Many of the stories and poems you have read in this book were submitted by readers like you who had read earlier *Chicken Soup for the Soul* books. We publish at least five or six *Chicken Soup for the Soul* books every year. We invite you to contribute a story to one of these future volumes.

Stories may be up to 1,200 words and must uplift or inspire. You may submit an original piece, something you have read or your favorite quotation on your refrigerator door.

To obtain a copy of our submission guidelines and a listing of upcoming *Chicken Soup* books, please write, fax or check our Web sites. Please send your submissions to:

Chicken Soup for the Soul
P.O. Box 30880
Santa Barbara, CA 93130
fax: 805-563-2945
Web site: *www.chickensoup.com*

Just send a copy of your stories and other pieces to the above address. We will be sure that both you and the author are credited for your submission.

For information about speaking engagements, other books, audiotapes, workshops and training programs, please contact any of our authors directly.

Dress for Success

Continuing the tradition of supporting worthwhile non-profits, the publisher and authors of *Chicken Soup for the Shopper's Soul* are pleased to donate five cents for every book sold to Dress for Success.

The mission of Dress for Success is to advance low-income women's economic and social development and to encourage self-sufficiency through career development and employment retention. Dress for Success provides programs that help economically disadvantaged women acquire jobs, retain their new positions and succeed in the mainstream workplace. Since 1997, Dress for Success has served almost 300,000 women around the world through seventy-nine local affiliates in the United States, Canada, the United Kingdom and New Zealand.

Dress for Success clients come from a continually expanding and diverse group of over 2,500 non-profit and government agencies, including homeless shelters, immigration services, job-training programs, educational institutions and domestic-violence shelters.

On her initial visit, after an interview is scheduled, a woman receives a suit appropriate for the industry in which she is interviewing and, if available, accessories. Once a woman finds a job, she returns to Dress for Success for additional clothing that can be mixed and matched to make several outfits, providing her with the foundation for a professional wardrobe.

While Dress for Success may be best known for providing suits to women, employment-retention programs are the cornerstone of the organization. Finding a job is only one step in a woman's journey toward economic independence; remaining employed and building a rewarding career are equally important. The Professional Women's Group program provides ongoing support to enable women to successfully transition into the workforce, build thriving careers and prosper in the mainstream workplace. In addition, Career Corner, a Dress for Success initiative, offers women career guidance, the chance to acquire technology skills and assistance in their job searches.

www.dressforsuccess.org
Dress for Success Worldwide
32 East 31st Street, 7th Floor • New York, NY 10016
phone: 212-532-1922 • fax: 212-684-9563

Who Is Jack Canfield?

Jack Canfield is one of America's leading experts in the development of human potential and personal effectiveness. He is both a dynamic, entertaining speaker and a highly sought-after trainer. Jack has a wonderful ability to inform and inspire audiences toward increased levels of self-esteem and peak performance. Jack most recently released a book for success entitled *The Success Principles: How to Get from Where You Are to Where You Want to Be.*

He is the author and narrator of several bestselling audio- and videocassette programs, including *Self-Esteem and Peak Performance, How to Build High Self-Esteem, Self-Esteem in the Classroom* and *Chicken Soup for the Soul—Live.* He is regularly seen on television shows such as *Good Morning America, 20/20* and *NBC Nightly News.* Jack has co-authored numerous books, including the *Chicken Soup for the Soul* series, *Dare to Win* and *The Aladdin Factor* (all with Mark Victor Hansen), *100 Ways to Build Self-Concept in the Classroom* (with Harold C. Wells), *Heart at Work* (with Jacqueline Miller), and *The Power of Focus* (with Les Hewitt and Mark Victor Hansen).

Jack is a regularly featured speaker for professional associations, school districts, government agencies, churches, hospitals, sales organizations and corporations. His clients have included the American Dental Association, the American Management Association, AT&T, Campbell's Soup, Clairol, Domino's Pizza, GE, Hartford Insurance, ITT, Johnson & Johnson, the Million Dollar Roundtable, NCR, New England Telephone, Re/Max, Scott Paper, TRW and Virgin Records. Jack has taught on the faculty of Income Builders International, a school for entrepreneurs.

Jack conducts an annual seven-day training called Breakthrough to Success. It attracts entrepreneurs, educators, counselors, parenting trainers, corporate trainers, professsional speakers, ministers and others interested in improving their lives and the lives of others.

For free gifts from Jack and information on all his material and availability, go to:

www.jackcanfield.com
Self-Esteem Seminars
P.O. Box 30880 • Santa Barbara, CA 93130
phone: 805-563-2935 • fax: 805-563-2945

Who Is Mark Victor Hansen?

In the area of human potential, no one is more respected than Mark Victor Hansen. For more than thirty years, Mark has focused solely on helping people from all walks of life reshape their personal vision of what's possible. His powerful messages of possibility, opportunity and action have created powerful change in thousands of organizations and millions of individuals worldwide.

He is a sought-after keynote speaker, bestselling author and marketing maven. Mark's credentials include a lifetime of entrepreneurial success and an extensive academic background. He is a prolific writer with many bestselling books such as *The One Minute Millionaire, The Power of Focus, The Aladdin Factor* and *Dare to Win*, in addition to the *Chicken Soup for the Soul* series. Mark has made a profound influence through his library of audios, videos and articles in the areas of big thinking, sales achievement, wealth building, publishing success, and personal and professional development.

Mark is also the founder of MEGA Seminar Series. MEGA Book Marketing University and Building Your MEGA Speaking Empire are annual conferences where Mark coaches and teaches new and aspiring authors, speakers and experts on building lucrative publishing and speaking careers. Other MEGA events include MEGA Marketing Magic and My MEGA Life. He has appeared on television (*Oprah, CNN* and *The Today Show*), in print (*Time, U.S. News & World Report, USA Today, New York Times* and *Entrepreneur*) and on countless radio interviews, assuring our planet's people that, "You can easily create the life you deserve."

As a philanthropist and humanitarian, Mark works tirelessly for organizations such as Habitat for Humanity, American Red Cross, March of Dimes, Childhelp USA and many others. He is the recipient of numerous awards that honor his entrepreneurial spirit, philanthropic heart and business acumen. He is a lifetime member of the Horatio Alger Association of Distinguished Americans, an organization that honored Mark with the prestigious Horatio Alger Award for his extraordinary life achievements.

www.markvictorhansen.com
Mark Victor Hansen & Associates, Inc.
P.O. Box 7665 • Newport Beach, CA 92658
phone: 949-764-2640 • fax: 949-722-6912

Who Is Theresa Peluso?

Theresa has always felt drawn to a page and the power of words. Books represent knowledge, expression, freedom, adventure, creativity and escape—so it's no surprise that her life has evolved around books.

Theresa's career began over thirty years ago in a large publisher's book club operation. In 1981, she joined Health Communications, a fledging book publisher, which grew to become the country's #1 self-help publisher and home to ground-breaking *New York Times* best-sellers as well as the series recognized as a publishing phenomenon, *Chicken Soup for the Soul*.

After twenty years spent in the day-to-day operations of a thriving publishing company, Theresa is now developing books as a writer, compiler and editor.

She is the coauthor of *Chicken Soup for the Horse Lover's Soul, Chicken Soup for the Horse Lover's Soul II, Chicken Soup for the Recovering Soul* and its companion, *Chicken Soup for the Recovering Soul Daily Inspirations*.

In addition to other *Chicken Soup* books waiting to be hatched, Theresa is developing titles in the *Read a Little Bit About . . .* series. *Read a Little Bit* books help teens and young adults build literacy skills while focusing on relevant, contemporary topics and issues, such as buying a car or getting a job. Theresa is also working on *Sonic Boomers, That Sound You Hear Is YOU Making a Difference*, a book featuring unsung heroes of the baby boomer generation who have found fulfillment and growth in their lives by helping others.

Theresa lives in South Florida with her husband, Brian, and enjoys life in perpetual sunshine and high humidity. Her shopping Achilles' heel is shoes, and she confesses to being a fan of the local home-improvement center, which just happens to be next door to the designer shoe warehouse. You can contact Theresa at:

teri@shopperssoul.com
Health Communications, Inc.
3201 S.W. 15th Street
Deerfield Beach, FL 33442
phone: 954-360-0909 • fax: 954-418-0844

Contributors

If you would like to contact any of the contributors for information about their writing or to invite them to speak in your community, look for their contact information included in their biography.

D. K. Abbott resides in Meyersdale, Pennsylvania.

Lea Ann Atherton is a writer by nature and a teacher of writing by calling. New to the freelance writing community, she currently teaches middle-school language arts and encourages children to see the gifts they possess within the written word. You can reach Lea Ann at *latherton@hotmail.com*.

Kelly Austin writes from northeast Pennsylvania where she lives with her husband and works as an arboretum curator and a horticultural therapist. She writes science, history and gardening articles and essays for various publications, including *GreenPrints*, *Learning Through History*, and scholarly journals.

Vicki Austin lives with her husband of nearly thirty-six years in Hartford, Maine, where she works as a child-care aide. Vicki is also a seamstress and an equestrian who enjoys long-distance riding. Vicki has taught riding for thirty-seven years and is also a certified member of the Mid-Maine Equestrian Search and Rescue Unit with her horses King and Baby.

Suzanne Baginskie recently retired from her job as a law office manager/paralegal after twenty-five years. She has been published in other *Chicken Soup for the Soul* books, *Cat's Magazine*, *True Romance* and several non-fiction articles. She lives on the west coast of Florida with her husband, Al.

Susan Bauer taught in Africa for six years. Her work appears in *Transitions Abroad*, *Women's Independent Press*, *The Georgetown Review*, *The Rambler* and the anthology, *A Matter of Choice: 25 People Who Transformed Their Lives* (Seal Press, 2004). She writes about her African friends from her home in North Carolina.

Lanita Bradley Boyd is from a family of writers. Her maternal grandfather wrote a popular newspaper column for forty years. Lanita and her mother, Mary Ralph Bradley, have published stories in popular series such as *God Allows U-Turns* and *Rocking Chair Reader,* as well as newspapers and magazines.

Angelique Caffrey lives in Pennsylvania where she and her son frequently "do errands" (aka shop). Their outings are always labeled "adventures" and typically result in amusing anecdotes that are enthusiastically shared with Daddy over dinner.

Kathe Campbell lives in Montana with her husband where they raise national champion spotted asses. Kathe has contributed to newspapers and national magazines on Alzheimer's disease, and her stories are found on many e-zines. She is currently featured in several *Chicken Soup for the Soul* books, in *Releasing Times, Rocking Chair Reader* and *Medhunters Journal*. You can e-mail Kathe at *bigskyadj@in-tch.com*.

Yogesh Chabria is a die-hard bargain hunter and a freelance journalist who has written for publications across the globe, including the United Kingdom, Germany, India and Iran. His most recent credits include articles and essays in publications such as *Spotlight, JAM, The Times of India* and *Iran News*.

Stacey Chillemi has a B.A. in marketing and has worked for NBC, *Dateline* and *News 4* in New York. Stacey is the author of nine books, lectures, appears as a TV guest/expert and is a dedicated advocate helping to educate the public about epilepsy. She is a H.O.P.E. Mentor for the Epilepsy Foundation. Visit Stacey at *www.inspirationallivingonline.com*.

Pamela N. Danziger (introduction) founded Unity Marketing, a consulting firm specializing in consumer insights for luxury marketers in 1992. She is the author of *Why People Buy Things They Don't Need: Understanding and Predicting Consumer Behavior* and *Let Them Eat Cake: Marketing Luxury to the Masses—as Well as the Classes*. Her latest book, *Shopping: Why We Love It and How Retailers Can Create the Ultimate Shopping Experience*, will be released in the fall of 2006.

Renee Holland Davidson lives in southern California with her husband, Mark, and their two mischievous mutts, Josie and Kinsey. She dedicates her flash memoir, *Nothing at All*, to her mother, Elizabeth Curtius, who passed away in June 2004. "I love you, Mom."

Avis Drucker retired to Cape Cod with husband, Al, as "washashores" in 2001. Leaving behind a corporate career, she quickly discovered writing, her new passion. Her memoir and poetry have been published in *Chicken Soup for the Soul, Primetime, the Aurorean, the Philosophical Mother*, the "On the Road Series" of the *Cape Cod Times* and an upcoming Cape Code Literary Press anthology. She has two daughters, Leslie and Vicki.

Terri Duncan received her bachelor's, master's, and specialist degrees in education from Augusta State University. She is an educational specialist in Evans, Georgia, and is also a wife and the mother of two delightful teenagers. Terri enjoys spending time with her family, reading, writing and, of course, shopping!

Norma Favor splits her time between the mountains of Idaho and Surrey, British Columbia, Canada. A widow, seventy-two years young, Norma has been published in *Chicken Soup for the Grandma's Soul*. Writing and her twenty-two grandchildren keep her busy.

Dara Fleischer is a New York–based shopping editor for Canada's *LOULOU* magazine and is also the founder of *FashionJunkie.com*, a fashion and beauty webzine and personal shopping service. Planning a trip to the Big Apple? E-mail *dara@fashionjunkie.com* to book your customized private or group shopping safari.

William Geen is a retired business executive who lives in upstate New York. Bill enjoys traveling to refill the creative reservoir for his writing. A contributor to *Chicken Soup for the Horse Lover's Soul*, he is currently working on a manuscript about Alaska and finding a publisher for his collection of essays, *Manure Memories*, about his early years as a stable hand.

Dianna Graveman is a college instructor and writer. Her stories have appeared in many national publications, including *Letters to My Teacher* (Adams Media) and *St. Anthony Messenger*. She lives with her husband and two daughters, Beth and Teresa, and is happy to report her son visits home often.

Rachel Green has been writing for quite a few years, though working two "day jobs" has certainly put a damper on things. Rachel has written for school newspapers, with one short story published in Valparaiso University's student literary magazine, and has written a children's book for a college course that she hopes to publish.

Norah Griggs lives in Ohio. Her recently published book, *No Going Back*, is historical fiction coauthored with Barbara Paulson. Previous works include *Rocklady, The Building of a Labyrinth*, a non-fiction book. Articles she has written have been featured by various e-zines as well as the LuminQuest e-book and CD, *Spiritual Symbology*.

Marilyn Haight is the author of *The Instruction Writer's Guide: How to Explain How to Do Anything*, and the bestselling career advice book, *Who's Afraid of the Big Bad Boss? 13 Types and How to Survive Them*. For more information on

Marilyn's work, visit her Web sites, *www.wordedwrite.com* and *www.bigbadboss.com*.

Jodie Haley has been writing for several years and is now taking a college writing course. She has written several short stories and hopes to someday write a novel.

Jonny Hawkins' cartoons have been in over 300 publications and in over 100 books over the last twenty years. His calendars, *Medical Cartoon-A-Day, Fishing Cartoon-A-Day* and *Cartoons for Teachers,* are available everywhere. He can be reached at *jonnyhawkins2nz@yahoo.com.* These cartoons are dedicated to his shopping goddess wife, Carissa.

Miriam Hill is the coauthor of *Fabulous Florida* and a frequent contributor to *Chicken Soup for the Soul* books. Her work has appeared in *The Christian Science Monitor, Grit Magazine, St. Petersburg Times* and *Poynter Online.* Miriam's work was judged First Place for Inspirational Writing at the Southeastern Writers Conference in 2002 and 2004.

Dawn Howard-Hirsch is a former Realtor and freelance writer who contributes to *Principal Broker Online, Miami Realtor* and other real-estate journals. She is currently producing *Democratic Family Magazine* for Howard-Hirsch Publishing.

Patricia Carroll Johnson is a freelance writer and a special features editor with three newspapers. She is the mother of three and grandmother of seven with another grandchild expected soon. She enjoys reading, knitting, spinning and weaving, and never misses an opportunity to shop or go to the library.

Susan A. Karas owns and operates a business with her husband. In her free time she shops and enjoys visiting with her two grown children, who just moved into their own places. Susan is a regular contributor to *Guideposts Magazine,* and has been published in *Sweet 16, PLUS Magazine* and *Guideposts 4 Kids.* She can be reached at *Mssusankaras@yahoo.com.*

Judith Keenan is a professional freelance writer specializing in internal communications. Judith has been writing fiction and non-fiction for a number of years and has just begun to submit her work to publishers.

Mimi Greenwood Knight is a freelance writer and artist-in-residence living with her husband, four kids, four cats, four dogs and an ill-tempered bird in what's left of south Louisiana. Her work has appeared in *Parents Magazine, Working Mother, American Baby, Christian Parenting Today, Today's Christian Woman* and, she's proud to say, several *Chicken Soup for the Soul* books. Reach Mimi at *djknight@airmail.net.*

Kathryn Lay lives with her husband and daughter in Texas. She is a full-time writer and author, including a children's novel, *Crown Me!* and a non-fiction book, *The Organized Writer Is a Selling Writer*. She also enjoys speaking to school kids and writer's groups. Learn more at *www.kathrynlay.com*.

Terry Lilley is a freelance humorist who makes her home in New Mexico. Her credits include work in various corporate newsletters and publication in *The SouthWest Sage*, the newsletter for the SouthWest Writers Workshop. Terry is an avid shopper with an affinity for shoes and big straw hats.

Patricia Lorenz is a nationally known inspirational, art-of-living writer and speaker. An award-winning newspaper columnist, Patricia is one of the most frequent contributors to the *Chicken Soup for the Soul* series. She is the author of six books and the coauthor of *Chicken Soup for the Dieter's Soul, Daily Inspirations*. Visit *www.patricialorenz.com* for more information.

Karen Lynch, a freelance writer and journalist, has been putting pen to paper since she was thirteen years old. Writing is in her soul; it's her God-given gift. Karen lives in Connecticut with her husband and their three children. E-mail Karen at *karenmlynch@gmail.com* or visit her Web site, *www.lynch.st/karen*.

Kenneth C. Lynch is a retired military officer from the U.S. Navy, having served twenty-seven years. Ken is currently a substitute schoolteacher for the Pennridge School District and a freelance stringer for *Navy Times*, a subsidiary publication for Army Times Publications, a position Kenneth has held since January 1996.

Michelle Mach lives and shops in Colorado. Her work has appeared in several anthologies, including *Simple Pleasures of Friendship, KnitLit the Third* and *Short Attention Span Mysteries*. Please visit her Web site at *www.michellemach.com*.

Deepana Mallik admits she has an ordinary life but adds that it's through her ordinary life that she has had some extraordinary experiences. Someone once said, "To meet, to know and then to part is the saddest tale of human heart . . ." to which Deepana would add, "but till the day upon this earth we stay, sweet memories lay, never to fade away."

Staci Mauney holds a B.A. in English from Southwestern Oklahoma State University. She and her husband of nine years, Michael, reside in Clinton, Oklahoma. Staci grew up in Oklahoma, and she and Michael returned there after Michael was honorably discharged from the Army in 2000.

Stacy Lytwyn Maxwell has written about grammar school, cafeteria workers as well as such luminaries as Ella Fitzgerald and is currently serving as CEO for Cat Tales Press, Inc., a Connecticut-based publishing company, which has published its debut travel guidebook, *Consummate Connecticut: Day Trips with Panache.* Visit *www.cattalespress.com* or e-mail *cattalespress@snet.net.*

Melissa Mayntz is a Utah-based freelance writer and frequent thrift-store shopper. Her favorite store is now Deseret Industries Thrift Store, where she often finds unique holiday decorations and plenty of warm clothes. Melissa's writing credentials include newspaper, magazine and Web site articles.

J. A. McDougall is a business graduate of the University of Calgary and a former sales and marketing professional. She writes fiction and creative non-fiction from her home in Calgary, Canada, while raising her four beautiful children.

Roberta McGovern is the mother of two and a grandmother of four who relocated from Massachusetts to Florida with her husband in 1979. Roberta is a registered nurse who is looking forward to retirement so she can indulge her passion for bargain hunting and thrift-store shopping.

Esme Mills can be found at her computer writing, when not going on adventures with her two boys or taking an occasional break for some online shopping. She is presently working on a teen novel (and buying books online when she gets stumped).

Shana Moore's spunky and irreverent annual Christmas letter segued into her fun and highly relatable "Why IS It That . . .?" column at the coaxing of family and friends. By popular demand, her essays were woven together to create her first book, *Caffeinated Ponderings on Life, Laughter & Lattes.* Contact information: *www.caffeinatedponderings.com.*

Irma Newland is a retired public schoolteacher with a bachelor's degree in Education. She is a contributing author to *Chicken Soup for the Soul Daily Inspirations for Recovery* and writes children's stories. She and her husband, Donald, a retired pastor, are the parents of three adult sons.

Mark Parisi's "Off the Mark" comic panel has been syndicated since 1987 and is distributed by United Media. Mark's humor also graces greeting cards, T-shirts, calendars, magazines, newsletters and books. Please visit his Web site at *www.offthemark.com.* Lynn is his wife/business partner and their daughter, Jenny, contributes with inspiration (as do three cats).

Maria Pascucci is a full-time freelance writer based in Buffalo, New York. She specializes in health and wellness, creative non-fiction and any topic that serves to empower women and men to love their imperfect selves. Visit her Web site that she shares with her graphic-designer husband, Shaun, at *www.creativetypeco.com*. Contact her at *Maria@creativetypeco.com*.

Ava Pennington is a writer, Bible study teacher, public speaker and former Human Resources Director. With an M.B.A. from St. John's University in New York, and a Bible Studies Certificate from Moody Bible Institute in Chicago, Ava divides her time between teaching, writing, speaking and volunteering. Contact her at *rusavapen@yahoo.com*.

M. J. Plaster has been a freelance writer for the past two decades, juggling a dual life in the airline and high-tech fast lanes. She traded in the glamour of it all—whirlwind travel, speaking, training and jet lag—to write full time and serve as editor for *www.adventurous-cooking.com*.

Eileen Rafferty is from Yardley, Pennsylvania. She graduated from Villanova University in May 2006 with a degree in English, concentrated in Irish Studies and Writing & Rhetoric, as well as a business minor. She is planning a future career in the field of writing.

Peggy Reeves is an inspirational speaker, singer, worship leader and writer. Published in *Experiencing God Magazine, Open Windows* and *Chicken Soup for the Recovering Soul, Daily Inspirations,* Peggy is the mother of two, Shauna and Kyle. Peggy and her husband, Tom, own a recording studio and production company. They have been married for over twenty-five years.

Carol McAdoo Rehme favors out-of-the-way antique shops and hole-in-the-wall flea markets for her shopping sprees. She is a longtime author and editor for the *Chicken Soup for the Soul* series. The newly released *Chicken Soup for the Soul Christmas Virtues* is her first book. Contact her at *carol@rehme.com* or *www.rehme.com*.

C. L. Robinson (pseudonym) has written for the online *Inside Out Travel Magazine,* the magazines *France Today* and *Destinations Abroad,* and recently placed eleventh in the 74th Annual Writer's Digest Writing Competition, for which there were almost 18,000 entries.

Gwen Rockwood writes a humor column called "The Rockwood Files" for a family magazine as well as several newspapers in Arkansas and Missouri. She has been a weekly columnist for eleven years and lives in Arkansas with her husband and two sons.

Nan Schindler Russell is living her dream in Montana after twenty years in management on the East Coast. Currently writing her first book, *Winning at Working: 10 Lessons Shared,* Nan is a writer, columnist and speaker. More of Nan's work can be read at *www.nanrussell.com.*

Jodi L. Severson resides in Wisconsin with her husband and three children and is employed by the State Public Defender's Office. Read more of her stories in these *Chicken Soup* books: *Sister's Soul, Working Woman's Soul, Chicken Soup Celebrates Sisters* and *Girlfriend's Soul.* She is currently seeking a publisher for her children's book. Reach her at *jodis@charter.net.*

Sarah Smiley is the author of "Shore Duty," a syndicated newspaper column, and of the memoir *Going Overboard* (NAL 2005), which was optioned by Paramount Television and Kelsey Grammar, and is now in development to be a half-hour sitcom on CBS. Learn more about Sarah at *www.SarahSmiley.com.*

Morgan St. James earned recognition for *Writer's Digest* submissions and articles spanning interior design, human-interest, travel and business topics. Morgan coauthored *A Corpse in the Soup* (Wings ePress) with her sister Phyllice Bradner. For more information on Morgan and the *Silver Sisters Mysteries* series, visit *www.silversistersmysteries.com.*

Joyce Stark lives in Scotland and has recently retired to concentrate on her writing. Her projects include a book on traveling in the cities and small towns of the United States and a children's series set in Spain, which will also teach very young children a little Spanish.

Elva Stoelers is an award-winning Canadian writer. Most recently her work appeared in *Chicken Soup for the Recovering Soul* and *Recovering Soul Daily Inspirations.* Elva is broadcast on CBC Radio and has been published internationally in a variety of small press parenting magazines. She currently teaches Creative Writing for Surrey Continuing Education.

Marti Kramer Suddarth is a freelance writer from southeastern Indiana, where she lives with her husband, three children, two fire-bellied toads, a newt and a beagle named Splash. She's the composer/playwright of *Mini-Musicals for Special Days* and *The Adventures of Quinn Quarternote* and the *Wooden Spoon Orchestra.*

Tsgoyna Tanzman is a *Chicken Soup* contributor and author of numerous articles and essays for books and newspapers. Tsgoyna now claims mother/wife as her career of choice. She also volunteers as a speaker and Child Safety Educator and is the director of "Characters Come Alive," a program bringing historical characters to life in elementary classrooms. Contact: *tnzmn@cox.net*.

B. J. Taylor is a *Guideposts* special correspondent/writer and has been published in numerous magazines, newspapers and many *Chicken Soup* books. She shares her home with three cats, one dog and a wonderful husband. They have four children and two adorable grandsons. You can reach B. J. at *bj.taylor@verizon.net*.

Tena Thompson writes about life and shares her experiences with a touch of humor. Tena left her hometown in Ohio and now resides in Las Vegas where she works as a freelance writer. Her column, "A Citizen's View," appears in the *West Valley News*.

Cristy Trandahl lives with her husband and their six children in rural Minnesota, fifty miles from any major mall. Cristy's work is published in *Cup of Comfort for Mothers-to-Be, Chicken Soup for the Soul, Recipes for Busy Moms, Teacher Miracles* and various regional anthologies. E-mail her at *davecristy@frontiernet.net*.

Anne Culbreath Watkins is the author of *The Conure Handbook*, as well as scores of published articles and essays including stories in *Chicken Soup for the Dog Lover's Soul* and *Chicken Soup for the Soul Celebrates Grandmothers*. She and her husband, musician Allen Watkins, live in north Alabama. E-mail her at *featherheart1@yahoo.com*.

Kim Weiss has been a public-relations director for a renowned book publisher for over twelve years. Prior to that she had her own PR agency in Boca Raton, Florida, where she worked with corporations, artists and municipalities. Kim's passion is music, and she currently studies operatic singing and plays in an acoustic rock band. She's also mom to two orange cats and two small birds.

Bonnie West has published short stories and essays in national literary and women's magazines, and she was published in *Chicken Soup to Inspire a Woman's Soul*. She has produced an audio CD, *Yoga for Writers*, which is available on *Amazon.com* or directly from Bonnie. Contact her at *yogabonnie@yahoo.com*.

Ferida Wolff is a frequent contributor to the *Chicken Soup for the Soul* series and several other anthologies. Ferida is the author of *Listening Outside Listening Inside, The Adventures of Swamp Woman, Menopause: Essays on the Edge* and sixteen books for children. Her work has appeared in *The New York Times, The Philadelphia Inquirer, The Christian Science Monitor, Moment Magazine* and several poetry journals.

My Wish List

My Wish List

Guaranteed
to make you smile!

Chicken Soup for the **Sister's Soul 2**

Celebrating
Love and Laughter
Throughout Our Lives

Jack Canfield, Mark Victor Hansen,
Patty Aubery and Kelly Mitchell Zimmerman

Code #5512 • $14.95

Chicken Soup for the **Girlfriend's Soul**

Celebrating the Friends
Who Cheer Us Up,
Cheer Us On
and Make Our
Lives Complete

Jack Canfield, Mark Victor Hansen,
Mark & Chrissy Donnelly and Stefanie Adrian

Code #1541 • $14.95

Take time for you.

Code #5210 • $14.95

Code #1592 • $14.95

Also Available

Chicken Soup African American Soul
Chicken Soup African American Woman's Soul
Chicken Soup Breast Cancer Survivor's Soul
Chicken Soup Bride's Soul
Chicken Soup Caregiver's Soul
Chicken Soup Cat Lover's Soul
Chicken Soup Christian Family Soul
Chicken Soup College Soul
Chicken Soup Couple's Soul
Chicken Soup Dieter's Soul
Chicken Soup Dog Lover's Soul
Chicken Soup Entrepreneur's Soul
Chicken Soup Expectant Mother's Soul
Chicken Soup Father's Soul
Chicken Soup Fisherman's Soul
Chicken Soup Girlfriend's Soul
Chicken Soup Golden Soul
Chicken Soup Golfer's Soul, Vol. I, II
Chicken Soup Horse Lover's Soul, Vol. I, II
Chicken Soup Inspire a Woman's Soul
Chicken Soup Kid's Soul, Vol. I, II
Chicken Soup Mother's Soul, Vol. I, II
Chicken Soup Parent's Soul
Chicken Soup Pet Lover's Soul
Chicken Soup Preteen Soul, Vol. I, II
Chicken Soup Scrapbooker's Soul
Chicken Soup Sister's Soul, Vol. I, II
Chicken Soup Shopper's
Chicken Soup Soul, Vol. I-VI
Chicken Soup at Work
Chicken Soup Sports Fan's Soul
Chicken Soup Teenage Soul, Vol. I-IV
Chicken Soup Woman's Soul, Vol. I, II